GODDESSES AND WOMEN

in the Indic Religious Tradition

Edited by
Arvind Sharma

INDICA

Published in 2007 by

Indica Books
D 40/18 Godowlia
Varanasi - 221 001 (U.P.)
India
E-mail: indicabooks@satyam.net.in

ISBN: 81-86569-69-3

Printed in India by First Impression
011-22481754, 09811224048

in memory of

David Kinsley
(1939-2000)

who passed away while this volume was in preparation

CONTENTS

INTRODUCTION

ARVIND SHARMA

Fokke Dijkema approached me several years ago to put together a book on the theme of goddesses and women in the Indic religious tradition. At the time, I was inclined to demur for fear that the field may have been harvested to the point of diminishing returns. But now that the volume is ready I am glad that I allowed myself to be persuaded. This transformation in my attitude is the result of what the distinguished contributors to this volume have accomplished in these essays. Apparently the field is more fecund than I had taken it to be.

In the first essay we are offered a glimpse of how even initially unpromising material of the kind associated with ritual minutiae can reward scholarly perseverance. Stephanie W. Jamison demonstrates how such investigation sheds new light on the status of women. It also allows us to see earlier conclusions in this respect in a new light.

With the second essay we enter a magic garden, as it were, inhabited by the Buddhist "fairies." This paper explores a realm often neglected, the realm which lies between the mundane and the transcendent. Victoria K. Urubshurow dis-closes how vital a role *ḍākinīs*, who inhabit this in-between world, play in the ascent from the mundane to the transcendent in Tibetan Buddhism.

The third essay deals with "embodied knowledge," wherein Kartikeya C. Patel offers a new paradigm of viewing the relationship between women, earth and the Goddess.

The fourth essay, by comparison, is more conventional and deals with women and the worship of the Goddess, at the end of which Hillary Rodrigues offers the interesting conclusion that the entire period of festivities brings about "a temporary status elevation" for women. It represents a period during which "woman hood is transformed and purified, elevated in auspiciousness and venerated."

The fifth essay discusses what happens to ordinary women of the family when the families become God-intoxicated. Vidyut Aklujkar illustrates their fate with the help of biographical details from the lives of Nāmdev and Tukārām.

The final essay examines in textual and hermeneutical detail the position of Śaṅkara on the accessibility of salvation to woman and *śūdras*. The issue is important because it is Śaṅkara's position that the Vedas are inaccessible to women and *śūdras*, and further that the Vedas are the primary means of attaining salvific knowledge about Brahman. An important point in Śaṅkara's thought is involved here—that Śaṅkara allows for a universal soteriology within allowing for universal accessibility to the Vedas. Katherine K. Young spells out how precisely Śaṅkara manages to hold on hermeneutically to these apparently divergent positions.

These essays point to a hermeneutics of surprise, both individually as well as collectively. That is to say, they surprise us by belying our academic expectations. To offer just two examples: Menstruation often possesses negative associations in Hinduism and yet it seems to acquire an almost celebratory air in chapter three when the earth is feminized in this way—an outcome one would hardly expect in the light of the earlier association. Similarly, one would expect the family of a devout devotee to be suffused with domestiv felicity as an expression of such piety, and yet the next-of-kin of the saint seem to have a hard time in chapter five. And so on.

I hope I have said enough to induce the reader to keep reading further for more surprises.

CHAPTER ONE

ROLES FOR WOMEN IN VEDIC ŚRAUTA RITUAL[1]

STEPHANIE W. JAMISON

One of the neglected sources for the study of women in ancient India is the vast storehouse of materials relating to Śrauta ritual, i.e. solemn Vedic ritual. The extent of the textual material is immense: Our very earliest texts, the four Vedas themselves, are ritual-internal texts, consisting of formulae, both poetry and prose, to be pronounced during rituals. In addition to these liturgical texts, we have an enormous body of ritual-external texts. The class of texts known as Brāhmaṇas consists of exegesis—explanations for ritual procedure that turn on mythological, practical, or mystical justifications. And perhaps most remarkable of all, there are extremely detailed ritual manuals, the Śrauta Sūtras, which specify every step of the procedure—every hand position, every muttered word, every wiping of every spoon—from the point of view of a variety of ritual participants. Each type of text exists in many versions, the products of different priestly traditions and theological schools. The whole comes to many thousands of pages.

This material is relevant to the study of women and gender because one of the necessary participants in solemn ritual is a woman, the so-called "Sacrificer's Wife." The performance of even the simplest Śrauta ritual requires a number of participants, whom I will briefly introduce. The setter-in-motion of the sacrifice is the misleadingly named "Sacrificer" (*yajamāna*). He arranges for the performance, chooses the priests, and pays for the "gifts" that are equivalent to priestly wages. He also receives all the benefit (or malefit) of the

[1] A previous version of this paper was presented in the Harvard Divinity School Women's Studies in Religion lecture series, in Feb. 1993, and most of the research was conducted while I was a Visiting Lecturer and Research Associate at the Harvard Divinity School. The material is discussed in detail in my book, *Sacrificed Wife/Sacrificer's Wife: Women, Ritual, and Hospitality in Ancient India* (New York: Oxford University Press, 1996).

ritual: there are no rites performed purely for social or public ends. What he does not do is *sacrifice*, in the narrow sense. Most of the action, both physical and verbal, is the province of the various priests he has assembled. All but the simplest rituals require several priests, representing the different Vedas, and each may have several assistants. The more elaborate rites could become very populous indeed.

At the prompting of the priests the Sacrificer goes from place to place and occasionally says something or makes an offering, but his participation consists primarily of being there and, in some rituals, undergoing a preliminary consecration (*dīkṣā*). His companion in the ritual process is his wife. One of the main technical requirements for being a Sacrificer is that he must be a householder (*gṛhastha*); he must be married. Not only that but the presence and participation of his wife is required in all the solemn rituals. Sacrificer's Wife (*patnī*) is a *structural role* in ritual with particular duties and activities that cannot ordinarily be performed by anyone else.

Though treatments (or rather mentions) of the Sacrificer's Wife in modern secondary literature tend to minimize the importance of her role,[2] there is much evidence to suggest the opposite. We might begin by noting the term by which she is invariably referred to. Though there are a number of words for 'wife' current in Vedic Sanskrit of the period (e.g. *jāyā, bharyā* [lit. 'the one to be supported']), only one is used of her in her ritual role: *patnī*, the feminine counterpart of *pati* 'master'. If the English word did not have misleading connotations, 'Mistress' would be a better rendering than 'Sacrificer's Wife'. Her husband is not mentioned in her nomenclature: she is simply the female 'Master' of the rites.[3]

The exegetical texts specifically mention her importance to ritual performance—a ritual without a wife is no ritual at all—and the wife is half of oneself.[4] The first major duty of a wife is to serve as ritual partner, and this requirement is so strong that, according to some legal authorities, a wife may not be repudiated once they have jointly kindled

2 See e.g. Lṝvi, p. 157, n. 1; Hubert and Mauss, n. 263; Hopkins, p. 338.
3 Interestingly enough the sacrificer is not called a *pati*.
4 Cf. e.g. ŚB I.3.1.12; BŚS XXIX.9 (381: 2); MŚS VIII.23.10, 12-13.

the fires that establish them as sacrificers.[5]

There is also a whole machinery to deal with any temporary inability of the wife to take part because she is menstruating or in childbirth.[6] In the former case, though she is banished from the ritual area, she may be required to leave behind a token of her presence[7] or sit close by on a heap of sand until her menstrual period is over[8]: her presence is so necessary that even when she is polluting she must oversee the ritual from a safe distance. Meanwhile someone else may be assigned to speak her lines and perform her acts, or they may be omitted—there is much debate on the subject among the theologians.[9] There is also some debate about whether a pregnant woman may engage in ritual, but the question is resolved in favor of her participation.[10]

Despite this testimony to her importance, it must be admitted that the wife's activities are somewhat circumscribed. Her movement around the ritual ground is more restricted than her husband's, and for long stretches of the ritual she does nothing at all but sit in her assigned spot. However, she acts independently of her husband; she is not merely his double or shadow in ritual performance. Furthermore, though she is inactive for much of most rituals, when she does act it is often at crucial and climactic moments, as we will see.

The treatment of the wife's activities in the ritual manuals seems to me a promising place to begin probing the vexed question of women in ancient India.[11] The treatments are descriptive, not interpretive. They dispassionately tell where she sits, what she wears, what she does with her hands, what she says, what kind of basket she carries and what it

---

[5] Cf. ĀpDS II.5.23-24.

[6] Cf. e.g. TB III.7.1.9 [KS XXXV.18 (64:17)]; KŚS XXV.11.17, BŚS XXIX.11 (384:3).

[7] Cf. ĀpŚS IX.2.1-2.

[8] Cf. KŚS (XXV.11.13-16); BŚS (XXIX.10-11).

[9] Cf. e.g. BŚS XXIX.11 (384:5); XX.10 (23:7); ĀpŚS VI.12.5.

[10] KŚS XXV.11.18-19.

[11] But they have been remarkably little used for this purpose. The only systematic exception I know of is a recent (1991) article of F. M. Smith. Smith reaches very different conclusions from mine, but a full discussion is beyond the scope of this article. The promisingly titled "The wife in the Vedic ritual" of J. B. Chaudhuri is almost entirely descriptive; what little analysis it contains is directed towards establishing the ritual supremacy of the chief wife and, by extension, the monogamous bent of ancient Indian society -- sometimes to the detriment of the evidence. Winternitz 1920 devotes relatively little space to the wife's ritual behavior.

contains, and so on. Insofar as any text can be considered "objective," these seem to be. There is no overt ideological shaping, simply a minute-by-minute account of everyone's activities, from which the wife's occasional participation can be extracted. But once extracted, this material makes it clear that the tasks of women in ritual were not haphazardly assigned. By examining the mandated religious activities of women as chronicled by the remarkable "ritual scripts" of the Śrauta Sūtras, we can begin to grasp the conceptual space women fill in religious practise. Though the wife does relatively little, her duties frame the ritual and ensure her contact with every important portion of it. Moreover, her tasks fall into functional roles that help define the position of women in religious ideology and also define the religious ideology as in part a function of the conceptual position of women.

What I will do now is give a *thematic overview* of the wife's roles in ritual, trying to avoid as much as possible the technical minutiae that has made this field so impenetrable to those who might find its implications valuable. However, there are occasions when only technical detail can clarify what is going on. Given limitations of space, I forbear to quote the texts, but ample references are given in the notes.[12]

A few of the wife's actions she undertakes jointly with her husband. In particular, in rituals in which her husband is first consecrated, she undergoes a *dīkṣā* entirely parallel to that of her husband, involving the same privations with regard to food and physical comfort.[13] This consecration makes her eligible to participate as the full ritual partner of her husband.

Unlike her husband, she is also bound temporarily with a cord even during rituals not requiring his consecration, in a ceremony known as the *patnīsaṃnahana* 'the girding of the wife.'[14] The girding occurs at the beginning of the ritual, and the cord is loosened at the end. Though

---

[12] Full textual citations are given in the book mentioned in n. 1.

[13] The actual procedures of the Dīkṣā are well-discussed in the standard secondary literature (e.g. Caland-Henry, pp. 11-26; Hillebrandt 1897, pp. 125-6; Kane, pp. 1135-41).

[14] The pattern for this girding is given in the description of the model Iṣṭi, the Darśapūrṇamāsa ritual, and it is used for all other Iṣṭis and as the basis for the more elaborate consecration ceremonies. A synopsis of the action can be found in Hillebrandt's 1879 treatment of the Darśapūrṇamāsa ritual, pp. 59-61.

this girding has been seen[15] (wrongly in my view) as a symbol of the wife's dominated state and loss of independence, in fact it is another procedure to bring her to temporary ritual equality with her husband. When he was initiated as a boy, he was tied with a girdle and invested with a sacred cord (*upavīta*), which he always wears. The binding of the wife gives her the status of an initiate for the duration of the ritual, as the accompanying mantras and the theological exegesis makes quite clear. The binding and unbinding of the wife also provide a perceptual frame, within which the principal activity of the ritual performance occurs.

From our point of view the independent actions of the wife are more interesting than those undertaken with her husband. Some of the wife's roles are fairly predictable from her secular life, activities that connect her with the household and with housekeeping tasks. Actions like threshing and grinding the grain for the Iṣṭi[16] or fashioning a pot to hold the fire in the ritual of the Piling of the Fire Altar (*agnicayana*)[17] seem simply sacralized equivalents of real-life domestic duties—though other conceptual associations can also spill over onto these simple tasks. For example, since pots are often conceived of as surrogate wombs,[18] her shaping of the fire pot connects her to the fertility functions we will discuss below.

Let us also note her usual position on the demarcated place of the ritual, the ritual ground, a conceptually complex geography bounded especially by three functionally distinct sacred fires. The various parts of the ritual ground have rich symbolic associations, and moving from place to place in this little cosmos is as significant an action as pouring a libation or reciting a mantra. The "world" or place of the wife (*patnīloka*) is south-west of the so-called "Householder's Fire" (*gārhapatya*), which sits at the western end of the ritual ground. This is where she stays throughout the ritual except when she is led elsewhere to perform some specific task. Many of the actions performed with regard to her, or to female divinities, happen here at the Householder's

[15] By F. M. Smith, art. cit. (above, n. 11).

[16] Cf. e.g. MŚS I.1.2.4, 16; KŚS II.4.14; ĀpŚS I.7.10; I.20.12; 21.8-9; VārŚS I.2.4.49, 69.

[17] Cf. e.g. MŚS VI.1.2.4-12; ĀpŚS XVI.4.3.

[18] On this concept, see Jamison, *Hyenas* pp. 228-242.

Fire. This again links the wife clearly to the domestic and mundane sphere.

Most of the sacral activity occurs elsewhere, around the Offering Fire (*āhavanīya*) to the east. So, in one sense, the wife is physically marginalized in her "wife's world." But the "Householder's Fire" is not only the "home" of the wife; it is also the *homebase* of the whole ritual procedure: the male participants begin there, fare forth to the east for the crucial actions in the middle of the performance, but return to the west to wind down with a series of actions that in some ways reverse the opening activities. So, though not geographically central, the Householder's Fire and the wife anchor the sacrificer and the priests to the human world and provide a means of re-entry at the end of the ritual. The wife's function as linkage we will return to below.

Perhaps even more important than this linking of the mundane and the sacred is her role in injecting sexuality into the perfect, ordered world of the ritual. One of the abiding concerns of all Vedic rituals, no matter what else they are directed towards, is fertility, the increase of prosperity through the generation of offspring and cattle and the assurance of good pasturage and crops through abundant rain. This fertility, on whatever level, is often conceived of as sexual in nature, as resulting from sexual activity. Indeed, many other desirable events and states in the natural and social world, like the rising of the sun, are also considered to be the direct result of sexual activity. Now, for reasons I do not have space to detail here, I think we must see women as the primary locus of active sexuality in ancient India, and therefore they act as the conduit to introduce sexual energy into the potentially sterile world of the orderly ritual. Their very presence traps sexuality and its power for ritual use.

The exegetical texts explicitly state this rather tediously often. It is the only reason for women in ritual that they consistently recognize. Over and over it is repeated,

yad vai patnī yajñe karóti tan mithunam

What the wife does in ritual is sexual pairing.[19]

---

[19] MS III.7.9 (88: 6). Cf. MS III.8.7, IV.1.12; TS VI.2.1.2; TB III.3.4.2, etc., as well as the equivalent KS comment after describing an action of the wife:

Activities with the most banal and innocuous aspect, like the wife's looking at a pot of melted butter, can be exegetically tortured into bearing sexual meanings—giving one great respect for the ingenuity of the exegetes.

How is this injection of the wife's sexuality manifested ritually? There is a continuum from the most attenuated and subtle suggestions to the most dramatic displays. Let us begin with the subtle ones. Returning briefly to the wife's place on the western end of the ritual ground, we may note that, because of the east-facing Vedic spatial orientation, this western part of the territory is known as the "hind end" (*jaghana*) and is explicitly connected both with the female posterior and with sexuality and generation. The wife is then called the "hind end" of the ritual.[20]

There is also a ritual posture known as "taking hold of from behind" (*anvārambha*[*na*]). This involves touching someone or something from behind, either with the hand or with some intermediary material like a grass blade or even a meat-skewer, while the other person is performing some action like pouring an oblation. The purpose seems to be on the one hand to increase the power and effectiveness of the libation (or whatever) by making available to it the power of a second performer, who is linked to the first through physical contact. On the other hand, it also spreads the sacrality of the action or object back to those in contact with it.

Though in performance this posture is the special province of the sacrificer, the exegetical texts classify almost every action of the wife—looking at the melted butter, conversing with her husband—as mystically equivalent to "taking hold *of the ritual* from behind."[21] They then frequently liken her "taking hold of from behind" to sexual intercourse. In these cases, her sexual potential is clearly being both tapped and enhanced. On the one hand, her sexuality and fertility are being spread to the entire ritual by this theoretical contact. On the other,

---

atho mithunam eva yajñamukhe dadhāti prajananāya

Then he places sexual pairing in the mouth/front of the worship, for progeneration [KS XIV.8 (202: 7), XXIV.4, XXIV.8, XXV.8, XXXI.9].

[20] Cf. e.g. ŚB I.3.1.12, I.9.2.3, II.5.2.29, V.2.1.8.

[21] Cf. e.g. MS I.11.8 (169: 15), IV.1.12 (15: 7).

the power unleashed by the ritual because of *its* contact with the divine is spread back to her, to increase her generative capacity. Her various actions, however minor they may appear and however far from the center of ritual activity they may occur, are classified as physical contact—and not merely with one participant or object in the ritual, but with the very ritual itself. She encompasses the ritual in some sense whenever she performs the smallest sacral action. Thus, though she is physically marginalized during the ritual performance, her forces can be brought into contact with it, through this theoretical "touching from behind." Such reclassification of action is not made for any other participant.

More explicit reference to sexuality is found on the occasions when she ceremonially receives from her husband or a priest tokens with sexual symbolism—e.g. a broom, a bow, or a fire-drilling apparatus. Though these particular objects may not seem suggestive to us, they are culturally and religiously laden, and their symbolic burden is announced in the mantras that accompany the transfer. For example, at the end of the twice-monthly New and Full Moon Sacrifice, the broom that has been ritually employed is tossed into the wife's lap or put between her thighs, and it is said that she will give birth to a son.[22] The exegetical texts explicitly call the contact between wife and broom to a "procreative sexual pairing," since the wife is female, the broom male. In fact, certain aspects of the treatment of the broom show that it functions in the ritual as a surrogate husband.

Such are some of the *symbolic* representations of sexuality in Vedic ritual. We come now to the actual, the lurid, in fact to a ceremony so striking that it has become notorious even outside of this field (though not particularly far outside). It occurs in a royal ritual, the Horse Sacrifice (*aśvamedha*), which is performed for an already powerful king, to extend, consolidate, and display his power. In royal rituals the king is Sacrificer, and his wives act as *patnī*, particularly his chief queen, the *mahiṣī* or 'Great Female Buffalo.' At the climax of this lengthy and elaborate ritual (the preliminaries take a year), the chief queen copulates with the just slaughtered horse. Though she is covered by a linen garment, the texts leave no doubt as to what physically she is

---

[22] Cf. e.g. MŚS I.3.5.15-16; ĀpŚS III.10.3; BŚS III.30 (104:12); ŚŚS I.15.14; KB III.8.

supposed to do, and it is not merely symbolic. As she lies there, she mockingly slights the horse's sexual performance, and she and the lesser wives of the king engage in obscene banter with the priests, while hundreds of female attendants of the queens, their hair unbound, circle the horse and the unfortunate lady, singing, dancing, and slapping their thighs. The verbal part of the ceremony is so explicit that most translators omit it or take refuge in scholarly Latin.[23]

"Ribald dialogue" also takes place at the New Year's Ceremony at the end of a year-long ritual called the Progress of the Cows (*gavāmayana*). Here the dialogue is between a prostitute (*puṃścalī*) and a chaste student (*brahmacārin*), with some texts specifying ritual copulation between them as well.[24] Meanwhile the sacrificer's wives play flutes and lutes, and maid servants sing, dance, and slap their thighs as above.

In both cases it is hard not to see this showcasing of extreme public sexuality, not only physically enacted but verbally encoded, as an attempt to capture sexual power in order to enhance the ritual effect and to promote fertility. In fact, this aspect of the Horse Sacrifice has been so exhaustively discussed, by ancient commentators and modern ones, that I will not at present add further to it. However, I hope I have shown that rather than being the freakish and aberrant spectacle it is sometimes presented as, it is the logical, if extreme, fulfillment of women's ritual function.

Somewhat more difficult cases are presented by several examples of what, for want of a better term, I will call "negative sexuality," but here the same explanations can also prevail.

Let us begin with a curious incident in one of the yearly Seasonal Rituals (*cāturmāsyāni*), the Varuṇapraghāsa ('Devouring of Varuṇa'), which occurs at the beginning of the rainy season. At a point in the course of this ritual, the priest asks the wife either (depending on the text) "Who is your lover?" or "How many lovers do you have?"[25] She is supposed to name him or point to him or to hold up as many grass

---

[23] Cf. Eggeling (ŚB XIII.5.2.2ff.); Keith (TS VII.4.19 d-k); Griffith (VS XXIII.20-31); Caland (ĀpŚS XX.18.4).

[24] Cf. e.g. MŚS VII.2.7.13; KŚS XIII.3.6, 9; BŚS XVI.21 (267:10), 22 (268:10); ĀpŚS XXI.17.18, 19, 9.5, 6.

[25] Cf. e.g. MŚS I.7.4.11; ĀpŚS VIII.6.20 [=HirŚS V.2 (Einoo 106), BhārŚS VIII.9.4, VaikhŚS VIII.12]; BŚS V.7 (136:15); KŚS V.5.5; VārŚS I.7.2.27.

blades as she has lovers. After this confession, there is a brief expiation with a curse laid on the lover, and the ritual continues. Most people[26] who have discussed this episode see it as representing a need for confession and purification before embarking on important religious acts, an impulse that is nearly universal. No doubt there is something to this, as there is to the theory that it banishes evil from the ritual by scapegoating the lover.

But why does this happen only in this ritual? No similar interrogation and confession occurs elsewhere in the system. Why in the middle of the ritual, not the beginning? Would not the spiritual force of what went before be annulled because impurity had not yet been banished? And why is only the wife involved, when other participants should be equally pure to be effective? Moreover, no one seems to have commented on the presupposition at the heart of the question: the wife is presupposed to have a lover; she has no option to announce that she has none. But nothing in the legal system or in the narrative literature suggests that wifely unchastity was the norm.

All of this leads me to suppose that to serve ritual purposes she *needs* to have a lover—or at least the fiction of one. It seems to me possible that eminently respectable, middle-aged brahmin ladies "confessed" to lovers they did not have, for the sake of ritual effectiveness. Why? Perhaps because illicit sex may bring a bigger jolt of sexual energy into the arena than proper marital sexual conduct, and the wife, as locus of sexuality, was charged to provide this. (The student and the whore mentioned above function likewise.) A kind of "animal passion" outside of socially sanctioned norms is what's wanted, and I think it is no accident that the interrogation of the wife takes place at the ritual that ushers in the rainy season, which begins the cycle of fertility. Moreover, this question and answer session is embedded in the middle of another episode in that ritual, in which a pair of statuettes of ram and ewe, cunningly fashioned of barley meal with their sexual organs especially prominent, are offered. Animal passion indeed! Both the barley meal figurines and the wife with her quite possibly fictitious lover are tidy and controllable simulacra of rampant sexuality, in a yearly repeated ritual where the real thing, in the mode of the Horse

[26] Beginning with the exegetes themselves. Cf. e.g. MS I.10.11(151:3) [= KS XXXVI.6]; ŚB II.5.2.20.

Sacrifice, might be too much.

A mirror-image figure to the lady and her phantom lover is a wife who plays an important part in several royal rituals. Recall in our discussion of the Horse Sacrifice that, while the chief queen is under the linen with the horse, several other wives of the king stand by making dirty jokes. These subsidiary wives have other roles. In the ceremonies immediately preceding the sacrifice of the horse, they join the chief queen in anointing the horse and adorning it by weaving hundreds of beads into its hair. After it is killed and the copulation is over, they insert needles into the dead animal, to guide the paths of the knives in cutting up the victim.

One of these wives is the so-called Rejected or Avoided Wife (*parivṛktī*), one no longer favored by the king, perhaps because she has failed to bear a son.[27] The particular part of the horse she has charge of is the hind end, called by the same word as the wife's place in the ritual ground. This part, of course, contains the generative organs and is explicitly connected with sexuality. The Rejected Wife also appears in the ritual of the Consecration of the King (*rājasūya*): an offering is made in her house, one of a series performed in the dwellings of a set of important social figures known as the "Bejewelled" (*ratnin*). The Rejected Wife's oblation is dedicated to the Goddess of Disorder (Nirṛti) and consists of "black rice grains split by the (finger) nails."[28] It is perhaps not only to modern sensibilities that this conjures up a picture of a scarlet-nailed harpy, driven by jealous rage, systematically assassinating rice grains, one by one.

Why is such a presumably inauspicious person allotted important roles in rituals that affect not only the king but the security, power, and fertility of his kingdom? A person whose very title names her despised position. Is this simply a case of inviting the bad fairy to the feast, so she will not crash and spoil it? I think it is more than that—that, like the wife with the supposed lover, the Rejected Wife is a woman who lives outside of socio-sexual norms and who therefore has access to more charged sexual energy than others do. In her case, sexual frustration/rejection is felt to build up unreleased passion—to see that this is a

---

[27] So ŚB V.3.1.13.

[28] Cf. e.g. MŚS IX.1.1.36; BŚS XII.5 (92: 1); KŚS XV.3.14; MS IV.3.8; KS XV.4 (211:16); TB I.7.3.4; ŚB V.3.1.13.

widely held view we need look no further than modern models like the movie Fatal Attraction. This passion can be channelled into the ritual and utilized to increase the king's power. It is not surprising that the Rejected Wife is associated with the army in some texts: her sexual fury can be ritually transformed into martial fervor.

Let us now leave the sexual realm and turn to an area where the role of the wife seems to me at least as important, though not as explicitly recognized by contemporary exegetes. This is the area of hospitality and exchange relations—a crucial mechanism in ancient India, governing the relations between people (or rather, to be realistic, men) as well as those between the human and the divine, the living and the dead. Hospitality—its obligations and dangers—and gift exchange, the delicate negotiations involved in giving and receiving presents, are endlessly repeated themes throughout Indian literature and religious practise. Women figure prominently in both areas, as dispensers of hospitality on the one hand and, more important, as the ultimate exchange token in the most fundamental exchange relation, that of marriage. Needless to say, her importance in these areas is symbolically represented in the ritual, again in a continuum from subtle to dramatic. Many of her activities in these spheres are especially clearly highlighted in the most elaborate of the non-royal rituals, the Soma Sacrifice—a ritual in which the *plant* soma, made into the inspiriting *drink* soma, is both ceremonially received as king and god and then as ceremonially sacrificed. The complex of exchange relations in this ambivalent treatment of the central substance, soma, is reflected in the wife's several roles.

First let us note that when King Soma is ritually received as guest in the Hospitality Rite (*ātithya*), the wife—unusually—participates in the oblation, which is made through the medium of her hand.[29] (Most actual offering otherwise is done by a priest.) This rite is conducted exactly as if the dry bundle of sticks from the soma plant were an especially distinguished human visitor: he is brought in on a cart, solicitously taken down, offered a seat and comestibles. The wife's role is, in many ways, just a ritual enactment of household duty. The exegetical texts mention that she "has control of the household goods,"[30] and so her permission and participation in this guest reception is required.

[29] Cf. e.g. MŚS II.1.5.3; ĀpŚS X.30.6; MS III.7.9 (88: 5).
[30] MS III.7.9 (88:5); KS XXIV.8, TS VI.2.1.1.

The wife also has ritual dominion over the "Foot-washing water (*pannejanī*)." In the secular realm a major requirement for the reception of a guest is to provide him with water to wash his feet. The Soma Sacrifice also has foot-washing water, destined for the reception of the visiting gods or for washing the limbs of the dead animal victim subsidiarily sacrificed at this elaborate ritual. The foot-washing water marks not merely the gods but also the victim as a guest, and this water is in the wife's sole charge. She carries it wherever it needs to go on the ritual ground, and at the end of the pressing day, she places the pot between her thighs and pours some of the water along her thighs: an interesting yoking of her sexual and hospitable functions. This same linkage is played out elsewhere, in a number of narratives we cannot explore here.

Women's role as exchange token is quite remarkably enacted in the Soma ritual as well, but through such a series of transfers and representations that I think it has escaped notice before. The situation is this: before Soma the king can be received as a guest, Soma the plant must be purchased. The purchase is part of the ritual—even the bargaining is scripted—and the purchase price is a cow. Needless to say, given the elaboration of every other part of the procedure, the cow is not just produced and handed over. There is a series of actions that prepare her, too, for the exchange. These actions connect her both with the wife and with the sacrificer in a bizarre sort of switch.

On the one hand, the wife and the cow participate in two nearly simultaneous exchanges. They are made to look at each other, to exchange glances, and the wife is given the sand from the footprint of the cow, sand which she will later distribute ritually.[31] Though there is no physical contact by our standards, both gazes and footprints are symbolically charged in this culture, as has been amply demonstrated by others. Mutual gazes "count" as physical contact and are frequently used in ritual to transfer forces, as we saw above with the melted butter. Footprints are so representative of the person or animal that made them that they are objects of worship to this day.

What is even more interesting is the particular footprint from which the sand has been extracted. Just previously the priests have caused the

---

[31] Cf. e.g. BŚS VI.13 (169:19).

cow to take seven steps.[32] It is the footprint from the seventh step that provides the sand that the wife receives. What is the significance of this seventh step? Let us consider an important ritual belonging to the domestic sphere, the marriage ceremony. This ritual has a number of parts, but the climactic moment, the action after which the marriage is legally irrevocable, is the "Seven Steps," which the bride makes, led or accompanied by the groom.[33] So when the soma cow makes the seven steps, she becomes symbolically a bride; she *marries* the sacrificer. The exchange of the glances and of the sand between wife and cow simply cements their interchange of roles. Wife becomes cow, cow wife. Indeed, in at least one text the sacrificer addresses the cow with the same mantras the groom uses to the bride under the same circumstances at the wedding: "We have become companions at the seventh step."[34]

So the cow now represents the sacrificer's wife, and as soon as she does so, he sets out to *exchange* her for the soma plant that is to become successively Soma the king, honored guest, and Soma the drink, the sacrificial victim. The wife, both directly and in the guise of the cow, mediates between the sacrificer and his guest and the sacrificer and his victim.

We can also see this mediation in one last ritual task of the wife, the tending and preparation of the animal victim, once it has been sacrificed. In animal sacrifices all the principal actors stay strictly away from the actual killing of the animal; they physically remove themselves and turn their backs while someone else does the inauspicious deed. But once the animal is dead, it must be rearranged, cut up, cooked, and offered. In the first step of the process, when the fearful forces bound up in the killing have not yet been dissipated, the wife is led near, to bathe the animal and verbally reinvigorate it.[35] She touches the victim and is said in one text to "perform much that is dirty and ritually impure (*amedhya*)"[36]—while her husband, the sacrificer, remains unsullied. Remember also that in the Horse Sacrifice, when the time comes to cut up the animal, the wives (already overworked, as we have seen) prepare

[32] Cf. e.g. BŚS VI.12, 13 (169:15).
[33] Cf. e.g. ŚGS I.14.5.
[34] Cf. ĀpŚS X.23.1.
[35] Cf. e.g. MŚS I.8.4.4; ĀpŚS VII.18.6-7; BŚS IV.6 (118: 12); KŚS VI.6.2; VārŚS I.6.5.14-15.
[36] MS III.10.1 (128: 8).

the paths of the knives to cut up the victim.

In both these instances the sacrificer's wife, by touching the dead animal, creates the necessary contact between the human and the divine realms, between the living and the dead, that is a major aim of the sacrifice. She gains access to powerful and dangerous forces unleashed by the killing and can direct them to her husband and the success of his ritual, without his putting himself at risk. The husband himself never touches the animal; even when it was still alive, he made contact only by touching it from behind with a meat skewer.[37] The wife's general role in the mundane world as mediator, as central token in the system of exchanges, allows her to perform this same function in the ritual realm.

In this brief and rather breathless tour of the most striking of the wife's ritual activities, I have tried to unify under a few conceptual rubrics the varied and often bizarre-seeming tasks she is called upon to perform. I have not been able to touch on them all, or to explore the often telling variations from text to text—nor have I done any justice to what must have been her main *experience* of ritual, hours and days of extreme tedium sitting quietly in her *patnīloka* while the priests muttered, chanted, and poured, with this tedium broken only by her being led off to perform some peculiar and often humiliating task at the margins of the action. Nonetheless, I hope to have demonstrated the ideological importance of the wife in Śrauta ritual and the value of this evidence for a general understanding of the roles of women in ancient India.

[37] Cf. e.g. BŚS IV.6 (117:11); ĀpŚS VII.15.7.

BIBLIOGRAPHY: SECONDARY LITERATURE

Caland,W. 1928. *Das Śrautasūtra des Āpastamba*,Vol. III.

Caland, W. and V. Henry. 1906. *L'Agniṣṭoma.*

Chaudhuri, J. B. 1940. "The wife in the Vedic ritual," *IHQ* 16, pp. 70-98.

Eggeling, J. 1900. *The Śatapatha-Brāhmaṇa*, Part V (SBE 44).

Einoo, S. 1988. *Die Cāturmāsya.*

Griffith, R. T. H. 1899 (3rd ed. 1957). *The texts of the White Yajurveda* [=VS] *translated with a popular commentary.*

Hillebrandt, A. 1879. *Das altindische Neu- und Vollmondsopfer.*

____. 1897. *Ritual-litteratur: Vedische Opfer und Zauber.*

Hopkins, E. W. 1889. "The social and military position of the ruling caste in ancient India, as represented by the Sanskrit epic," *JAOS* 13.

Hubert, H. and M. Mauss. 1964 (translation of 1898 text). *Sacrifice: Its nature and function* (transl. W. D. Hall).

Jamison, S. W. 1991. *The ravenous hyenas and the wounded sun: Myth and ritual in ancient India.*

____. 1996. *Sacrificed Wife/Sacrificer's Wife: Women, Ritual, and Hospitality in Ancient India.*

Kane, P. V. 1974. *History of Dharmaśāstra* Vol. II,

Part 2. (2nd ed.)

Keith, A. B. 1914. *The Veda of the Black Yajus School Entitled Taittiriya Sanhita*, Part II.

Lṝvi, S. 1898 (2nd ed. 1966). *La doctrine du sacrifice dans les Brahmanas.*

F. M. Smith. 1991. "Indra's Curse, Varuṇa's Noose, and the Suppression of Women in Vedic *Śrauta* Ritual," in *Roles and Rituals for Hindu Women* (ed. J. Leslie), pp. 17-45.

Winternitz, M. 1920. *Die Frau in den indischen Religionen. Teil I Die Frau im Brahmanismus.*

PRIMARY SOURCES: TEXTUAL ABBREVIATIONS

ĀpDS	Āpastamba Dharma Sūtra
ĀpŚS	Āpastamba Śrauta Sūtra
BhārŚS	Bhāradvāja Śrauta Sūtra
BŚS	Baudhāyana Śrauta Sūtra
HirŚS	Hiraṇyakeśi Śrauta Sūtra
KB	Kauṣītaki Brāhmaṇa
KS	Kāṭhaka Saṃhitā
KŚS	Kātyāyana Śrauta Sūtra
MS	Maitrāyaṇī Saṃhitā
MŚS	Mānava Śrauta Sūtra
ŚB	Śatapatha Brāhmaṇa
ŚGS	Śāṅkhāyana Gṛhya Sūtra
ŚŚS	Śāṅkhāyana Śrauta Sūtra
TB	Taittirīya Brāhmaṇa
TS	Taittirīya Saṃhitā
VaikhŚS	Vaikhānasa Śrauta Sūtra
VārŚS	Vārāha Śrauta Sūtra
VS	Vājasaneyi Saṃhitā

CHAPTER TWO

TIBETAN FAIRY GLIMMERINGS: *ḌĀKINĪS* IN BUDDHIST SPIRITUAL BIOGRAPHY

VICTORIA KENNICK URUBSHUROW

I. *Fairies: West and East*[1]

Who are the fairies? What is their nature? And what might be the measure of their relationship with us? To obtain a glimmer of understanding on these points it is useful to approach the Tibetan Buddhist tradition that devotes a slice of its world view to one type of these subtle feminine presences. But before turning from home base in search of such beings, let us hear an account from a well-respected Irish man. It may suggest that what is still alive among Tibetans may not be too long-gone in the so-called "west" for those with a little imagination.

William Butler Yeats (1865-1939) yearned to encounter and comprehend the ways of the Good People, the Forgetful People, the Sidhe—that is the fairies. He befriended old Irish peasants and visionaries to inquire after them. Yeats wrote of an encounter in which he made personal contact with a woman he called the "queen of the little people." What follows is Yeats' account from *The Celtic Twilight* (1893) entitled "Regina, Regina Pigmorum, Veni":[2]

> One night a middle-aged man, who had lived all his life far from the noise of cab-wheels, a young girl, a relation of his, who was reported to be

---

[1] This essay is based upon a presentation made by the author at the Smithsonian Institution, Washington, DC on April 30, 1994 in a course entitled "The Goddess in Myth and Religion."

[2] Yeats adds in 1924 a note indicating that these words were "used as an evocation in Windsor Forest by Lilly, the astrologer." William Butler Yeats, *Mythologies* (New York: Macmillan, Collier Books, 1969 (c. 1959)), p. 54. The passage contains two footnotes, marked here by asterisks. See note 3 below for their content.

enough of a seeress to catch a glimpse of unaccountable lights moving over the fields among the cattle, and myself were walking along a far western sandy shore. We talked of the Forgetful People, as the faery people are sometimes called, and came in the midst of our talk to a notable haunt of theirs, a shallow cave amidst black rocks, with its reflection under it in the wet sea sand. I asked the young girl if she could see anything, for I had quite a number of things to ask the Forgetful People. She stood still for a few minutes, and I saw that she was passing into a kind of waking trance, in which the cold sea breeze no longer troubled her, nor the dull boom of the sea distracted her attention. I then called aloud the names of the great faeries, and in a moment or two she said that she could hear music far inside the rocks, and then a sound of confused talking, and of people stamping their feet as if to applaud some unseen performer. Up to this my other friend had been walking to and fro some yards off, but now he passed close to us, and as he did so said suddenly that we were going to be interrupted, for he heard the laughter of children somewhere beyond the rocks. We were, however, quite alone. The spirits of the place had begun to cast their influence over him also. In a moment he was corroborated by the girl, who said that bursts of laughter had begun to mingle with the music, the confused talking, and the noise of feet. She next saw a bright light streaming out of the cave, which seemed to have grown much deeper, and a quantity of little people,* in various coloured dresses, red predominating, dancing to a tune which she did not recognise.

I then bade her call out to the queen of the little people to come and talk with us. There was, however, no answer to her command. I therefore repeated the words aloud myself, and in a moment she described a very beautiful tall woman, who came out of the cave. I too had by this time fallen into a kind of trance,** in which what we call the unreal had begun to take upon itself a masterful reality, and I had an impression, not anything I could call an actual vision, of gold ornaments and dark hair. I then bade the girl tell this tall queen to marshal her followers according to their natural divisions, that we might see them. I found as before that I had to repeat the command myself. The beings then came out of the cave, and drew themselves up, if I remember rightly, in four bands. One of these bands, according to her description, carried boughs of mountain-ash in their hands, and another had necklaces made apparently of serpents' scales, but their dress I cannot remember. I asked their queen to tell the seeress whether these caves were the greatest faery haunts in the neighborhood. Her lips moved, but the answer was inaudible. I bade the seeress lay her hand upon the breast of the queen, and after that she heard every word quite distinctly. No, this was not the greatest faery haunt, for there was a greater one a little farther ahead. I then asked her whether it was true that she and her people carried away mortals, and if so, whether they put another soul in the place of the one they had taken. 'We change

> the bodies,' was her answer. 'Are any of you ever born into mortal life?' 'Yes.' 'Do I know any who were among your people before birth?' 'You do.' 'Who are they?' 'It would not be lawful for you to know.' I then asked whether she and her people were not 'dramatisations of our moods'? 'She does not understand,' said my friend, 'but says that her people are much like human beings, and do most of the things human beings do.' I asked her other questions, as to her nature, and her purpose in the universe, but only seemed to puzzle her. At last she appeared to lose patience, for she wrote this message for me upon the sands—the sands of vision—'Be careful, and do not seek to know too much about us.' Seeing that I had offended her, I thanked her for what she had shown and told, and let her depart again into her cave. In a little while the young girl awoke out of her trance, and felt the cold wind from the sea, and began to shiver.[3]

"Be careful, and do not seek to know too much about us," said the glamourous—a word favored by Yeats—lady from the cave. Now, if we take this dictum inscribed on the sands of Yeat's vision to heart we find ourselves in an awkward position. With Yeats we wish to ask precisely the kind of questions that seemed to puzzle and offend the queen of the little people—questions as to the nature of fairies, their purpose in the universe, and so on. But we are human, and it is our nature to make such inquiry. So we shall proceed—hopefully in a manner that both respects the integrity of such feminine presences, and fulfills our native sense of wonder and desire to know.

Fairy lore in European-based cultures has been relegated largely to legends and traditions. "[I]n spite of the fact that in English we are likely to speak of all tales of wonder as fairy tales, the truth is that

---

[3] Ibid., pp. 54-56. The notes read as follow:

* "The people and faeries in Ireland are sometimes as big as we are, sometimes, bigger, and sometimes, as I have been told, about three feet high. The old Mayo woman I so often quote thinks that it is something in our eyes that makes them seem big or little."

** "The word 'trance' gives a wrong impression. I had learned from MacGregor Mathers and his pupils to so suspend the will that the imagination moved of itself. The girl was, however, fully entranced, and the man so affected by her that he heard the children's voices as if with his physical ears. On two occasions, later on, her trance so affected me that I also heard or saw some part of what she did as if with physical eyes and ears." (1924)

fairies appear rarely in such stories."[4] Speaking of the belief in marvelous creatures, Stith Thompson noted nearly a half century ago that "[o]ne of the most widely accepted of all such beliefs, particularly in the countries of western Europe, concerns fairies."[5] Yet, few people of "western" culture take the fairies seriously any more; and written accounts of them remain meager. The esoteric work of Yeats might inspire a glimmer of curiosity; and perhaps the fairy queen Titania in Shakespeare's *A Midsummer Night's Dream* fleetingly awakens childlike wonder. Yet, the day when fairies are counted as vital beings in our culture apparently is nowhere afoot. On the other hand, Tibetan Buddhist tantric literature[6] for centuries has presented earnest accounts of ethereal female beings. They are considered to be enlightened compilers of tantric teachings, and are thought to assist adepts with their spiritual practice. Looking into the lives of Indo-Tibetan Buddhist adepts we encounter an awesome slice of the universe inhabited by fairies known as "sky dancers" (S: *ḍākinī*; T: *mkha'gro ma*).[7] For example, *ḍākinīs* figure prominently in

[4] Stith Thompson, *The Folktale* (Berkeley, CA: University of California Press, 1977; copyright 1946), p. 49. Thompson goes on to say, "Occasionally in some literary reworking of a tale, one hears of a fairy godmother, but most accounts of fairies appear as legends or traditions." [Ibid.]

[5] Ibid., p. 246.

[6] Tantra is a subdivision of the Tibetan Mahayana Buddhist tradition. The spiritual biographies treated in this essay are associated with the class of tantra known as "highest yoga tantra," (S: *anuttarayogatantra*; T: *bla med kyi rgyud*).* This class of *tantra* involves the practice of moving subtle winds into the central channel of the subtle body in meditation. See *Ḍākinī as Subtle Wind* below. For a succinct description of the relationship between *tantra* and Tibetan Buddhist meditation see Jeffrey Hopkins, *Meditation on Emptiness* (London: Wisdom, 1983), pp. 111-115.

* Parenthetical terms in Sanskrit and Tibetan are preceeded by an "S:" or a "T:". Although the subject of this essay is Tibetan literature, Sanskrit terms are used more often because they are relatively better known to the public. Diacritical marks have been omitted.

[7] Before proceeding with an analysis of the nature and function of the *ḍākinī* in Tibetan spiritual biography, it is important to note that not all extraordinary manifestations of feminine energy are equivalent: some are beneficent and some are malevolent; some are more powerful than others, and so on. Tibetan tradition takes account of both positive and negative feminine manifestations called *ḍākinī* and *ma mo* respectively. [Klong chen rab 'byams pa, *Kindly Bent to Ease Us, Part two: Meditation*, Herbert V. Guenther, (trans.) (Emeryville, CA: Dharma Publishing, 1976), p. 99, n. 9.]

Among the *ḍākinīs* or beneficent forces two types are acknowledged in Tibetan

the life stories of Yeshe Tsogyel (757-817), Naropa (1016-1100), and Milarepa (1040-1123) who stand as models of spiritual accomplishment for Tibetan Buddhists to this day.[8]

Stith Thompson astutely noted that "an accurate translation of folk tradition from one [country to another] is all but impossible" due to the variance and "shading off" of concepts.[9] Yet, despite a wide range of inconstant characteristics attributed to fairies across cultures, legends and traditions of the west may be enlivened by reading many Tibetan Buddhist life stories in which fairies play a significant role and have not degenerated into mere entertainment and heresay. Looking into a living tradition in which fairies play a prominent role provides clues as to their nature and function.[10] In the Tibetan

---

religious life—transcendental and worldly. The transcendental *ḍākinīs* are considered to be "fully enlightened Buddhas manifesting in female form;" while the worldly *ḍākinīs* "are not spiritually superior to ordinary sentient beings." [Garma C. Chang, (trans.) *The Hundred Thousand Songs of Milarepa*, 2 vols. (Seacaucus, NJ: University Books, 1962), p. 331, n. 8.] Vajra Yogini (T: *rdo rje rnal 'byor ma*), whose encounters with Yeshe Tsogyel and Naropa are discussed in this essay, typically is considered to be of the transcendental type. Often *ḍākinīs* appearing in the biographies are not named; and the category into which they fall must be interpreted by context. In general, the *ḍākinīs* are "in constant attendance upon the yogin." They function "to instruct and bring the highest bliss to the Guru [yogin]. [Keith Dowman, (trans.), *The Legend of the Great Stūpa and The Life Story of the Lotus Born Guru* (Emeryville, CA: Dharma Press, 1973), p. 123.] In a commentary on the origins of the Tibetan Buddhist teachings, Geshe Wangyal defines *ḍākinīs* as "[f]emale enlightened beings who assist others in their practice," and notes that "[t]he Mahayana teachings of secret mantra (*tantrayana*) were compiled by Vajrapani and the dakinis." [Geshe Wangyal, *The Jewelled Staircase* (Ithaca, NY: Snow Lion, 1986), pp. 165, 47.]

[8] Yeshe Tsogyel was an advanced meditator and consort of Padmasaṃbhava, founder of the Nyingma sect of Tibetan Buddhism. Naropa was a Bengali pandit-turned-yogi from whom the Kagyu sect of Tibetan Buddhism springs. Milarepa, a disciple of Marpa the translator who studied with Naropa, extended the Kagyu lineage through his songs. The biographical materials upon which this essay is based include: Keith Dowman, (trans.), *Sky Dancer: The Secret Life and Songs of the Lady Yeshe Tsogyel* (London: Routledge & Kegan Paul, 1984), p. 65. The original text was composed by Stag sam Nus ldan rdo rje, b. 1655.) Herbert V. Guenther, (trans.), *The Life and Teaching of Naropa*, (Oxford: Oxford University Press, 1963). The original text was written by lHa'i btsun pa Rin chen rnam rgyal of Brag dkar in the twelfth century. Lobsang P. Lhalungpa (trans.), *The Life of Milarepa* (New York: E. P. Dutton, 1977). The original was written by Gtsang smyon Heruka (1452-1507).

[9] Thompson, *Folktale*, p. 247.

[10] While not all characteristics of fairies noted by Stith Thompson fully accord with the accounts examined in this essay, two points are well-supported in the Tibetan

Buddhist tradition, *ḍākinīs* have an ambivalent nature, appearing to be subjective or objective phenomena depending upon what aspect of religious experience is highlighted. The function of *dākinīs* is to promote spiritual transformation of Tantric adepts by purifying their mind/body continuum, inspiring religious practice, and demonstrating the synchronous nature of the world. The life stories of Yeshe Tsogyel, Milarepa, and Naropa (to which we now turn) suggest that without the fairies, human life is deprived of an edifying dimension of experience.

II. Ḍākinī *as Subtle Wind*

Tibetan spiritual biographies known as tales of liberation (T: *rnam par thar pa*) refer often to feminine beings who "dance in the sky" in connection with the practice of Tantric yoga. This yoga involves meditation on a subtle body comprised of three major channels (S: *nāḍi*; T: *rtsa*) located along the spinal column in a form resembling the caduceus of Hermes, and several energy centers (S: *cakra*; T: *'khor lo*) situated at the gut, heart, throat, and brow-point).[11] In meditation tantric adepts gather their wind energy (S: *prāṇa*; T: *rlung*) into the central channel. The wind moves up the central channel, gradually opening the energy centers along the way. The practice involves a reciprocal relationship between mind and body: mind moves wind and wind effects a state of mind. The opening of each energy center is correlated with a particular type of experience. For example, when Milarepa opened or untied the knot at his throat

---

Buddhist materials: (a) "the fairies are usually thought of as living in a land of their own," and (b) "[f]airies are normally invisible to the generality of men." [Ibid., p. 247.] Thompson further notes that "The dealings of fairies with mortals are sometimes advantageous to people, but they are nearly always fraught with danger." [Ibid., p. 248.] In the Tibetan Buddhist tantric literature, *ḍākinīs* can take on a frightening appearance, but the type with which the *yogis* and *yoginīs* sport are not portrayed as harmful to human beings. They are considered to be helpful beings—though dealing with them is not for the fainthearted.

[11] Sometimes the crown of the head is mentioned, and the gut is omitted if the centers are enumerated as a customary four. Hindu tantra enumerates seven energy centers including two at the base of the spine, at positions roughly corresponding to the anus and genital organ. On the Tantric use of the centers, channels, and winds see Kelsang Gyatso, *Clear Light of Bliss: Mahāmudrā in Vajrayāna Buddhism*, trans. Tenzin Norbu, ed. Jonathan Landaw (London: Wisdom Publications, 1982), pp. 17-66.

center, he could sing energetic and compelling songs. When the winds enter fully into the heart center, the yogi's mind of clear light directly cognizes emptiness, which is profound wisdom according to Buddhist theory.

The Tibetan tales of liberation show that the appearance of *ḍākinīs* is correlated with purification of the flow of energy through the central channel: Yeshe Tsogyel perceived her "psychic nerves and energy flows as the *Ḍākinī's maṇḍala* [or microcosm],"[12] and saw numerous *ḍākinīs* in the conjugal *yab yum* (male-female) configuration, manifesting in white at her forehead, yellow at her throat, blue-black at her heart, and red at her gut.[13] When Milarepa had trouble controlling the movement of his subtle wind, *ḍākinīs* demonstrated remedial yoga postures. Assuming the postures, he gained "mental harmony through the vital powers of the self-releasing snake's coil" as wind ascended his central channel.[14] The vital heat (T: *gtu mo*) produced from the navel center in tantric meditation spread through his body, giving vocal energy control as wind reached the throat center. In gratitude to Lama Marpa and the *ḍākinīs*, Milarepa sang:

> ...I invoked my lama with great concentration, and one night I perceived, in an inner state of lucidity (T: *od gsal gyi nyams snang*), a multitide of women officiating at a sacrificial feast, who surrounded me and said, "Marpa has sent us to tell you that if you do not feel the Fire of Tummo, you may use these methods of body, speech, and mind until the blissful warmth arises within you."[15]

Another time, when Milarepa was fasting the *ḍākinīs* brought food from their "house of heaven" by opening a cloud gate and riding the

---

[12] In his commentary on the biography of Yeshe Tsogyel, Dowman notes that "besides the common definitions of *maṇḍala* [T: *dKyil 'khor*]—(1) a simple symmetrical *yantra*; (2) an external, symbolical, ideal representation of the mind; (3) an internal, visualised place with principal deity and retinue—*maṇḍala* can also denote: (4) the body-mind or the Guru or *Dākinī*, etc.; (5) the female organ (*bhaga*); (6) an offering plate; (7) a globe, sphere or disc. The defining characteristics of a *maṇḍala* are its centre and circumference." [Dowman, *Sky Dancer*, p. 190.]

[13] Ibid., pp. 40-41. According to Dowman, "The Dakini is understood as structural patterns of energy (*rtsa*), the dynamic energies that play within that structure (*rlung*), and ultimate non-dual awareness (*thig-le*)." [Ibid., p. 200, n. 1.]

[14] Lhalungpa, *Life of Milarepa*, p. 117.

[15] Ibid.

sun's rays down to him. After stabilizing his mind, "five bewitchingly lovely maidens" circumambulated and offered Milarepa a blue gem spoon filled with yogurt of wild ox-milk. The yogi thought, "I have never seen such a precious and unique spoon, nor is there in the world any food comparable to this wonderful yogurt!"[16] The *ḍākinīs* told Milarepa of the Blue Queen Snow Mountain from whence they came.

> On the right side of this valley,
> Fashioned like a triangle,
> Stands a high snow mountain.
> On the summit of the central peak we dwell.
> The crowning ornament of our house
> Is a crystal-like ice-mirror
> Reflecting rays of sun and moon...
> This is Blue Queen Snow Mountain,
> The famous place, our home.[17]

The song of these *ḍākinīs* carries double meaning as it refers both to their home and to an inner geography which is the subtle body of the yogi.[18] The high snow mountain is Milarepa's subtle body which

---

[16] Chang, *Songs of Milarepa*, p. 313; 331 n. 3.

[17] Ibid., p. 318.

[18] The speech of *ḍākinīs* is known in the tantric tradition as "twilight language" (S: *sandhyābhāṣā*). For a better sense of the inner/outer dialectic revealed through twilight language see the first two chapters Dowman's commentary in *Sky Dancer*, "The Path of Inner Tantra," and "Woman and *Ḍākinī*." Dowman notes the difficulty of translating such language in the biography of Yeshe Tsogyel.

> "Another problem in the translation of *The Life* has been to maintain the ambiguity of twilight language (*sandhyābhāṣā*). For instance, when sexual union and mystical union are implied by the same words the translation must not stress one level at the expense of the other; it must contain the same potential for multi-levelled interpretation as the original." [Dowman, *Sky Dancer*, p. xviii.]

The tradition of twilight language is present among the "Eighty-Four Siddhas" of Indian Tantric yoga. For example, Karma Phrin las pa (fifteenth century) tells of an arrowsmith woman to whom the yogi Saraha exclaimed, "'You are not an ordinary arrowsmith woman; you are a teacher of symbols.'" The exclamation itself plays on a double meaning of the sound of the aurally identical words for "female arrowsmith" (T: *mda' mkhan_ma*) and "woman well versed in symbols" (T: *brda mkhan ma*). Further, according to Herbert V. Guenther, "symbol terms...must not be confused with the connotations these words have in ordinary language." Guenther, (trans.), *The Royal Song of Saraha: A Study in the History of Buddhist Thought* (Berkeley, CA: Shambhala, 1973), p. 6.

mystically interpenetrates the "famous place" of the *ḍākinīs*. The ox-milk yogurt ladled from a blue gem spoon is the nectar of blissful meditation, drunk by Milarepa as the subtle wind coursed freely through his central channel.[19]

Ḍākinīs also sustained Yeshe Tsogyel in periods of fasting. For one year the *yoginī* "had nothing to eat, not even a single grain of barley; for food [she] relied upon stones and for drink upon water." At the point of near starvation she prayed to her teacher and "visualised an unbroken stream of offerings to the *Ḍākinī*."[20] Yeshe Tsogyel tells how one *ḍākinī* came to help in response to her petition:

> Then I had a vision of a red woman, naked, lacking even the covering of bone ornaments, who thrust her *bhaga* against my mouth, and I drank deeply from her copious flow of blood. My entire being was filled with health and well-being, I felt as strong as a snow-lion, and I realised profound absorption to be inexpressible truth.[21]

Thereafter the *yoginī* practiced meditation for another year, sustaining herself on air alone. She incurred terrible pains and physical hardship as a result. Padmasaṃbhava came to her in a vision to lend this advice:

> You are too repressed and too fervent in your practice. You should use essential elixirs of herbs and shrubs to cultivate the play of your intelligence and restore your body to health.[22]

Following the teacher's precept, Yeshe Tsogyel began to extract and imbibe the essences of certain medicinal herbs, shrubs, and minerals

---

[19] Once when the disciple Gampopa had a vision of nectar raining down but found himself unable to drink, Milarepa explained:

> "The raining down of the nectar was due to the Tig Le (Bindu)[drop] increasing in the Right and Left channels (Roma and Jhunma) at the Throat Center. Your inability to drink the nectar was because your Central Channel has not yet opened." [Chang, *Songs of Milarepa*, p. 478.]

After months of tantric practice Gampopa succeeded in untying the knots and clearing the channels of his subtle body. His whole body then appeared to be full of sentient beings, some of whom were drinking milk drawn from stars. Milarepa noted Gampopa's success in "driv[ing] all the Tig Le into the hundreds of thousands of Nadis [channels] throughout [his] entire body." [Ibid., p. 479]

[20] Dowman, *Sky Dancer*, p. 71.

[21] Ibid.

[22] Ibid., p. 73.

to transform her body into a *vajra* or diamond body. *Ḍākinīs* were involved in this alchemical (S: *rasāyana*; T: *bcud led mdzad pa*) "extraction of essence or nectar" which promoted synergistic reactions in the *yoginī*. The process involved both gross and subtle aspects of the substances in conjunction with gross and subtle aspects of Yeshe Tsogyel's body. Thus, the medicinal regimen was "both chemical and metaphysical, although...no distinction is made between the two in '*Dākinī* talk'."[23]

The *ḍākinīs* appearing in conjunction with the movement of subtle winds in the meditations of Yeshe Tsogyel and Milarepa have a psycho-physical nature; and they function to purify the adepts' mind/body continuum. The *ḍākinīs* facilitate the gathering of subtle wind into the central channel, and thus promote the subtle mind of clear light that cognizes emptiness.

III. Ḍākinī *as Inspiration*

Ḍākinīs often appear to tantric adepts decked in bright, colorful brocades with ornaments and streamers of light. For instance, Milarepa dreamed of "a green girl with golden hair and shining eyebrows,"[24] or again, saw a group of *ḍākinīs* who wore "splendid silk garments which fluttered lightly in the breeze, and [were] adorned with jeweled bracelets, necklaces, and various other ornaments of precious stones."[25] The luminous nature of *ḍākinīs* is evident also in Padmasaṃbhava's instruction on prayer to one's spiritual teacher (S: *guru yoga*), which includes sitting "[i]n the midst of shimmering *Ḍākinīs* of five-fold rainbow light, [s]hining, glowing, clear as the light of the mind." Moreover, at the time of Padmasaṃbhava's passing away numerous *ḍākinīs* (along with their male counterparts or *ḍākas*—about whom little is said in these texts) appeared "making music and song, carrying canopies [and] victory banners."[26] These magnificent-looking *ḍākinīs* generally appear in

---

[23] Ibid., p. 201, n. 13.
[24] Chang, *Songs of Milarepa*, p. 159.
[25] Ibid., p. 323.
[26] Dowman, *Sky Dancer*, pp. 129, 131.

conjunction with successful meditation practice. They inspire further practice through pleasant encouragement.

Although their form is often beautiful and efflorescent, *ḍākinīs* also assume fierce, ugly forms. In their wrathful aspect the *ḍākinīs* are particularly effective in testing an adept's understanding and providing inspirational shocks. Once when Milarepa was deep in meditation, five maidens came "clad in shrouds of light" riding on their "horses"—glittering rays of crystal-pure moonlight. Seeing this, the yogi was "undistracted for even a single moment." He then recognized them as the same *ḍākinīs* who, some months before, had caused armies of demons to try to "harm [him] in all sorts of ways" with their missiles.[27] At that time Milarepa generated compassion for the demons, knowing that harmful acts carry suffering in their wake. Impressed with the yogi's ability to turn hardship into an occasion for the practice of virtue, the *ḍākinīs* came back to request teachings related to Milarepa's conquest of anger and impatience. They explained:

> As to our demonstration of malignant and wrathful forms before you a while ago, it was to make a crucial test of your realization. Since we are protectors of Dharma, we would not do anything truly harmful to people. But now we pray you to give us the [Precept] for raising the Bodhi-Mind [of compassion].[28]

Whereas *ḍākinīs* rode their "horses" of crystal moonlight to visit Milarepa as he sat in meditation near a river bank in the land of Tibet, Yeshe Tsogyel went in meditation to visit the *ḍākinīs* in their own land. Once in "a vivid vision of radiant light," the *yoginī* found herself in a fearsome place called Orgyen Khandro Ling, the Land of the *Ḍākinīs*:

> In this land the fruit trees were like razors, the ground was plastered with meat, the mountains were bristling piles of skeletons, and the clods of earth and stone were scattered fragments of bone. In the centre of this *maṇḍala* [microcosm] was an immeasurable palace built of skulls and wet and dry heads, and the ceilings and door-blinds were made of human skin.[29]

---

[27] Chang, *Songs of Milarepa*, pp. 319-20.
[28] Ibid., p. 322.
[29] Dowman, *Sky Dancer*, pp. 65-66.

Yeshe Tsogyel went into the palace and "found many *ḍākinīs* in human form, carrying various offerings to [Vajra Yogini] the principal *ḍākinī*," including shreds of their own flesh, blood from their veins, their eyeballs, noses, tongues, ears, hearts, and lungs. She asked the *ḍākinīs* why they were pursuing such pain; and they replied, "Procrastinating [in religious practice], merit is lost—[d]elay, and hindrances and obstacles multiply."[30] Moved by the immediacy of this lurid display, Yeshe Tsogyel generated a wish "to practice something of that kind of austerity." Hearing of this, Padmasaṃbhava advised:

> All that was only symbolic vision....It is not necessary for you now to make an actual offering of the flesh. Better than that, practice [the eight] austerities [of diet, dress, speech, body, mind, teaching, compassion, and benevolence].[31]

Yeshe Tsogyel's encounter in the Land of the *Ḍākinīs*, and her vision of Vajra Yogini standing at the center of the palace *maṇḍala* "in a blaze of light so intense that is was almost unbearable to gaze upon,"[32] inspired an intensive practice of the eight austerities. Eventually she developed compassion enough to emulate the *ḍākinīs* directly by cutting off her knee caps to help a man in need.[33]

Pandit Naropa encountered the fearsome aspect of the *ḍākinī* right in his office at Nalanda University in north India. One day as Naropa was absorbed in academic study with his back to the sun, the "terrifying shadow" of a hag fell upon his books. She was a manifestation of Vajra Yoginī who came to exhort the scholar to attain highest enlightenment and to spread the "intrinsic message of

---

[30] Ibid., p. 66.

[31] Ibid., p. 67. Padmasaṃbhava does not belittle Yeshe Tsogyel's experience by calling it symbolic. His reference to "symbolic vision" does not indicate that the *yoginī's* encounter with *ḍākinīs* is fictive, as the *ḍākinīs* are taken with full seriousness in the "tale of liberation" genre. *Ḍākinī* talk and action is *normally* symbolic with a double meaning structure (see note 18 above). Here, Padmasaṃbhava helps Yeshe Tsogyel to interpret her *ḍākinī* encounter at the appropriate level of meaning. He realizes that the *ḍākinīs* are teaching Yeshe Tsogyel to practice giving and effort on the spritual path, and counsels her on the suitable means of doing so for that time and circumstance. As her practice of compassion deepened Yeshe Tsogyel apparently reinterpreted the "symbolic vision" when she cut off her kneecaps to help someone.

[32] Ibid., p. 67.

[33] Ibid., p. 136.

the Doctrine."[34] In standard Tibetan iconography depicting her visionary subtle form (S: *saṃbhogakāya*), Vajra Yoginī carries a hooked knife in her right hand, and a skull cap in her left. To Naropa, she appeared as a grotesque human lady who was lame and hump-backed with "red and deep-hollowed" eyes, "disheveled" hair, a "large and protruding" forehead, "long and lumpy" ears, a "yellow beard streaked with white," and decayed teeth in her sucking, chewing, panting mouth.[35] The hag demanded an honest evaluation of his study; and Naropa realized that his intellect was too dry. He asked to be put in touch with someone who understood the sense—not just the words—of his books. The hag sent him to search for her brother, and disappeared like a rainbow.

Alone again, Naropa mulled over the details of her grotesque form, recalling thirty-seven kinds of dissatisfaction causing the misery of cyclic existence (S: *saṃsāra*), thirty-seven impure substances that comprise the perishable body, and thirty-seven pathways of the subtle body that promote spontaneous awareness of the co-emergence of appearance and reality (S: *sahajajñāna*).[36] Sensing the depth of his encounter, Naropa was deeply moved, and resolved to find the hag's brother. He gave up the academic post at Nalanda, and set out on a harrowing journey, which culminated in full Buddhist realization under the guidance of *guru* Tilopa.

The *ḍākinīs* function to inspire religious practice. They appear in magnificent displays to enhance the luminous grandeur of tantric meditations. They appear in maleficent displays to test the mettle of tantric adepts and remove obstacles to religious practice. Serving in this inspirational capacity, the "objective"—or at least semi-autonomous—nature of the *ḍākinīs* is highlighted, as they appear in their own land or surprise the tantric adepts with a visit.

IV. Ḍākinī *as Psychological Archetype*

The *ḍākinī* who paid Naropa a surprise visit in the form of a hag is

---

[34] Guenther, *Life and Teaching of Naropa*, p. 24.
[35] Ibid., p. 24.
[36] Ibid., pp. 25-26.

presented with a measure of automony in the biographical account, as it is conceivable in the context of the tantric tradition that Naropa encountered Vajra Yoginī in the form of an everyday human woman. However, the hag can also be counted as a psychological phenomenon. The biography of Naropa lends itself well to a psychoanalytic interpretation after the work of Carl Gustav Jung. A Jungian perspective highlights the subjective aspect of the *ḍākinīs*' ambivalent nature. From a psychoanalytical point of view, the sudden appearance of a hag over Naropa's shoulder signals a confrontation with his anima, a figure from the collective unconscious that appears to men early in the healthy process of integrating conscious and unconscious psychic contents. As his anima, the decrepit woman showed the feminine aspect of Naropa's psyche that was ascending in the midst of intellectual disappointment. She appeared when the great scholar became receptive to direct, intuitive awareness of the nature of reality. Once Naropa recognized his lack of intuitive awareness, the hag vanished—as a psychological projection ceases the moment it becomes conscious.

When Naropa was psychologically disposed to experience his anima projection, the hag appeared to expose a mode of spirituality that went beyond his intellectual comprehension. The hag who inspired Naropa's quest for direct realization was the first in a series of psychic projections experienced by Naropa. In time, he encounterd three more archetypes of his collective unconscious: the shadow in the form of numerous ghastly characters; the wise old man in the form of a dark-skinned man; and the cosmic person, in the form of a celestial vision of *guru* Tilopa.[37] Accordingly, it might be presumed that the *ḍākinī* is an image derived from the psyche, whose nature is non-material, and whose function is to enhance non-rational, intuitive patterns of thought.

The biographies of Yeshe Tsogyel, Milarepa, and Naropa show that *ḍākinīs* do not manifest in the context of subtle, not gross, material experience. A psychoanalytic interpretation of the *ḍākinī*

---

[37] For a fuller analysis of the life of Naropa along Jungian lines, see Victoria Kennick Urubshurow, "The Vajrayana Buddhist Alchemy of Spiritual Development: Jungian Symbols of Transformation in Naropa's Tale of Liberation," *Journal of the Psychology of Religion*, 1 (1992), 53-80.

highlights one aspect of their subjective nature. But it does not exhaust their meaning. *Ḍākinīs* correspond to inspired "psychological" attitudes as the shockingly beautiful or gruesome *ḍākinīs* prompt intensive religious practice. But they also appear "physically" in conjunction with purification of the subtle body as wind moves through the centers and channels, and as herbal essences synergystically react in the body. Thus, different aspects of their ambivalent nature—subtle physical or psychological—are highlighted in the texts according to the side of tantric experience emphasized.

Even when an assessment of the nature and function of *ḍākinīs* moves beyond psychology to the mind/body dynamic, their meaning is not exhausted. Although the *ḍākinī* corresponds to various subjective conditions, a flatly solipsistic interpretation of her nature is defied. In Tibetan Buddhism not only is mind viewed in relation to body; but also a person is viewed in relation to the cosmos. Thus, two relationships operate in dynamic tension: mind/body and person/cosmos. In a cosmic context, the *ḍākinīs'* nature looks somewhat objective, although it remains subtle. *Ḍākinīs* appear in moments of meaningful coincidence, as they "arrange" structural correspondences between outer and inner events. They are "objective" insofar as they coordinate outer circumstances with the mind/body process. They are "subjective" insofar as they appear in the context of non-ordinary sequences of events that call for intuitive awareness on the part of tantric adepts.[38]

In light of this mind/body/cosmos dynamic, Naropa's experience with the hag can be interpreted as an instance of the cosmos "responding" to his ripeness for intuitive awareness with the emergence of a *ḍākinī* upon whom his anima was projected.[39] Thus,

---

[38] The tentative attitude toward objectivity and subjectivity reflects a fundamental ambivalence of all symbols of transformation, which operate "betwixt and between" the subject and the object. *Ḍākinīs* are symbols of transformation insofar as they are images or forms that con-fuse a person (!) and the environment. It is simply not clear how and whether *ḍākinīs* "arrange" outer events; but they are spoken of in the texts as taking part in the con-fusion. See note 62 below.

[39] Milarepa and Yeshe Tsogyel encountered *ḍākinīs* during moments of intuitive awareness that were not necessarily radical initial revulsions from stalwart intellects. The *ḍākinīs* appear to them—and to Naropa later on—whenever intuitive awareness is at

the manifestation of Naropa's anima coincides with the appearance of a hag, who was a *ḍākinī* coming to help him grow to spiritual maturity. The multi-valent nature of *ḍākinīs* is indicated here as psychological, subtle physical, and cosmic dimensions are evidenced.

V. Ḍākinī *and Synchronicity*

Carl G. Jung's work on synchronicity provides a framework for understanding the function of *ḍākinīs* to promote awareness of (or "arrange") subtle connections between external events and the

---

play.

In a woman's psyche, the female figure can be the archetype of the Self, indicating wholeness and integration. In men's experience she usually is associated with the anima archetype. However, the same figure can function in different capacities, and must not be reduced to a single interpretation. For example, with reference to votaries of the Eleusinian Mysteries, Jung noted:

> "[T]he Demeter-Kore myth is far too feminine to have been merely the result of an anima-projection. Although the anima can, as we have said, experience herself in Demeter-Kore, she is yet of a wholly different nature. She [the anima-projection] is in the highest degree *femme a homme*, whereas Demeter-Kore exists on the plane of mother-daughter experience, which is alien to man and shuts him out. In fact, the psychology of the Demeter cult bears all the features of a matriarchal order of society, where the man is an indispensable but on the whole disturbing factor." ["The Psychological Aspects of the Kore," in C. G. Jung and C. Kerenyi, *Essays on a Science of Mythology*, pp. 156-77, trans. R. F. C. Hull (Princeton: Princeton University Press, 1973, c. 1949), p. 177.]

Supporting the view that feminine figures are not necessarily anima-projections, Jungian analyst Dora Kalff comments on the significance of the Buddhist Tara and the Christian Black Madonna:

> When the Black Madonna comes, I usually see this as the first impulse of the good feminine. When she appears, then we can guess that the psyche is beginning to grow in a spiritual direction, spiritual as together with the everyday life, with the body, the earth...
>
> Tara and the Black Madonna are the carriers of this development in the psyche. We're seeing a dawning of the feminine now. Women are beginning to realize that to follow the man's way is not working. We must develop our own capacities, not follow men. The Black Madonna is beginning to break through [in the psyches of women]. [China Galland, *Longing for Darkness: Tara and the Black Madonna*, (New York: Penguin, 1990), p. 142.]

Like Demeter-Kore, Tara, and the Black Madonna, the tantric *dākinīs* might be far too feminine, and of a wholly different nature from the anima, though they may at times function in that capacity.

condition of an adept's mind/body process. The concept of synchronicity suits the ambivalent nature of *ḍākinīs* who bridge subjective and objective dimensions of "reality." Jung defined synchronicity as an a-causal connecting principle that integrates a person with the cosmos.

> [S]ynchronicity takes the coincidence of events in space and time as meaning something more than mere chance, namely, a peculiar interdependence of objective events among themselves as well as with the subjective (psychic) states of the observer or observers.[40]

> [S]ynchronistic phenomena occur, for instance, when an inwardly perceived event (dream, vision, premonition, etc.) is seen to have a correspondence in external reality.[41]

Synchronicity refers to a connecting principle that does not pertain to linear causality. And though the scientific worldview that permeates "western civilization" tends to favor logical empirical explanations,[42] the Tibetan Buddhist world view incorporates synchronicity into its understanding of events and their meaning.[43] The life stories of tantric adepts refer to the meaningful confluence of circumstances as *rten 'brel* (S: *saṃyoga*), which indicates a combination of interrelated portentous factors that forms the basis of omens and other meaningful coincidences.[44] In the tantric tradition, *ḍākinīs* are readily associated

[40] See Urubshurow, "Vajrayana Symbols," p. 70. Citation is from C. G. Jung, "Foreword" to the *I Ching or Book of Changes*, trans. Richard Wilhelm (Princeton: Princeton University Press, 1950, 1971), p. xxiv.

[41] Carl G. Jung, *Memories, Dreams, Reflections*, ed. Aniela Jaffe, trans. Richard and Clara Winston (New York: Pantheon Books, 1963), p. 388.

[42] Jeremy W. Hayward provides an account of the scientific method and the emergence of western logical empiricism in the context of dialogue with the Dalai Lama, whose Tibetan Buddhist reflections shed light on the topic of synchronicity. Hayward points out some post-modern scientific views that challenge classical scientific assumptions, and thus bring western views more in line with traditional Tibetan views. See "Scientific Method and Validation" and "Questions of Method: A Conversation" in Jeremy W. Hayward, and Francisco J. Varella, (eds.), *Gentle Bridges: Conversations with the Dalai Lama on the Sciences of Mind* (Boston, MA: Shambhala, 1992), pp. 6-49.

[43] This is the case whether one considers the principles of Mind-Only or Middle Way thought in Indo-Tibetan philosophy. Although the degree of reality accorded to the "external" world is greater among Middle Way thinkers, both philosophies take into account the structure of events.

[44] Dowman, *Sky Dancer*, pp. 199-200, n. 60. Dowman translates *rten 'brel* as synchronicity.

with *rten 'brel.* They promote spiritual transformation by coordinating external events, primarily by bringing people together at suitable moments to inspire insight or faith. They tie up what might be called the "loose threads of history," by drawing people together at appropriate moments against all odds, or presenting adepts with what they need—even outside a normal chain of events.[45] Their appearance corresponds to moments of heightened intuitive awareness when adepts create meaning from the juxtaposition of normally unassociated events.[46]

Ḍākinīs frequently bring people together by urging adepts to ask their human teachers for specific instructions in moments of ripeness for those teachings. For example, one night Milarepa was visited in a dream by "a young girl...blue as the sky, and beautiful in her brocade dress and bone ornaments, her eyebrows sparkling with light" who told Milarepa to ask his teacher for Naropa's precepts on consciousness transference. Again, a *ḍākinī* urged Rechung to ask his teacher Milarepa for the story of his life.[47] *Ḍākinīs* also promote fresh encounters between people who are ripe for a meeting. For instance,

---

[45] The nature of *ḍākinīs* is ambivalent, as they empower both sides of the person/cosmos, subjective/objective dynamic. *Ḍākinīs* function in what we might call a "twilight world" in which their words, gestures, and rhythms convey multiple suggestions. See note 18 above in reference to the "twilight language" of *ḍākinīs*.

Ḍākinīs function as symbols when they are multi-valent, expose what is not obvious to everyday sense perception, and promote insight about the mind/body and person/cosmos relationships. On symbols, see "The Work of Condensation," in Sigmund Freud, *The Interpretation of Dreams*, trans. and ed. James Strachey (London: Allen & Unwin, 1954), pp. 279-304; "Methodological Remarks on the Study of Religious Symbolism," in Mircea Eliade and Joseph M. Kitagawa, eds. *The History of Religions: Essays in Methodology*, pp. 86-107; "Two Kinds of Thinking" in C. G. Jung, *Symbols of Transformation*, trans. R. F. C. Hull, Princeton: Princeton University Press, 1956, 1970), pp. 7-33; "Notes on Processual Symbolic Analysis," in Victor Turner, *Process, Performance, and Pilgrimage: A Study in Comparative Symbology* (New Delhi: Concept Publishing Co., 1979), pp. 143-149.

[46] The synchronistic creation of meaning resembles the "act of creation" identified by Arthur Koestler in his study of moments of ingenious insight, when two normally unassociated planes of meaning intersect to reveal new connections. A famous example cited by Koestler is the "eureka" experience of Archimedes who while sitting in a tub of water noticed for the first time—*in a new context*—his body's displacement of water. This event became meaningful to the mathematician as he sought a solution to the problem of determining whether or not the crown of a king was gold. See Arthur Koestler, *The Act of Creation* (New York: Macmillan, 1974).

[47] Lhalungpa, *Life of Milarepa*, pp. 81, 10-11.

"two women who said they came from Ugyen in the north"[48] showed Lama Marpa where to run into Milarepa for the first time. Later on, Milarepa regularly got directives from *ḍākinīs* on where to meet future disciples.

Often the people whose encounter is presaged by *ḍākinīs* display some recognition of each other. For example, Yeshe Tsogyel found a willing consort, following the advice of Padmasaṃbhava who told her:

> [G]o to the Valley of Nepal where there is a sixteen-year old youth with a mole on his right breast . . . called Atsara Sale. . . Find him and make him your ally. . . .[49]

Once in the valley, Yeshe Tsogyel offered a handful of gold dust at a *stūpa*, and received a vision of her teacher surrounded by many *ḍākinīs* who said: "Now, do not wander here for long. Return to Tibet with the consort you need." Then, through a meaningful coincidence, she encountered the youth. Yeshe Tsogyel tells of their meeting:

> Wandering slowly, since I had no precise knowledge of the whereabouts of the object of my search, I found myself in the neighbourhood of the large market-place near the southern gate of the city of Bhaktapur (Kho-khom-han). There a youth boldly approached me. He was handsome and attractive and a red mole on his chest threw out brilliant lustre. . . . His intelligent eyes were haloed with a red tint, his nose was pointed and his eyes were azure. . . .
>
> "Lady, from where have you come?" he enquired. . . . "Have you come to set me free?"[50]

Indeed, he was the appropriate youth; and together they went to Tibet. Another time, Yeshe Tsogyel met a Bhutanese girl through meaningful

---

[48] Ibid., p. 44. Ugyen (O-rgyan) here probably refers to the Land of the *Ḍākinīs* in which Yeshe Tsogyel found herself [see note 29 above]. Keith Dowman notes that "O-rgyan, Oddiyana, is the ancient kingdom of the Swat Valley in northern Pakistan. Before the Muslim invasion it was a centre of tantric practice, and as Guru Pema's [Padmasaṃbhava's] birthplace it became known as the *Ḍākinīs* Paradise, a *nirmāṇakāya* Buddhafield (O-rgyan mkha'-'gro gling)." Dowman, *Sky Dancer*, p. 189, n. 3. Dowman's comment reflects the typical ambivalence associated with *ḍākinīs*. The place is both an everyday geographical location, and a *ḍākinī* land. This ambivalence is repeated when the wife of Milarepa's teacher sees two ladies from Ugyen in her dream. The two *ḍākinīs* are associated with the dream consciousness and their own land. [Lhalungpa, *Life of Milarepa*, p. 44.]

[49] Ibid., p. 44.

[50] Ibid., p. 48.

coincidence. Speaking of *rten 'brel* she said that

> [t]hrough a synchronistic coincidence of external events and inner needs, a human girl called Khyidren visited me and offered me a large quantity of honey [when I was sorely in need of food].[51]

Noting that the girl had "all the marks and signs of an Awareness Ḍākinī," Yeshe Tsogyel delivered her to Padmasaṃbhava.[52]

Participation in *rten 'brel* calls for intuitive openness and mental flexibility. For example, since Yeshe Tsogyel had "no precise knowledge of the whereabouts of [her] search," she wandered slowly with heightened receptivity to synchronistic connections. Such openness was cultivated by Yeshe Tsogyel, Milarepa, and (eventually) Naropa through tantric vizualization practice that enhanced their imaginations. Vizualization practice heightened their awareness of color, sound, and other energy patterns, and attuned them to the *ḍākinī's* presence.

VI. Ḍākinī *and Imagination*

Synchronistic events pertain to non-linear causality. As such, they are recognized largely by imaginative modes of apprehension. Evidence gleaned from the lives of Yeshe Tsogyel, Milarepa, and Naropa suggests that two complementary modes of imagination are engaged in the encounter with *ḍākinīs*. On one hand, the imagination serves as a tool for integrating the mind-body process. On the other hand,

---

[51] Ibid., p. 77.

[52] Ibid., p. 88. Examples of synchronicity are found also contemporary spiritual biographies, such as Andrew Harvey's account of his relationship with the Indian *guru* Mother Meera. Her gestures, appearance, and words readily dovetail into Harvey's experience, taking it out of the linear mode. For example, one day Mr. Reddy (uncle and disciple of Mother Meera) was telling Harvey the story of his first encounter with Mother Meera. Just as Mr. Reddy came to the part when Mother Meera entered the story, Mother Meera actually entered the room. Mr. Reddy then mentioned to Mother Meera the coincidence, whereupon she replied, "That is natural" as a crow from the garden squeaked louder. Later, Mother Meera's attendant Adhilakshmi noted, "One day all the things that seem so wild and strange to you now will seem normal." Andrew Harvey, *Hidden Journey: A Spiritual Awakening* (New York: Henry Holt & Co., 1991), p. 75.

imagination promotes synchronistic interaction between person and cosmos.[53]

In the context of his work on the psychological process of individuation, Carl G. Jung used the term "active imagination" to describe a technique of integrating conscious and unconscious psychic contents.[54] The unconscious and conscious aspects of a person's psyche come into dynamic relationship through the appearance of archetypal projections, or images from the collective unconscious that show up in imaginative circumstances such as dreams. According to Jung, psychic wholeness is indicated when "active imagination" engenders the archetype of the Self, as a result of the free-flowing integration of unconscious contents into conscious awareness. For example, the Self archetype was experienced by Naropa as a cosmic person at the climax of his spiritual journey when Tilopa appeared radiant in the sky singing to him of non-duality.[55] As the psyche becomes increasingly integrated, the relationship between the whole psyche and the cosmos becomes increasingly integrated as well. Once the archetype of the Self manifests, experiences of synchronicity tend to arise readily.[56] The regularity with which tantric adepts participate in synchronous events suggests that their religious practice promotes a healthy and balanced management of the psyche.

The Jungian paradigm of the psyche with unconscious and

---

[53] To comprehend the complex function of religious imagination, it is useful to consider three perspectives—the psychological, the (tantric) subtle physical, and the metaphysical. Because of a Buddhist insistence on the interdependence of mind, body, and cosmos some aspects of the non-Buddhist perspectives should be adjusted to suit the tantric adepts' experience of *ḍākinīs*. Yet, the foreign perspectives provide suggestions that complement the tantric presentation of religious imagination, and render it more comprehensible. To enrich the psychological and metaphysical perspectives, some ideas of C. G. Jung and Ibn al-'Arabi are examined here.

[54] On "active imagination" see, for example, "The Psychic Nature of the Alchemical Work" (originally published in 1944) in C. G. Jung, *Psychology and Alchemy*, trans. R. F. C. Hull (Princeton: Princeton University Press, 1968), pp. 242-287.

[55] Guenther, *Life and Teachings of Naropa*, p. 90.

[56] Describing synchronicity, M-L. von Franz reports that "the older [Dr. Jung] became the more he got the information he needed for whatever he was thinking about or was working on; it simply ran after him." She suggests that Jung's experience of synchronicity was an "experience of expansion, or perhaps it is not even an expansion, of the archetype of Self." Marie-Louise von Franz, *Alchemical Active Imagination* (Dallas: Spring Publications, 1979), p. 44.

conscious aspects does not fully accord with the tantric Buddhist presentation, although the fruits of "active imagination" correspond to some elements of tantric experience. The yogic system does not bifurcate the psyche into known and unknown contents. Rather, it emphasizes the relationship between mental consciousness and activity of the subtle wind. The appearance of *ḍākinīs* is associated with the force of wind entering and dissolving into the central channel. The clarity and enduring quality of the appearance of *ḍākinīs* depends upon the extent to which the adept has gained proficiency in tantric practice of vizualization and movement of winds.[57] When the subtle wind courses freely through the centers and

---

[57] See the section on *Ḍākinī as Subtle Wind* above, where the appearance of *ḍākinīs* to tantric adepts is discussed in terms of meditative stabilization that results from subtle wind entering into the central channel. Commenting on the experience of meditative stabilization (S: *samādhi*; T: *ting nge 'dzin*), Geshe Gedun Lodro identifies three circumstances that give rise to "pure appearances.":

> "(1) Sometimes, through the force of winds' entering into channels in which they usually do not course, appearances arise that do not occur otherwise. There are various good and bad appearances. Some people have hallucinations or go crazy, and there are many cases of pure appearances dawning for such people.
>
> (2) There is a dawning to the mind of meditative visions....[S]uch an appearance would be due to the force of that person's familiarity with meditative stabilization. It would occur not only during the session but outside it also, without the person's even seeking to think about [it]....Such appearances are spontaneous. They are innate and like our usual appearances but are such that they would start to disappear upon analysis, whereas, without too much attention, they are very clear. Such appearances occur without a person's specific intention, in the course of usual activities.
>
> (3) The third type of pure appearance is of a sense consciousness actually perceiving pure appearances. For example, people speak of seeing the face of a deity; this means that they see the deity, not just the face. It might be said that a certain person has seen the face of the goddess Sarasvati. This is a case of his or her directly seeing the deity with the eye consciousness." [Geshe Gedun Lodro, *Walking Through Walls: A Presentation of Tibetan Meditation*, trans. and ed. Jeffrey Hopkins (New York: Snow Lion Publications, 1992), pp. 252-53.]

Geshe Gedun Lodro does not speak specifically of *ḍākinīs*, nor does he explain the means by which the third type of appearance (by sense consciousness) is produced. Yet, we can presume that Yeshe Tsogyel, Milarepa, and Naropa experienced pure appearances due to their intensive practice of Highest Yoga Tantra which "causes the winds to enter and dissolve into the central channel." [Ibid., pp. 254-55.] Due to their reputed greatness, we might also presume that they experienced pure appearances by way of the sense consciousness.

The distinction between meditative visions and sensory perceptions of pure

channels of the adept's body a spontaneous intuitive awareness arises that perceives the cosmos as a *maṇḍala* in which synchronous events are normal.

To describe the connection between the workings of the mind-body process and the synchronous events promoted by *ḍākinīs* it is useful to turn to the concept of "creative imagination," a type of imagination that links the integrated subject with the cosmos. Henry Corbin, based on his study of the Muslim mystic Ibn al-Arabi (1165-1240), used the term "creative imagination" to describe a function of perception correlated with a visionary world.[58] Despite discrepancies between Buddhist and Muslim metaphysics, the treatment of imagination by Ibn al-Arabi suggests one way in which the *ḍākinīs* experienced by tantric adepts can be understood. Corbin notes that creative imagination is distinct from the operation of fantasy or aesthetic creation. It is

> a faculty of perception and mediation very different from the demonstrative or historical reasoning which judges the sensible and finite data relating to rationally defined dogmas or to the irreversible events of material history.[59]

According to Corbin, this perception exposes an imaginal realm that is not generally accessed through the senses. It brings to light a mystic geography of the body, and beings of an imaginal world through the operation of a special human organ of perception.

Ibn al-'Arabi makes a distinction between contiguous imagination (Arabic: *al-khayal al-muttasil*) and discontiguous imagination (Arabic: *al-khayal al-mutlaq*) that is helpful in thinking about the appearance of *ḍākinīs*. He speaks of the imagination (Arabic: *khayal*)

---

appearances parallels a distinction made by the Muslim mystic Ibn al-Arabi (1165-1240) who speaks of an intermediate world of "discontiguous imagination" that exists independently of the viewer, and a faculty of "contiguous imagination" connected to the viewing subject. See discussion below.

[58] On "creative imagination" see Henry Corbin, *Creative Imagination in the Sufism of Ibn 'Arabi*, trans Ralph Manheim (Princeton: Princeton University Press, 1969); Ibid., "*Mundus Imaginalis,*" or the Imaginary and the Imaginal," trans. Ruth Horine, *Spring: An Annual of Archetypal Psychology and Jungian Thought* (1972), pp. 1-19. See also, William C. Chittick, *The Sufi Path of Knowledge: Ibn al-Arabi's Metaphysics of Imagination* (Albany: SUNY Press, 1989), pp. 112-124.

[59] Corbin, *Creative Imagination*, p. 153.

as a presence that on one hand coincides with human perception, and on the other hand remains autonomous:

> God created another creature. If you say concerning it that it is existent, you will have spoken the truth, and if you say it is nonexistent, you will have spoken the truth. If you say that it is neither existent nor nonexistent, you will have spoken the truth. It is imagination, and it has two states: a state of contiguity, which it possesses through man and certain animals, and a state of discontiguity. To the latter outward perception becomes connected while remaining separate from it in actual fact, as in the case of Gabriel's appearance in the form of Dihya [Kalbi, a beautiful human contemporary of the Prophet], or a jinn or an angel which becomes manifest from the world of curtaining.
>
> The difference between contiguous imagination and discontiguous imagination is that the contiguous kind disappears with the disappearance of the imaginer, while the discontiguous kind is an autonomous presence, constantly receptive toward meanings and spirits. It embodies them in accordance with its own characteristics, nothing else. Contiguous imagination derives from the discontiguous kind.[60]

The Tibetan tantric worldview recognizes both discontiguous and contiguous aspects of imagination in relation to *ḍākinīs*, who are central to the imaginative process of deciphering "twilight language." A contemporary Buddhist commentator explains:

> [T]he "twilight language" is an actual cipher which can only be understood by those blessed by the wisdom *ḍākinī*. The way the language is translated is not with a dictionary and a grammar book, but through "another way of knowing" which comes from a space which is far from the sunlit rational world dominated by the logos, and at the same time it is not from the dark abyss of the unconscious but rather a twilight world where another function of the mind is possible. This is not merely the intuitive part of the mind, because even very sensitive people cannot understand the language of the *ḍākinī*. It is a realm governed by the *ḍākinīs*, and only those who can integrate into the symbolic world of the *ḍākinī* can understand their half-concealed language.[61]

From the perspective of tantric yoga, the mystic geography of the subtle mind/body process and the *ḍākinīs* are viewed as

---

[60] Chittick, *The Sufi Path of Knowledge*, p. 117.

[61] Tsultrim Allione, *Women of Wisdom* (London and New York: Arkana, 1984, reprint 1984), p. 44.

interdependent.[62] In Ibn al-'Arabi's terms it might be said that tantric adepts encounter *ḍākinīs* in the contiguous imagination, while the *ḍākiṇīs* maintain a kind of autonomous presence—with their own characteristics in their own land—in the discontiguous imagination. The adepts cultivate an intuitive spontaneous awareness through the contiguous imagination, and the cosmos responds with *ḍākinī* presences through the discontiguous imagination.

In the Tibetan context, the double-edged creative imagination is evidenced in relation to the generation of so-called "self-arisen" (T: *rang jung*) deities whose figures appear in rocks. Causes governing the appearance of *ḍākinīs* may be a parallel phenomenon. Journalist China Galland inquired after a peculiar self-arisen figure of Tara growing from a rock in the Himalayas at Pharping from a height of some four inches to a height of ten or twelve inches. In response to her queries, a Tibetan lama replied: "Is it so strange to imagine that the mind when concentrated could do this....The power of devotion calls Tara out of the rock, yes?"[63] When asked whether or not he believed in "this Tara growing out of the rock at Pharping" the Dalai Lama elaborated as follows:

> "Oh yes. These things depend on many factors, many. . . . There's a great sort of interrelationship between the appropriateness of the time, the place, and also a person intimately related to it. All these factors must be taken into account. When suitable people remain there, the image

---

[62] The degree of "objectivity" accorded to visionary appearances, and to conventionally existing objects is debated among the Mahāyāna Buddhist Mind Only and Middle Way philosophers, in the climate of whose assumptions the tantric adepts seek enlightenment. However, the principle of interdependence is commonly accepted, regardless of whether the emphasis is placed upon the perceiving agent or upon the interaction between the perceiving agent and a world that conventionally exists.

The Mind Only/Middle Way debate over the degree of objective existence of perceived phenomena is left unresolved in the life stories of Yeshe Tsogyel, Milarepa, and Naropa. The status of *ḍākinīs* in the *rnam thar* texts remains ambiguous, as the genre prefers narrative and poetry to philosophical argument. Yet, the authenticity of tantric adepts' experience of *ḍākinīs* is seriously presented, regardless of their ambiguity.

[63] China Galland, *Longing for Darkness: Tara and the Black Madonna, A Ten Year Journey* (Penguin Books: New York, 1990), p. 65. Galland is quoting Cho Kyi Nyima Rimpoche.

> remains. When there are no more suitable people there, the image also disappears."[64]

The case of the self-arisen images suggests that the devotees of Tara engage their faculty of contiguous imagination, to which the deity appears. Her form "called out of the rock" derives from the discontiguous imagination. Likewise, the *ḍākinīs* are semi-automonous presences of the discontiguous imagination that appear to the contiguous imagination of tantric adepts.

Ḍākinīs and self-arisen images have an esoteric nature because an adept must *interact* with them through the contiguous imagination. Milarepa said:

> To him who sees the mind's nature
> And dispels the mists of ignorance,
> The *Ḍākinīs* show their faces.[65]

Tantric adepts to whom the *ḍākinīs* show their faces open themselves to the experience by means of exacting techniques.

The tantric method of developing the contiguous imagination involves an intensive practice of visualization. During visualization an adept mentally constructs in detail the form and color of holy beings on the basis of canonical paintings. The figure is mentally constructed in conjunction with verbal recitation of sacred syllables and the performance of prescribed physical gestures. This exercise of body, speech, and mind leads to meditative stabilization with the movement of subtle wind into the adept's central channel. By the force of the wind's so entering, various "pure appearances" dawn.[66] Andrew Harvey's Tibetan lama explained the nature of visualization practice as follows:

> At first you will find the process of visualization hard. You have not been trained to it. You have been trained in a materialist way of imagining and seeing, which has its beauties and precisions, but has not accustomed you to the kind of inner projection that I am asking you to do....You must work every day. You must not be discouraged if for many months you can visualize very little. What you are beginning is a journey into a different world, into an awareness of a different reality; you cannot expect

---

[64] Ibid., p. 94.
[65] Chang, *Songs*, p. 661.
[66] See note 57 above.

to make that journey quickly. Nor, in a sense should you want to. The journey itself has its joys; the hardness of the journey has its lessons also, of perseverance and trust and humility, which you will need to learn.[67]

VII. *Conclusion*

More than a break from the everyday imagination or a technical mastery of subtle winds is needed to participate fully in what Andrew Harvey's Tibetan teacher called a "different reality"—or the imaginative universe (including contiguous and discontiguous aspects) described by Ibn al-'Arabi. Communion with *ḍākinīs* involves numerous trials and transformations—details of which are found not only in Tibetan tales of liberation, but also in accounts of shamanic and mystic initiation.[68] An overhaul of the personality, a re-orientation to the world at large, and the growth of sensitivity to the cosmic condition are requisite for spiritual maturity.

Initiatory transformation is demanding. So, it is not surprising that most people do not see *ḍākinīs*. For instance, Yeshe Tsogyel was recognized by tantric adepts as a *ḍākinī* in human form.[69] Yet, in spite of this glamorous nature, she endured considerable abuse from people seeking to take advantage of her as a mere woman. Yeshe Tsogyel encountered thieves, rapists, and other violent men who could not immediately discern her transcendent aspect. Thus, while *ḍākinīs* are intimates to the adepts, they remain unrecognized by others. And though William Butler Yeats and his friends on the Irish countryside encountered the Little People, most of his compatriots—believing or not—never saw any fairies. Recall Stith Thompson's observation that

---

[67] Andrew Harvey, *A Journey in Ladakh* (First published, Great Britain: William Collins & Sons, 1983); (London: Flamingo/Fontana Paperbacks, 1988), p. 234.

[68] One might like to call Naropa, Yeshe Tsogyel, and Milarepa "mystics" who deepen their realization of Buddhist views through meditation. However, with regard to *ḍākinī* encounters, their experiences are reminiscent of shamanic initiations, which include periods of great physical debility, celestial journeys, visions of spirits (*ḍākinīs*), use of a secret language, and so on. The question of the relationship between mystic and shamanic initiation is an interesting one; but shall not be taken up here. On shamanic patterns of initiation see Mircea Eliade, *Shamanism: Archaic Techniques of Ecstasy*, trans. Willard R. Trask (New York: Pantheon Books, 1964), pp. 110-144.

[69] Dowman, *Sky Dancer*, p. 224. Tantric adepts continue to see Yeshe Tsogyel as a manifestation of Vajra Yogini, who is accessible to the creative imagination through visualization practice.

"[f]airies are normally invisible to the generality of men."[70]

While the fairy tales and traditions familiar to Stith Thompson tell how "particular individuals may secure a magic soap or ointment which permits them to see the little folk" or tell how it is "sometimes possible to have a view of them...by treading on someone else's foot,"[71] the Tibetan tales of liberation tell how the *ḍākinīs* are encountered through tantric practice. Now we ask: How is it that fairies in European literature are known through magic, whereas fairies in Tibetan literature are known through meditation? What accounts for the disparity between "magic soap" and "meditative stabilization of calm abiding"? How can one compare the act of "treading on someone else's foot" with dissolving subtle wind in the central channel of a tantric adept's body?

The discrepancy between the naive magic of a fairy tale and the profound tradition of highest yoga tantra is resolved when one realizes a fact of culture noted by Rene Guenon: "[M]agic—we might even say sorcery—is the last thing to be left behind when traditions disappear."[72] The fairy and her symbolism have been degraded in the west, along with other traditional symbolisms. Speaking of the "language of the birds" or "angelic language" Guenon observes what also applies in the case of the fairy:

> [H]ow inept it is to make fun of stories that speak of the 'language of the birds.' It is all too easy and too simple to disdain as 'superstitions' everything one cannot understand; but the ancients themselves knew very well what they meant when they used symbolic language. The true superstition in the strictly etymological sense (*quod superstat*) is what outlives itself, that is, the 'dead letter'; but this survival, however lacking in interest it may seem, is nonetheless not so totally insignificant, for the Spirit that 'bloweth where it listeth' (and when it listeth) can always come to breathe fresh life into the symbols and the rites and give them back their lost meaning and the fullness of their original virtue.[73]

The Tibetan tales of liberation provide a vital perspective on the

---

[70] See note 9 above.

[71] Thompson, *Folktale*, p. 247.

[72] Rene Guenon, "The Language of the Birds" in *The Sword of Gnosis: Metaphysics, Cosmology, Tradition, Symbolism*, pp. 299-303, ed. Jacob Needleman (London: Arkana, 1974), p. 303.

[73] Ibid.

nature and function of fairies—a perspective largely eclipsed in the tales of western culture. Yet, William Butler Yeats and some of his friends had not lost access to the fairies. Although they were not trained as tantric yogis, those Irish explorers of legendary fairy lands made use of the contiguous imagination accessible to all human beings. Twenty-two years after his encounter with the fairy queen (about which we spoke at the outset), Yeats appended a note to his account stating that his use of the word "trance" to describe the mental state of the young woman who summoned the fairies was misleading. He said:

> The word 'trance' gives a wrong impression. I had learned from MacGregor Mathers and his pupils to so suspend the will that the imagination moved of itself. The girl was, however, fully entranced, and the man so affected by her that he heard the children's voices as if with his physical ears. On two occasions, later on, her trance so affected me that I also heard or saw some part of what she did as if with physical eyes and ears.[74]

Perhaps for those who exercise only a gross material imagination the fairy has disappeared. Perhaps for those who accord hegemony to the intellect and ask too many questions the fairy has disappeared. Is this sacred presence in danger of being lost forever to human awareness? In the west, can fresh life be blown into the symbols and rites to retrieve the lost meaning and fullness of the fairy's original virtue?

Conversing with folklorist Evans Wentz in the early part of this century John Davies, an herb seller of Balsalla steeped in Celtic tradition suggested—in his own way—that modern education has contributed to the breakdown of the contiguous imagination, but not to the breakdown of the discontiguous imagination:

> Before education came into the island . . . more people could see the fairies; now very few people can see them. But they are as thick on the Isle of Man as ever they were. . . . There are as many kinds of fairies as populations in our world. I have seen some who were about two and a half feet high; and some who were as big as we are.[75]

Although aspects of modern education hinder the contiguous

[74] Yeats, *Mythologies*, p. 55, n. 2. See also note 3 above.

[75] K. M Briggs, *The Fairies in Tradition and Literature* (London: Routledge & Kegan Paul, 1967), p. 145.

imagination, methods for its cultivation are still available through some forms of psychotherapy and religious practice, as this essay suggests. Oddly enough, from time to time the ethereal feminine appears to break out of the discontiguous imagination. As a fluke she shows herself in the everyday world. But without cultivation of the contiguous imagination it is not possible to maintain communion with her.

In closing, let us consider the ancient Greek goddess Demeter, who for nine days was so overcome with grief at the rape of her daughter that her body wrinkled up. In nine days she turned into an old hag, and the ground withered with her. No plants issued forth until the fruit of her womb Persephone was recovered from the underworld. After recovering her daughter, who was thenceforth obliged to spend certain months of each year in the underworld, Demeter demonstrated a rite that became the basis of the Eleusinian mysteries, inaugurated in the fifteenth century BCE. The rites were celebrated for nearly two thousand years, until the king of the Goths (Alaric) burned the sanctuary at Eleusis in 396 CE, marking the "official" end of paganism. In Eleusis an uncanonized Saint Demetra continued to be venerated by peasants who ritually covered her with flowers to insure fertility of their fields. In 1820 the statue was forcibly removed, and then presented to Cambridge University.[76]

Did the goddess Demeter perish with the demise of the Eleusinian mysteries? Have the Celtic Little People vanished? Are the *ḍākinīs* bound to be forgotten? Mircea Eliade recounts the following episode, reported by the Athenian press in February 1940:

> At one of the bus stops between Athens and Corinth there came on board an old woman, "thin and dried up but with very big and keen eyes." Since she had no money to pay her fare, the driver made her leave the bus at the next stop—which was, precisely, Eleusis. But the driver could not get the motor started again; finally the passengers decided to chip in and pay the old woman's fare. She got back on board, and this time the bus set off. Then the old woman said to them: "You ought to have done it sooner, but you are egoists; and, since I am among you I will tell you something else: you will be punished for the way you live, you will be deprived even of plants and water!" She had not finished threatening them," the author of

[76] See Mircea Eliade, *A History of Religious Ideas*, 3 vols., Willard Trask, (trans.) (Chicago: University of Chicago Press, 1982), vol. 2. p. 415.

> the article published in *Hestia* goes on, "before she vanished....No one had seen her get out. Then the passengers looked at one another, and they examined the ticket stubs again to make sure that a ticket had indeed been issued."[77]

Like the gruesome women encountered by Yeshe Tsogyel in the Land of the *Ḍākinīs*, the frightful *ḍākinīs* of Milarepa's meditation, or the hag who cast a shadow over Naropa's books, Demeter and other feminine presences of the west may yet have the power to inspire spiritual transformation. As long as the human imagination does not die, the ethereal feminine can recover the fullness of her original virtue.

BIBLIOGRAPHY

Allione, Tsultrim. *Women of Wisdom*. London: Arkana, 1984, reprinted 1986.

Briggs, K. M. *The Fairies in Tradition and Literature*. London: Routledge & Kegan Paul, 1967.

Chang, Garma C. (Trans.) *The Hundred Thousand Songs of Milarepa*, 2 vols. Seacaucus, NJ: University Books, 1962.

Chittick, William C. *The Sufi Path of Knowledge: Ibn al-Arabi's Metaphysics of Imagination*. Albany: SUNY Press, 1989.

Dowman, Keith. (Trans.) *The Legend of the Great Stupa and The Life Story of the Lotus Born Guru*. Emeryville, CA: Dharma Press, 1973.

_____. (Trans.) *Sky Dancer: The Secret Life and Songs of the Lady Yeshe Tsogyel*. London: Routledge & Kegan Paul, 1984.

Eliade, Mircea. *A History of Religious Ideas*. Volume 2. Translated by Willard Trask. Chicago: University of Chicago Press, 1982.

_____. "Methodological Remarks on the Study of Religious Symbolism." In *The History of Religions: Essays in Methodology*. Pp. 86-107. Edited by Mircea Eliade and Joseph M. Kitagawa. Chicago: University of Chicago Press, 1959.

_____. *Shamanism: Archaic Techniques of Ecstasy*. Translated by Willard R. Trask. New York: Pantheon Books, 1964.

Freud, Sigmund. *The Interpretation of Dreams*. Translated and edited by James Strachey. London: Allen & Unwin, 1954.

Guenon, Rene. "The Language of the Birds." In Jacob Needleman. *The Sword of Gnosis: Metaphysics, Cosmology, Tradition, Symbolism*. Pp. 299-303. London: Arkana, 1974.

Guenther, Herbert V. (Trans.) *Kindly Bent to Ease Us, Part Two: Meditation*

---

[77] Eliade, *History*, vol 2, p. 416.

by Klong-chen rab-'byams-pa. Emeryville, CA: Dharma Publishing, 1976.

_____. (Trans.) *The Life and Teaching of Naropa*. Oxford: Oxford University Press, 1963.

_____. (Trans.) *The Royal Song of Saraha: A Study in the History of Buddhist Thought*. Berkeley, CA: Shambhala, 1973.

Gyatso, Kelsang. *Clear Light of Bliss: Mahamudra in Vajrayana Buddhism*. Translated by Tenzin Norbu. Edited by Jonathan Landaw. London: Wisdom Publications, 1982.

Hayward, Jeremy W. and Varella, Francisco J. (Eds.) *Gentle Bridges: Conversations with the Dalai Lama on the Sciences of Mind*. Boston, MA: Shambhala, 1992.

Hopkins, Jeffrey. *Meditation on Emptiness*. London: Wisdom Publications, 1983.

Jung, Carl G. "The Psychological Aspects of the Kore." In Jung, Carl G. and Kerenyi, C. *Essays on a Science of Mythology*. Pp. 156-77. Translated by R. F. C. Hull. Princeton: Princeton University Press, 1973 (c. 1949).

_____. *Memories, Dreams, Reflections*. Recorded and edited by Aniela Jaffe. Translated by Richard and Clara Winston. New York: Pantheon Books, 1963.

_____. *Psychology and Alchemy*. Translated by R. F. C. Hull. Princeton: Princeton University Press, 1968.

_____. *Symbols of Transformation*. Translated by R. F. C. Hull. Princeton: Princeton University Press, 1970 (c. 1956).

Koestler, Arthur. *The Act of Creation*. New York: Macmillan, 1974.

Lhalungpa, Lobsang P. (Trans.) *The Life of Milarepa*. New York: E. P. Dutton, 1977.

Lodro, Geshe Gedun. *Walking Through Walls: A Presentation of Tibetan Meditation*. Translated and edited by Jeffrey Hopkins. New York: Snow Lion Publications, 1992.

Thompson, Stith. *The Folktale*. Berkeley: University of California Press, 1977; copyright 1946.

Turner, Victor. *Process, Performance, and Pilgrimage: A Study in Comparative Symbology*. New Delhi: Concept Publishing Co., 1979.

Urubshurow, Victoria Kennick. "The Vajrayana Buddhist Alchemy of Spiritual Development: Jungian Symbols of Transformation in Naropa's Tale of Liberation." *Journal of the Psychology of Religion*, 1 (1992): 53-80.

von Franz, Marie-Louise. *Alchemical Active Imagination*. Dallas: Spring Publications, 1979.

Wangyal, Geshe. *The Jewelled Staircase*. Ithaca, NY: Snow Lion Publications, 1986.

Yeats, William Butler. *Mythologies*. New York: Macmillan, Collier Books, 1969 (c. 1959).

CHAPTER THREE

WOMEN, EARTH, AND THE GODDESS: A ŚĀKTA-HINDU INTERPRETATION OF EMBODIED RELIGION

KARTIKEYA C. PATEL

*This essay explores the notion of female embodiment and its relation to the phenomenon of religion. It explains religious beliefs, acts, and events in terms of the worship of the female body. By elucidating this standpoint, this essay hopes to reclaim the centrality of the female body and its importance in the study of philosophy of religion.**

One can approach the topic of women and religion in two ways. On the one hand, one can produce detailed documentation to show how a given religious tradition has historically excluded and degraded women in religious life. On the other hand, one can approach a given religious tradition with the aim of retrieving what is feminist/womanist and respectful of women in that tradition. Even though the first approach may be effective in raising our awareness about past injustices to women, I find that such an orientation only replicates the misogynist attitude of a given tradition by repeating it. However, I find the second approach advantageous in that it helps us reconstruct a given tradition by exploring the various ways in which women's lives have shaped and defined its very nature.

In what follows, I aim to retrieve what is feminist/womanist in the

* I would like to thank Siddhartha Chakravarti, Arvind Sharma, Elinor Gadon, Rachel Fell McDermott, the anonymous reviewers at *Hypatia*, Nancy Frankenberry, and Marilyn Thie, the guest editors for this special issue, for their helpful comments on the earlier versions of this essay. I am most indebted to Frederique Apffel-Marglin for giving me access and permission to use unpublished works. An earlier version of this essay was published in the special issue on Feminist Philosophy of Religion by *Hypatia: A Journal of Feminist Philosophy* vol. 9, no. 4 (Fall 1994), pp. 69-87.

Śākta-Hindu tradition. To this end, I explain the divine as a female body of which women, earth, and the Goddess are but different manifestations. Further, I explain an embodied religion as that in which the presence of this female body of women, earth, and the Goddess is celebrated rather than denied. In what follows, I argue that it is the female body which provides meaning, form, and coherence to religious beliefs, acts, and relations that otherwise seem disparate, like some loosely woven threads of a cord. Since Indian traditions do not readily make a distinction between "religion" and "philosophy" we will use the phrase "embodied religion" to refer to both philosophy and religion.

In Section I, I discuss issues of interpretation and context, and offer definitions of some key concepts such as woman's own nature (*strīsvabhāva*) and woman's religion (*strīdharma*). Here, the concepts of woman's own nature and woman's religion are defined in terms of menstruation, and it is argued that menstruation which is woman's own nature can also be construed as woman's religion. The aim here is to forge a link between the notions of female embodiment and religion. Thus I hope to move away from the prevalent liberationist interpretation which explains the notion of woman's religion in terms of social duties - the fulfilment of which leads to women's liberation (*mokṣa*).

Section II explains the principle of interconnectedness of all existences as the Goddess principle and argues that it forms the basis of the Goddess culture of India. In this part relying on the *theagraphy* of the Śākta-Hindu places of pilgrimage and worship (*śākta-pīṭhas*), and the fieldwork done by anthropologist Frederique Apffel-Marglin and Purna Chandra Misra, I argue that the interrelatedness which is a hallmark of the Goddess culture is not some abstract philosophical principle but a lived reality which is manifested in interpersonal social relations, in humans' relation to their environment, and to the larger cosmic whole. This part, then, addresses the ecological concern of feminist spirituality.

Section III of this essay is concerned about the meaning of the religious (*dhārmic*) activities. It is argued that according to the Śākta-Hindu tradition, religious acts and events attain fruition only when performed as worship of the female body of the women-earth-Goddess. As one texts put it, "Where women are not worshipped there the activities do not attain fruition. The one who worships (praises) woman, worships (praises) the Goddess and so worships the three worlds" (Nene 1970, 3.56, and Krishnamacharya 1959, 43.64).[1] The aim of this part is to articulate the notion of religion as a beneficial direction—a direction which suggests that respect for and worship of the female body leads to the collective happiness of people.

Let us begin with certain facts which any satisfactory explanation of the notion of the sacredness of the female in the Hindu tradition must take into account. First, as Arvind Sharma argues, there are some obvious problems in defining Hinduism (Sharma 1993, 5). Hinduism is not a tradition, but rather a blanket term invented to account for various traditions, e.g. *Vedānta*, *Śaiva*, *Vaiṣṇava*, *Śākta*, etc. To a large extent these various traditions presuppose the scriptural authority of the Vedas and to some extent the *Dharmaśāstras*. Yet, each tradition embodies a different interpretation of these texts, reflecting the sociocultural milieu in which it thrived, as well as the interpretive interests of the tradition itself. In this essay, I explain the nature of the divine as feminine from a Śākta Hindu perspective. For a Śākta-Hindu, the scriptural injunctions, rites and rituals attain fruition only when construed as worship of the feminine.

Second, there are numerous variables, for example, linguistic, social, rural, urban, and so on, which complicate the task of interpreting Hindu beliefs, rites, and rituals. These variables play an important role in determining the meaning of these beliefs, rites, and rituals for a given stratum of society. Thus, people at different levels of social strata may have a very different understanding of the specific rites and rituals that explain the nature of reality as feminine. For instance, Richard Shweder's and Frederique Apffel-Marglin's investigations reveal that the Brahmins of Orissa have an altogether different understanding of the menstruation rituals than the farmers of Orissa have (Shweder 1991, 241-265, and Apffel-Marglin 1991a and 1991b). For these reasons, if we do not take into account the variable-

---

[1] The translations in this essay are my own unless otherwise indicated.

bound context, we cannot possibly offer an empirical definition of the notion of the feminine.

Third, as Marla Powers (1980) has argued, the contemporary analysis of the rites, rituals, and beliefs of a non-Western society often has a Western cultural bias. However, an explanation based on Western presuppositions does not provide us with a correct analysis. This is so since the conceptual framework, social constructs, necessitating interpersonal relations, and roads for spiritual fulfillment of a non-Western society strikingly differ from those of a Western society.

To avoid the problem of misinterpretation, I propose a framework in which our conceptual claims can be measured against the lived reality of the beliefs, rites, and rituals which are presently under consideration. To accomplish this, I propose to use the fieldwork done by Frederique Apffel-Marglin in collaboration with Purna Chandra Misra in the Indian state of Orissa as a yardstick against which the conceptual claims made in this essay can be critically evaluated (Apffel-Marglin and Misra 1991a, and 1991b). This move is also useful in delimiting the scope of this essay to a given stratum of society. Finally, I use various Hindu works in this essay which provide a common theme but belong to different historical times and traditions within the Śākta-Hindu tradition.

I

One way to go about the search for definitions of the key concepts is to find out from a contextual point of view what the notions of woman, female, and feminine mean in the *Śākta* universe of discourse. To this end, I begin with the concept of woman's own nature.

Etymologically, the Sanskrit term *strīsvabhāva* consists of *strī* (woman), and *svabhāva* (one's own nature), meaning thereby, a woman's own nature.[2] The term, "a woman's own nature" can be best explained as some essential quality naturally belonging to an entity or being which is a *sine qua non* characteristic of the entity in question. It can be contrasted with what is artificially created.[2] The

---

[2] For instance, in the sentence "*sa tasya svo bhāvaḥ prakṛtiniyatvādakṛtakaḥ*"

term "a woman's own nature" has been variously defined in different texts and has no single applicable meaning. It has been variously defined in terms of mobility (*cala*), good fortune, and menstruation. For instance, the *Mahābhārata* defines a woman's nature in terms of mobility when it says, "Women are by nature mobile, difficult to provide unconditional service to, their very qualities difficult to comprehend; as are the uttered sentences of the wise men so are women" (Sukthankar 1933-39, XII, ch. 38, verse 24). This passage is important since it recognizes the difficulty of comprehending and defining woman's nature. But still it attempts to define it, in part, in terms of mobility. This attempt has some validity because according to Hinduism, a man (*puruṣa*) by nature is said to be still, immobile and cannot function or perform any activity without a woman (*prakṛti*). Thus in the *Śiva Purāṇa*, Pārvatī says to Śiva, "With my blessings you become qualitative and embodied. Without me, you are attributeless and incompetent to perform any activity. Being always subservient to *prakṛti* you perform all activities" (Shastri 1970, III, ch. 13, verses 19-20). In a similar vein, the sage Nārada says to Rāma, "Listen, Rāma, She is always eternal, primeval, and everlasting. Nothing is able to stir without her aid" (Radhakrishnan 1969, 83).

The notion of a woman's own nature has also been defined in terms of menstruation. Thus in a sentence such as "Sixteen nights are known to women, for whom, menstruation is own nature" (*ṛtuḥ svābhāvikaḥ strīṇāṁ rātrayaḥ ṣoḍaśasmṛtāḥ*, Kale 1982, ch. 3, verse 46) a woman's nature is defined in terms of the essential quality of being a woman, that is, menstruation (*ṛtu*). However, menstruation itself is a loaded category in contemporary discourse and requires further explanation. In contemporary discourse, we often define "woman" as a biological entity, "female" as a cultural concept, and "feminine" as a psychological attribute. But if we use this framework then we have to characterize menstruation as an *essential* quality which separates the concept of female from that of the woman and feminine. This is so because we tend to regard menstruation only as a

(*Uttararāmacarita* 6.14) one's own nature which is constituted as such by nature is contrasted with what is artificially created.

biological fact. It is in this sense that some contemporary writers, for example, Julia Leslie, have tried to explain the notion of a woman's own nature (Leslie 1989, 8).

For a Śākta-Hindu, however, menstruation is not simply a biological fact, and for that reason it cannot be separated from the concepts of women, female, and the feminine, or for that matter, from what is cultural, psychological, and biological. Nor can it be used to separate the notions of "female," "feminine," and "woman" from each other. For a Śākta-Hindu menstruation (*ṛtu*) is a holistic concept. It is a religion (*dharma*). The term *ṛtu*, which signifies menstruation, also signifies the cyclical changes of the seasons as well as orderliness in the cosmos. Thus, it is believed that the menstrual cycle in the female body corresponds to, and represents, the cyclical change of the seasons and the orderliness in the universe. A woman's *ṛtudharma* is thus said not only to interrelate and integrate the concepts of woman, female, and feminine but also to interrelate humans to their environment, and to the socio-cultural reality in which their rites and rituals attain fruition. The concept of *ṛtudharma* needs further explanation because as one of the *dharmas*, it carries the ambiguity and plasticity that the notion of *dharma* generally carries.

The term *dharma* has been used in a variety of ways in Hindu literature. The three primary senses in which the term *dharma* is used are: (1) a rule (*niyama*) that *enforces* a law-like structure; (2) a direction given to the members of a society to sustain continuity in the cosmos and to fulfill their individual functions so that collective actions may attain fruition; and (3) a duty that the individual has in order to attain liberation. Although the third sense has been used in most philosophical works, it is in the first two senses that I will be using the term *dharma* in this essay.

The use of the term *dharma* in the first two senses is compatible with the texts as well as with the contemporary usage of the term. If we combine the first two senses, we can interpret the concept of *dharma* in a slightly different way. We can say that it is a beneficial direction given to the members of a society to maintain a law-like structure in the cosmos and to attain the fruits of some collective action geared toward maintaining continuity and orderliness in that society.[3]

Thus defined, *dharma* consists of a set of beneficial directions to the individuals, or groups which are conducive to the attainment and fulfillment of collective human goals. A *dharma*-based society issues directions to its members so that human endeavors may attain fruition. It is believed that if an individual's *dharma* is observed, it leads to the collective fruition of human goals.

Conversely, if an individual's *dharma* is not respected, chaos and possible destruction follow. In this sense, respect for, and observance of, a woman's own nature would lead to the attainment of human goals; conversely, if it is not respected, chaos and total annihilation may follow.[4] For example, when brought into the assembly hall while still menstruating, Draupadī asks, "If you permit these faults in the presence of the elders, my father-in-law, will the rain fall? Will the world survive?" (Hiltebeitel 1988, 265).

To conclude, menstruation, which is both woman's *dharma* and woman's nature is not simply a biological fact and for that reason does not allow us to reify the reality of women's being into woman/female/feminine. It is a *dhārmic* episode that provides us with a choreography in which collective acts and events of theological/philosophical and cosmological significance attain fruition. This point will be further explained in Section III.

II

In recent feminist work, it has been consistently argued that the inseparability of all existences, their interrelatedness and interconnection is the cornerstone of feminist ways of looking at reality.[5] In this Section I argue that this principle of interconnectedness, the inter-relatedness of the elements to one another, forms the basis of the Goddess culture of India. In what

---

[3] It is in this sense that Jaimini defines *dharma* as *codanālakṣaṇo'rtho dharmaḥ*, i.e. *dharma* consists in beneficial directions (Nyāyaratna 1889, 1.1.2).

[4] Manu seems to express the same idea when he says, "When violated, *dharma* destroys, when preserved, *dharma* preserves, therefore *dharma* should not be violated, lest violated *dharma* destroy us." (Nene 1970, 8.15).

[5] For a comprehensive account from a western perspective, see, Keller (1986).

follows, with the help of fieldwork done by anthropologist Frederique Apffel-Marglin in collaboration with Purna Chandra Misra, I contend that the interrelatedness is not confined to abstract philosophizing: it is realised in interpersonal social relations and in people's relationship to the environment and the larger cosmic whole.

There is a vast array of literature in the Śākta-Hindu tradition that explains the nature of the Goddess as an eternal all-pervading reality, manifesting herself in different and diverse but interrelated aspects of the world.[6] This interrelatedness of all existences is first explained by Gārgī, a woman philosopher of circa 800 BCE, in a dialogue with the famous Indian philosopher Yājñavalkya.

The dialogue itself is presented in an interesting way. Whereas Western scholars traditionally present Indian women as silent, or with a subdued and submissive voice, this dialogue presents Gārgī as a flamboyant, outspoken woman whose only concern is the knowledge of truth. Gārgī opens the dialogue with two questions. The questions that Gārgī asks are about the interconnectedness of different elements of the universe. Her philosophical thesis or proposition (*pratijñā*) characteristically exhibits her belief in the interconnectedness of this universe. She says, "Since all that is here is woven, like warp and woof," *(yad idam sarvam....otam ca protam ca)* what is it that weaves everything together?" (Radhakrishnan, 1969, *Bṛhadāraṇyaka Upaniṣad* ch. 3, verse 6).

Gārgī argues that the air, water, sky, the worlds of the Gandharvas, the worlds of the sun, the worlds of the moon, the worlds of the stars, the worlds of the gods, the worlds of Indra, the worlds of Prajāpati, the worlds of Brahmā are all interwoven and held together by a single principle. Nothing exists disparately. She asks, "That, O Yājñavalkya, of which they say, it is above the heaven, it is beneath the earth, that which the people call the past, the present and the future, across what is that woven, like warp and woof?" (Radhakrishnan 1969, *Bṛhadāraṇyaka Upaniṣad* 3.6.1; 3.8.1-12). Gārgī's main concern is to inquire about the nature of reality which

[6] The *Devī-Māhātmya*, *Devī-sūkta* of *Ṛgveda*, *Ānandalaharī*, *Lalitā-Sahasranāma*, *Lakṣmī Tantra*, and *Devī-Rahasya* are some of the main Hindu texts in which the Goddess is explained as a principle that interrelates and interconnects different elements of life.

appears to be a unitive whole, according to a principle transcendent but at the same time immanent. When Yājñavalkya eventually replies that it is by the indestructible that everything manifested in space is woven like warp and woof, Gārgī's endeavor to establish the thesis of interrelatedness is accomplished. Only at this point does she become silent.

It could be argued that the principle that interconnects and interrelates different existences of the world is really the principle of Brahman rather than the Goddess principle. Thus, when Yājñavalkya says that the indestructible binds and weaves all disparate elements he could be interpreted as talking about Brahman. This would be of course one commonly accepted way of looking at the dialogue. And indeed it is in this sense that Yājñavalkya himself explains the nature of the indestructible reality. In some Hindu texts, however, the indestructible reality is construed as the Goddess principle. Such an interpretation is not entirely off the mark in light of some of the early Vedic hymns that attempt to construct the pre-Upaniṣadic world-view as the Goddess principle. For instance, the *Devīsūkta* of *Ṛgveda* construes this world-view in terms of goddess Vāc, the daughter of sage Ambhṛṇa, as pervading the entire reality as a connected whole. She says:

> It is I who move in the form of the Rudras, the Vasus, the Ādityas and all the other gods; I support both Mitra and Varuna, Agni and Indra, and the two Ashvins. I support the foe-destroying Soma, Tvashtri, Pūsān and Bhaga; I bestow on the Institutor of the sacrifice, ready with oblations and offering homage to the gods.
>
> I am the sovereign power (over all the worlds),...and the first among those to whom sacrificial homage is to be offered; the gods in all places worship but me, who am diverse in form and permeate everything. Whoever eats food, or sees, or breathes, or hears what is spoken, does it through me.
>
> I pervade heaven and earth. I give birth to the infinite expanse overspreading the earth. I transcend the heaven above, I transcend the earth below. (Griffith 1920-26, 10.125)

Moreover, other Hindu texts argue that Brahman itself is a manifestation of the Goddess, that all attributes predicated of Brahman are really the predicates of the great Goddess. In the *Śrī Devyatharvaśīrṣa,* an Upaniṣadic text, it is argued that all existences are the manifestation of the Goddess who is the nature of Brahman.

The text says:

> Aum, all gods went near the Goddess and asked her, "O great goddess (Mahādevī) who art thou?" She said: I am the nature of the Brahman. Puruṣa and Prakṛti are born of me. This (world)- empty and not-empty -is born of me.
>
> I am the veda and also what is outside the veda. I am knowledge and I am ignorance, that which is *aja* and *anaja,* and that which is above and beneath and on all sides is the manifestation of me. (Kalyāṇ 1987, verses 2 and 4)

In a similar vein, other texts such as the *Devī-Māhātmya* argue for the various ways in which the goddess makes herself known, stating that the goddess is manifested as intelligence (*buddhi*), energy (*śakti*), peace (*śānti*), compassion (*dayā*), prosperity (*lakṣmī*), instinct (*vṛtti*), etc. The great Goddess embraces in her manifestations both the animate and inanimate, seen and unseen worlds. The thesis that everything is interrelated and that this interrelation is grounded in the Goddess principle may be termed *metaphysical feminism.*[7] Metaphysical feminism accepts the Goddess principle as the ultimate reality that binds together different and disparate elements of reality.

Critics of metaphysical feminism have objected that, from the idea that there is an ultimate reality and that there is a principle which interconnects and interrelates different elements, it does not follow that this ultimate reality is feminine in nature. For example, Thomas Coburn says:

> [T]he DM [*Devī-Māhātmya*] does not argue that ultimate reality is feminine...Feminine motifs are, of course, pervasive of the DM. But insofar as the DM is concerned to 'demonstrate' anything, it is that ultimate reality is really ultimate, not that it is feminine. (Coburn 1990, 3)

This line of argument has some validity since in the Western sense of the term "feminine" there is nothing substantial in *Devī-Māhātmya* which would suggest that the ultimate reality is feminine in nature. However, if one means by "feminine" that which pertains to the cultural, psychological, and physical modes of expression of women's being, then one can arguably say that the *Devī-Māhātmya*

---

[7] In contemporary literature the word has been used in a variety of ways. One may refer to Morgan (1982), and Walker (1989).

propounds the nature of reality which is feminine in nature. Not only does the text describe and explain the goddess as feminine, the *vidhi* (that is to say, the ritual) preceding the traditional reading *Devī-Māhātmya* mandates the invocation of the Goddess in the form of ten girls. The text says:

> Two-year-old girl is known as Kumārī, three-year-old as Trimūrti, four-year-old as Kalyāṇī, five-year-old as Rohiṇī, six-year-old as Kālikā, seven-year-old as Caṇḍīkā, eight-year-old as Sāmbhavī, nine-year-old as Durgā, and ten-year-old as Subhadrā. They should be invoked with the help of the following mantra: The embodiment of this mantra, the embodiment of Lakṣmī, the embodiment of mothers, and the embodiment of nine goddessess, I invoke you in this way.
>
> Then one should perform a *pūjā* of these girls reciting the following: O Goddess, you are manifesting yourself in all that is manifested; you are the essence of all things [animate as well as inanimate]; you are the *śakti* of all. O mother of this universe, please you may accept this *pūjā* (Sastri 1985, 21-22)

Thus, the Goddess is seen as feminine insofar as she is considered a woman incarnate and construed in terms of the psychophysical and spiritual aspects of women's beings. Indeed, one can say that it is precisely on the psychophysical and spiritual aspects of women's being that the Hindu psyche has constructed its goddess imagery. Of course, it is also true that her manifestation is not limited only to women's ways of being. Still, this recognition does not change the fact that, according to the *Devī-Māhātmya*, ultimate reality is manifested as feminine.

The existence of a Goddess principle which is in accordance with the women's ways of being—a way of being that interconnects and interrelates different and disparate elements—brings up the question of whether it can be demonstrated that this principle is not just an abstract interrelatedness. As Catherine Keller remarks, "Abstract interrelatedness only means anything when it becomes physically and soulfully almost tangible" (Keller 1986, 161). In other words, does the Goddess principle entail some concrete manifestation in the interaction of people who believe in it? Further, how do women relate to this Goddess principle in a particular culture? I believe these questions can be addressed with the help of the Śākta-Hindu concept of the places of pilgrimage and worship (*śākta-pīṭhas*), and with Frederique Apffel-Marglin's fieldwork in the Indian state of Orissa.

I argue that the Goddess principle is not simply an abstraction. It is realized in the interpersonal relationships between humans and in their interrelationship with the cosmos. I argue that women not only relate to the Goddess principle, but they also perceive themselves as parts *(aṃśa)* of the Goddess. In this sense they themselves are goddesses. These themes, that the Goddess principle provides relationality and continuity, that women relate to the Goddess, are prominent in the voices of Oriya women and men who hail from the community of farmers studied by Frederique Apffel-Marglin. Their voices show beyond doubt that for them the Goddess is not an abstr-action but a living reality, providing them with a sense of continuity and relationality in a religious (*dhārmic*) context.

In two recent essays (1991a and 1991b), Frederique Apffel-Marglin has critically presented her field work on the menstruation festival *(raja parba)* of the Goddess in the Indian state of Orissa. In brief, this is a festival of menstruation of the Goddess who is variously known as Harcaṇḍī, Pṛthibī, Ṭhākurāṇī, Basudhā, Draupadī.[8] Etymologically, the word *raja parba* consists of *raja* (menses) and *parba* (festival), meaning thereby, the festival of the menses of the goddess. Participants believe that the life movements in the environment, that is, the cyclical changes of the seasons and different states of the earth, entail and correspond to the joining and disjoining of humans (that is, wives and husbands).

During this period of June 14-18 the earth itself is said to be menstruating. Hence her separation from the environmental forces, e.g. humans, rain, etc., is observed. It is believed that if humans plough or dig the earth during the menstruation period violates her and makes her unhappy. Conversely, her separation from the environmental forces during her menstruation period would ensure happiness and continuity of the life cycle. This belief entails and corresponds to the belief that during their menstruation women must keep to themselves, and not engage in any kind of work. Doing so

[8] Notwithstanding their different forms and functions these goddesses are manifestations of the same reality. Basudhā is goddess earth, Draupadī is an epic heroine who is also a goddess, and Ṭhākurāṇī is a goddess who is the protector and head of these farming people.

ensures the happiness and continuity of the life cycle; disregard leads to possible chaos and destruction.

The main participants in this festival are women and men from the agricultural community, but other members from different strata of society also take part in this festival. The festival takes place for four days every June 14-18. Each day has its own significance. For instance, on the third day, women try not to walk barefoot on earth so as not to hurt her. During this festival men of some fifty villages go to the temple of Harcaṇḍī, whereas women stay in the villages and celebrate the festival there.

The participants of this festival believe in one Goddess (*iṣṭadevī*) who is known by four different forms. Each manifestation is thought to symbolize different aspects of the great Goddess. For instance, the goddess Harcaṇḍī is mother earth who is said to be menstruating (*raj-asthalā*) during this festival. On the other hand, the goddess Draupadī is remembered and worshipped as the heroine of the epic Mahābhārata. However, for the participants different manifestations of the Goddess are not always distinguishable, and Harcaṇḍī is frequently identified as Draupadī, leading devotees of both forms of the Goddess to speak about them interchangeably.

Women and men believe that both Draupadī the goddess incarnate as the epic heroine of the Mahābhārata, and Harcaṇḍī the goddess incarnate as earth, have menstruation in common. Moreover, women themselves identify with the Goddess, and consider themselves as parts (*aṃśa*) of the Goddess. They believe that they are the representatives (*pratinidhi*) of the Goddess and that their menstruation is from the Goddess. One of the women participants, Dibulata, says, "In this festival the Goddess is at her menses and we follow all these rules [*niyama*] as we are the same kind as her. She is a woman and we all are women" (Apffel-Marglin and Misra 1991b, 53). Another woman, Sishulata, says, "We have this [menses] from her" (Apffel-Marglin and Misra 1991b, 44).

It is not only women who believe in this women-earth-Goddess manifestation of an all pervading one reality: men point that out in even stronger terms. They repeatedly say that women are the representatives, the shadows, of the Goddess. Raghaba Sahu, one of the male participants says, "Mā is at her menses (*māsika*) and our women are her parts (*aṃśa*)...It is their festival; it is the festival of the women folk."[9] Another participant, twenty four year old Sadasiba Jena, says, "According to tradition (*paramparā*) we understand that women are reflections or shadows of Mā and Prithibī. Mā and Prithibī and women are the same thing in different forms" (Apffel-Marglin 1991b, 29).

From this fieldwork it is clear that menstruation, the *sine qua non* aspect of a woman's being, is a focal point around which the conception of the Goddess and the relationship of women to the Goddess is formed for both women and men. The experience of the participants also furnishes an important insight into the nature of the female body. For the participants in the festival, the concept of the female body encompasses more than what is biologically given in a human form. It encompasses a larger reality which is inclusive of the women, earth, and Goddess. This point can be illustrated with reference to conception of the places of pilgrimage and worship (*śākta-pīṭhas*) as presented in the Hindu literature.

As the written and oral traditions explain it, Satī, the daughter of Dakṣa Prajāpati, went uninvited to attend a sacrificial fire (*yajña*) ceremony at her father's house. When she was insulted by her father, she abandoned her body in the fire lit from her body through the power of yoga.[10] The different body parts of Satī's being fell over the land of India and the places at which these parts fell are known as the *śākta-pīṭhas*. For example, Satī's breasts fell at Jalandhar, her vulva (*yoni*) fell at Kamakhya in Assam, her tongue (*jihvā*) fell at Jvalamukhi (Sircar 1948, 42-66). The places of pligrimage and worship where Satī's body parts fell are themselves considered as the parts of the Goddess. In this sense the earth is the body of Satī. Thus, when one refers to Satī, one is at the same time referring to the being of Satī as woman, earth, and Goddess.[11]

---

[9] Other participants also repeatedly say that women are the representatives of the goddess (Apffel-Marglin and Misra 1991b, 21, 22, 24, 25, 26).

[10] There are two prominent versions of this story. One version is explained here and finds some support from the various Sanskrit texts, such as, the *Kumārasaṃbhava* (Kane 1981). According to the other version, Satī's body was cut into pieces by Viṣṇu so that in the absence of Satī's body, Śiva may overcome his grieving. It is in this sense that the *Pīṭhanirṇaya* (Sircar 1948, 42-66) explains the story.

[11] This idea of oneness of the female body has been variously presented in Hindu

This notion of the oneness or the unity of the female body is of fundamental importance in understanding the rites and rituals that center around the concept of one female body. One of the Tāntric texts, the *Pīṭhanirṇaya* (Sircar 1948), describes the goddess as a blood-colored rock (*raktapāṣāṇarūpiṇī*). At Kamakhya where Satī's vulva (*yoni*) fell, specific rites and rituals are performed which presuppose this notion of one female body. Here the blood-colored rock, a part of the earth, represents Satī. As Mookerjee writes:

> Satī's organ of generation fell at Kamakhya, and a temple was built on the hilltop there to mark the spot. It contains no image of the goddess, but in the depth of the shrine there is a yoni-shaped cleft in the rock, adored as the Yoni of Śakti. A natural spring within the cave keeps the cleft moist. During *Ambuvāchi* (July-August), after the first burst of the monsoon, a great ceremony takes place, for the water runs red with iron-oxide, and the ritual drink is symbolic of the *rajas* or *ritu* of the Devī, her menstrual blood. (1988, 30)

In a similar vein, the rites and rituals for the farming community of Orissa, revolve around the female body of the goddess Harcaṇḍī, whose menstruation is collectively celebrated as a religious festival. One of the women participants says:

> Harcaṇḍī is at her menses; three days are gone and tomorrow is Ṭhākurāṇī Gaduā. After taking bath as the girls will do, so also she will do. Red color will be thrown on her so it will appear as if she is bleeding. Pouring this red on her they will treat her as if she were menstruating...yes, that cloth on which the red is thrown will be put in a bucket of water so the water will be red. The priest will show it to the pilgrims and say 'this is the blood of Ṭhākurāṇī.' People out of joy and happiness will take that water. (Apffel-Marglin and Misra 1991b, 44).

---

literature. For example, Kavirāyar (1977, 86) explains this oneness of the female body when he says the following about Draupadī:

> To the five she is the goddess, to others she is the mother.
> She is the goddess Earth,she is Fire's self-manifestation.
> She is a speaker of truth, she is a woman of virtuous
> qualities.
> She is the goddess of this lineage.

III

The rites and rituals which center around the female body of women, earth, and the Goddess form the very conception of religious (*dhārmic*) life and *dharma* (religion) for the Śākta-Hindus. In this section, I consider the meaning of *dharma* as beneficial directions which are considered conducive to the collective happiness and continued well-being of the cosmos. I will explain this collective happiness and the continued well-being in terms of the worship of the female body. According to the *Lakṣmī Tantra*, "The one who despises women, despises Lakṣmī, the one who worships (praises) women, worships (praises) Lakṣmī, and so worships (praises) the three worlds" (Krishanamacharya 1959, 43.64). Once again, voices from the farming community will provide us with further insights into the meaning of religious activities and religion.

For the farming people in Frederique Apffel-Marglin's study, the conception of religion centers around the female body of women-earth-the Goddess. They describe the goddess Harcaṇḍī who is Draupadī as a flagpost, a symbol *(sanketika)* of religion which keeps everything going (Apffel-Marglin and Misra 1991b, 17). The continuity of religion depends on the happiness of women-earth-the Goddess. The participants believe that if the cyclical continuity of menstruation, that is, *strīdharma* is respected and that if women, the earth, and the Goddess are not disturbed during their menstruation period, then the cyclical continuity of life on earth, and happiness, will be ensured.

Conversely, if the female body of women-earth-the Goddess is disturbed during her menstruation, what follows is discontinuity and possible annihilation. The participants often point to the story of goddess Draupadī who was disturbed during her menstruation: what followed was a great battle and almost total annihilation of the tribe of the Kurus. Just as the disturbance of Draupadī's menstruation caused the destruction of the Kuru lineage, the disturbance of mother earth's menstruation period would cause the destruction of crops and other vegetation. Similarly, if women are disturbed during their menstruation by being touched, or forced to attend to regular chores, the family will possibly be destroyed.

Thus, one of the participants says:

A. Draupadī cursed Harcaṇḍī [the victor of the wager and foe to her husbands] and he died. The whole lineage of the Kurus [the Kaurava clan of Harcaṇḍī] was destroyed because of this sin.

Q. What sin?

A. She was disturbed during her *ṛtu* [term for menses]; she was taken by the hair and she was angry and the result was very bad. Everything was destroyed, blood was shed.

Q. Your observances during this festival, does it mean that you give rest to mother earth?

A. Yes. If we do not allow her to rest during her menses, the results will not be good. Our works will not be fruitful. So that's why our women are given lots of rest since they are the representative of mother earth.

Q. What would happen if we do the same thing that the Kauravas did and disturb the earth?

A. We will get afflictions (*dośa*).

Q. What type of afflictions?

A. Everything will be spoiled. If you plow, it will not give results. That is why we give sufficient rest to women during their menses. If they rest it will be good for them. They do no work; they are untouchable (*achūa*) we do not disturb them. So the mother goddess should take rest at this time. (Apffel-Marglin and Misra 1991a, 34)

Hence religious (*dhārmic*) happiness is directly linked to the happiness and worship of the feminine. Giving happiness to women, the earth, and the Goddess partly depends on not disturbing them during their menstruation. During the menstruation festival the earth must not be dug or plowed or one must not walk on the earth barefoot as that would hurt or disturb her.[12] In the same vein women should be given rest during their menstruation and should not be disturbed. One of the male participants says:

Watchman [W]: This is just like the menses of women.

Frederique Apffel-Marglin [FAM]: What does it mean?

---

[12] Sishulata, one of the women participants says, "On the day of *Bhuī Dahana* (burning earth, the 3rd day) we pee on a banana leaf...On that day Basudhā (the earth) will not be dug. We will walk carefully so as not to dig up the earth. It is said that on that day the earth *(bhūmī)* burns. Rubbing or digging the earth will make the earth go away. That is why we pee on a leaf. This is what we do in this area." (Apffel-Marglin and Misra 1991b, 48-49).

W: *Raja* means this: for three days, the *pahilīraja* [the first day], *saṅkranti* [the second day] and *bhuī dahana* [the third day] she is bleeding (oozing).

FAM: Do you see this?

W: No, but we know it. You don't know? The trees, plants, fruits, the crops come because of her menstruation. How did we take birth?

Purna Chandra Misra [PCM]: How do we observe this?

W: We should stop all work.

PCM: Who?

W: Both men and women. Men will stop farming. Women will rest at home and won't walk barefoot.

P: You know, I have become old but when my wife is at her menses she is allowed to stay in a corner and rest. Me and my son cook for ourselves. We do not let her work. We consider her untouchable at that time. If she is not given rest, she will not be in a good condition. (Apffel-Marglin and Misra 1991a, 35)

But giving rest to mother earth or to a woman during the menstruation period is only one way to make them happy. Other ways to make them happy, and thereby make religious (*dhārmic*) life happy, consists in worshipping the female body with offerings. The men at Harcaṇḍī offer sacrificial animals to the goddess to make her happy. According to one of the participants:

> We have finished ploughing and we are waiting for rain so the right time *(pagayoga)* for sowing will come. So this is the time we come to Harcaṇḍī to offer her animal sacrifice *(boda)* for her pleasure so that she will take care to give us proper rains so that we will have good crops. We come here because she is the most powerful goddess of the earth (*pruthibī*). She is the goddess who protects us from the sea; she is here on the sea because if she were not we would be under water. So we come here to take shelter under her feet for four days; we worship her to make her happy and this is the right time to do that. (Apffel-Marglin and Misra 1991b, 16-17)

Similarly, women are kept happy by being given clothes, ornaments, and leisure time. During this festival, women receive the *raja* basket containing clothes, etc. from their parents, and their husbands also provide them with clothes. One of the men explains:

> The *raja* basket comes from our father-in-law's place for them and it makes them very happy. They get new clothes from their parents. Sometimes seeing our financial situation we also give new clothes to our

> women. The women do not cook and they eat before sunset; they also play on swings, play cards, sing songs and keep themselves happy. If the father cannot send anything the husbands take care to purchase everything carefully for their wives, so they become happy. So also the goddess becomes glad at the gifts and presentations of the men who pray to her. She becomes glad at this, so also her representatives as women, they become glad, so *prakṛti* is happy and her representatives are also happy.

Like men, women also make the Goddess happy by praying to her and by decorating and keeping themselves happy, since they are goddesses themselves. Dibulata Devi says:

> She (i.e. the goddess) is a woman and we all are women. We do not work. We play on swings, tying ropes in trees; we play cards; we do not walk barefoot so as not to give her pain. We decorate ourselves during this festival. We walk with friends and sing together. This reminds us of our menarche festival when everyone keeps us happy. Now we make ourselves happy during raja. People also love us when we take care of our bodies. So also our men go to goddess Harcaṇḍī to worship her, to please her by offering goats and rams. We women also do the things to please mother earth, so that she will give us fruitfulness, and by that she becomes active and ready to bear fruit, by which we all live.

Central to these religious festivities is the belief that actions pertaining to religion attain fruition only if the female body is worshipped. The continuation of life on earth depends on the proper worship of mother earth, and the continuation of human life depends on the proper worship of women in society.

To conclude, then, for the Śākta-Hindus, the notion of religion gains significance only when the divine is worshipped as feminine in the form of women-earth-the Goddess. The cyclical changes in a woman's body correspond to and represent the cyclical changes in the seasons. Their religious belief and awareness does not separate the environment from humans; they find connections in these events. When mother earth has her menstruation period, women also believe that they have their menstruation periods. For men, the belief that during the menstruation festival goddess earth should be kept happy by worship and offerings, is directly related and translatable into the belief that women are parts of the goddess and they should also be worshipped. Thus, it is the Goddess principle that provides them with the understanding of both the interrelatedness of humans and their surroundings. It also provides them with the understanding of religion as a way of life that gives continuity and meaning to human endeavors.

Conclusion

In this essay taking the Goddess tradition of India as a paradigmatic example, I have argued that the divine envisaged as the female body is the all-pervading reality that interconnects and interrelates different and disparate elements of life. In Section I of this essay, I have discussed the problems of interpretation and context and offered a context-sensitive definition of women's nature in terms of menstruation. Here, I have argued that a woman's own nature (*strīsvabhāva*) can be construed as a woman's religion (*strīdharma*). My main aim here has been to forge a link between the notions of female embodiment and religion. To this end, I have defined a woman's religion (*strīdharma*) not in terms of the duties that liberate women, but in terms of menstruation.

In Section II, I have offered a theological framework within which the divine may be envisaged as feminine. I have argued that the principle that interconnects and interrelates different elements of life can be better explained as the Goddess than as Brahman. Further, I have argued that the Brahman itself can in turn be understood as a manifestation of the Goddess. In response to the objection that the Goddess, viewed as ultimate reality, need not be regarded as feminine, I have pointed out that the method of Goddess worship mandates worshipping the Goddess in the form of ten girls.

I have also argued that if one means by "feminine" that which pertains to the psychological, cultural and biological ways of women's being, then in Hinduism the Goddess is definitely feminine, since it is precisely on women's ways of being that a Śākta-Hindu has constructed its Goddess imagery. Further, I have argued that the Goddess principle so construed as interrelation and interconnection is not an empty abstraction, but has concrete meaning for people who believe in it. The Goddess principle not only provides meaning to the social interaction between men and women, but more important, it connects them to their environment. Women and men both regard women as parts, as manifestations of the Goddess. Further, the interconnection among the Goddess, the earth, and women in the family is linked through menstruation, the *sine qua non* aspect of the feminine. It is menstruation that provides the meaning to the divine as the feminine manifesting herself in form of women, earth, and the Goddess.

In Section III, I have argued that from a Śākta-Hindu perspective the notion of religion and religious life are themselves dependent on the worship of the feminine. As we have noted earlier, the Goddess is a symbol of religion (*dharma*). Thus the notion of female embodiment has a direct bearing on the phenomenon of religion. In fact, the phenomenon of religion cannot be sufficiently explained without understanding the importance of and centrality of the female body of women, earth, and the Goddess. As a new discipline, feminist/womanist approach can effectively contribute to the study of philosophy of religion by further investigating the role and centrality of the female body in religious experience.

BIBLIOGRAPHY

Amos, Valerie, and Pratibha Parmar. 1984. Challenging Imperial feminism. *Feminist Review* 17: 3-19.

Apffel-Marglin, Frederique, in collaboration with Purna Chandra Misra. 1991a. *Woman's Blood: Challenging the Discourse of Development*. Unpublished manuscript.

_____. 1991b. *Gender and the Unitary Self: Locating the Dominant When Listening to the Subaltern Voice*. Unpublished manuscript.

Avalon, Arthur, trans. 1984. *Ānandalaharī*. New Delhi: Abhinav Publications.

Brown, C. Mackenzie. 1990. *The Triumph of the Goddess*. Albany, New York: State University of New York Press.

Coburn, Thomas. 1984. *The Crystalization of the Goddess Tradition*. Delhi: Motilal Banarasidass.

_____. 1991. *Encountering the Goddess*. Albany, New York: State University of New York Press.

Griffith, R.T.H., trans. 1920-1926. *Ṛgveda*. Benaras: E.J. Lazarus & Company.

Gupta, Sanjukta. 1972. *Lakṣmī Tantra*. Leiden: E.J. Brill.

Hiltebeitel, Alf. 1988. *The Cult of Draupadī*. 2 vols. Chicago: The University of Chicago Press.

Kak, Ram Chandra, and Haribhatta Shastri, trans. 1985. *Devīrahasya*. Vadodara: Butala Publications.

Kale, Moreshvar, trans. 1981. *Kumārasaṃbhava*. Delhi: Motilal Banarasidass.

_____. (1934) 1982. *Uttararāmacharita of Bhavabhūti*. Delhi: Motilal Banarasidass.

Kavirayar, I. (1857) 1977. *Śrī Makāpārata Vilācam Cūtu-Tukilurital*. Madras: Irattiṉa Nāyakar and Sons.

Keller, Catherine. 1986. *From a Broken Web: Separation, Sexism, and Self.*

Boston: Beacon Press.
_____. 1989. Feminism and the Ethic of Inseparability. In *Weaving the visions*. See Plaskow and Christ 1989.
Kinsley, David. 1985. *The Hindu Goddesses.* Berkeley: University of California Press.
Krishnamacharya, V., ed. 1959. *Lakṣmī Tantra*. Madras: The Adyar Library and Research.
Leslie, Julia. 1989. *The Perfect Wife: The Orthodox Hindu Woman According to the Strīdharmapaddhati of Tryambakayajvan.* Delhi: Motilal Banarasidass.
Mookerjee, Ajit. 1988. *Kālī.* London: Thames and Hudson.
Morgan, Robin. 1982. Metaphysical Feminism. In *The Politics of Women's Spirituality*, ed. Charlene Spretnak. New York: Anchor Press.
Nene, Gopalsastri, trans. 1970. *Manusmṛti.* Varanasi: Chaukhamba Sanskrit Series.
Nyayaratna, M., ed. 1889. *Pūrva Mīmāṃsā Sūtra of Jaimini*. Calcutta: Asiatic Society.
Plaskow, Judith, and Carol Christ, eds. 1989. *Weaving the Visions*. San Francisco: Harper.
Powers, Marla. 1980. Menstruation and Reproduction: An Oglala Case. *Signs* 6.1 (Autumn): 54-65.
Radhakrishnan, Sarvapalli. (1953) 1969. *The Principal Upanṣiads*. London: Allen & Unwin.
Sastri, Sankardatta, trans. 1985. *Śrī Caṇḍīpāṭha*. Bombay: Sastu Sahitya.
Sastry, Ananthakrishna, trans. (1951) 1970. *Lalitā-sahasranāman.* Adyar: The Theosophical Publishing House.
Sharma, Arvind. 1993. *Hinduism*. In *Our Religions*, ed. Arvind Sharma. San Francisco: HarperCollins.
Shastri, J., trans. 1970. *Śiva Purāṇa*. 4 vols. Delhi: Motilal Banarasidass.
Shweder, Richard. 1991. *Thinking Through Cultures.* Cambridge: Harvard University Press.
Sircar, Dineshchandra. 1948. *Pīṭhanirṇaya*. In *The Śākta Pīṭhas. Journal of the Royal Asiatic Society of Bengal* XIV: 42-66.
Śrī devyathārvaśīrṣa. 1987. In *Kalyāṇ* 61.1: 15-19.
Sukthankar, V.S. et al., eds. 1933-1939. *Mahābhārata*. 19 vols. Poona: Bhandarkar Oriental Research Institute.
Swami, Jagadiswarananda, trans. (1953) 1986. *Devī Mahātmya.* Madras: Sri Ramakrishna Math.
Swami, Vijnanananda, trans. (1921-23) 1977. *Śrīmad Devī Bhāgwatam.* New Delhi: Oriental Books.
Walker, Alice. 1989. "God is Inside You and in Everybody Else". In *Weaving the Visions*. See Plaskow and Christ 1989.
Woodroffe, John. (1918) 1969. *Śakti and Śākta.* Madras: Ganesh and Company.

CHAPTER FOUR

WOMEN IN THE WORSHIP OF THE GREAT GODDESS

HILLARY RODRIGUES

Introduction

In the autumn month of Āśvina (September/October), during the first nine nights (*navarātra*) of the fortnight in which the moon waxes bright (*śukla pakṣa*), Hindus celebrate the festival of the Great Goddess (Mahādevī). This festival is often called the Āśvina Navarātra to distinguish it from the nine night spring festival to the Goddess, held in the month of Caitra (March/April). Although popular participation in the Āśvina Navarātra surpasses the Caitra celebrations, particularly in urban centres such as Banaras and Calcutta, these two festivals constitute the major periods in the yearly cycle when attention is focussed primarily on the Goddess. The Devī receives a rich assortment of devotional worship from both men and women during the Navarātras. In this chapter I describe salient varieties of worship practices performed by Hindu women to the Goddess. I then examine the images and roles of women during such rituals. I inquire into the ways in which women's roles, images, and activities differ from male worship patterns and proceed to reflect on the differences.[1] I suggest that the festivals of worship of the Great Goddess serve to elevate the "feminine" to a highly auspicious status, while simultaneously encouraging specific states of womanhood.

---

[1] This chapter draws on field research conducted primarily in Banaras (Vārāṇasī) during the years 1990 and 1991. I am particularly grateful to the Social Sciences and Humanities Research Council of Canada and the School of Graduate Studies at McMaster University, Hamilton, Ontario, for their generous financial support. One may consult Rodrigues (1993) for a more substantial study on goddess worship in Banaras.

Which Goddess?

During the Navarātras, it is common to see devotees crowding into virtually every goddess temple for *darśana*, profound perceptual interaction with the Divine. Besides worship at major goddess temples, devotees also worship at smaller shrines, at sacred water tanks, at rivers, and at goddess effigies established especially at these times of the year. The vast array of differently named goddesses that are worshipped during these Navarātras naturally raises the question whether just one deity is the object of devotion. To further complicate matters, even in a particular worship ritual, one may find that devotion is addressed to goddesses in different forms and epithets.[2] Nevertheless, despite this seeming profusion of images, names, and places of worship, through observation, inquiry, and close attention to the liturgy of rituals it becomes clear that devotion is offered to the Divine Feminine in her most supreme aspect, through the medium of any number of chosen goddess images or image clusters. I therefore suggest that the Navarātras are times of worship of the Great Goddess rather than any goddess in particular.[3]

In Banaras, a city which often mirrors and sometimes shapes the character of Hindu religiosity throughout India, the terms most often used by devotees for the object of their devotions during these festivals are simply Devī (Goddess) or Mahādevī (Great Goddess).[4] The most frequently encountered names used to address the Devī are Mā (mother), Durgā, or Mā Durgā.[5] As these epithets suggest, the most pervasive conceptual images of the Great Goddess during the Navarātras is that of a Cosmic Mother, creatrix, nourisher, and nurturer of the world, or that of the regal warrior goddess Durgā, whose many

---

[2] A detailed study of the variety of names and forms of the Devī during the Durgā Pūjā ritual may be found in my forthcoming article, tentatively entitled "Faces of the Goddess."

[3] I use the terms Great Goddess, Goddess, Devī, and Mahādevī, synonymously to refer to the supreme form of the Divine Feminine. For lesser forms, I use particular epithets, or the general terms, *devī* and goddess.

[4] For more on the Great Goddess of Hinduism see Brown 1990, Kinsley 1986, Kramrisch 1975, and Humes 1991. On the cycle of worship festivals to all deities throughout the year in Banaras see Eck 1982.

[5] Devotees may refer to the Great Goddess by other names such as Mahālakṣmī, or Mahākālī. However such epithets are far less frequently encountered.

arms wield a host of weapons.[6] Durgā is often portrayed astride her mount, a great lion, or engaged in crushing the Buffalo demon, Mahiṣa. In fact, of the many goddess festivals which occur throughout the year, such as the Kālī, Lakṣmī or Sarasvatī Pūjās, only the ritual worship festival of Durgā coincides with the autumn Navarātras, leading many worshippers to use the terms Durgā Pūjā and Āśvina Navarātra synonymously.[7]

Types of devotional activities

A. *Home shrine worship (*pūjā*)*

Offering a five-part service (*pañcopacāra*) to the Devī image in a home shrine is one of the simplest devotional activities performed by worshippers during the Navarātras. This image may be something as simple as a framed lithograph print of the Devī or a more elaborate stone sculpture. The five-part devotional service may be used in the worship of any deity and generally consists of offering fragrant anointing paste (*gandha*), fragrant fresh flowers (*puṣpa*), fragrant incense (*dhūpa*), the flame (*dīpa*) from a lamp, and a piece of food (*naivedya*). When combined with other devotional elements such as utterances (*mantra*) of praise and homage, and gestures of obeisance (*praṇāma*), such acts of worship are termed *pūjā*. Although worshippers may perform *pūjā* to the images in their home shrines throughout the year, during the Navarātras one discerns an intensification of the devotion. Few, if any, of the five offerings will be omitted, and special or higher quality items may be utilized. Also, although the Devī image may be that of Lakṣmī, or Kālī, goddesses who are worshipped under those epithets on their respective festival days, during the Navarātras these images represent

---

[6] For information on the Goddess as Mother or as Durgā, see Bandyopadyay 1987, Bhattacharyya 1971, Brown 1974, Divakaran 1984, and Kinsley 1986.

[7] My own use of the term Durgā Pūjā is restricted to refer to the celebrations which take place mainly during the last days of the autumn Navarātras. These celebrations involve the worship of Durgā and attending deities in large, colourful clay images which are set up in temporarily erected shrines. After the *pūjā*, the images are delivered into a venerated body of water, such as the river Gaṅgā. For the cycle of goddess festivals celebrated throughout the year in Banaras, see Rodrigues 1993. For a detailed study of the Durgā Pūjā ritual, see the *Purohita Darpaṇa*, a Bengali ritual text. Also consult Ghosha 1871, Ostor 1980, and Rodrigues 1993.

subsidiary forms of the Great Goddess who is the actual object of devotion.

B. *Temple visits (*darśana*)*

It is quite common for devotees to include regular visits to Devī temples during the Navarātras. Such worship may consist of a daily visit to the same nearby or favorite Devī temple or to nine different temples during the nine days of Navarātras. Thus, for instance, a devotee living near Banaras's Daśāśvamedha Ghat, might visit the famous temple of Annapūrṇādevī on each of the nine days. Alternatively, she may choose to perform the Nine Durgā Pilgrimage (*navadurgā yātrā*), visiting a different Durgā temple on each of the nine days. The temple of Annapūrṇā Devī, incidentally, is one of these nine Durgā temples.

The central act of worship at temples is *darśana*, a word which means "view" or "vision" in its broadest sense. During *darśana*, paralleling a visit to a monarch, devotees seek to have a successful and intimate audience with the Devī. These visits may be gestures of respectful homage, but more often they are motivated by hopes and fears. Worshippers often come seeking some favour from the Goddess who is thought to be particularly accessible during the Navarātras. Her power oozes out of the earth and water and radiates from any shrine where her seat/throne (*pīṭha*) has been established. There, the Devī's grace may fall upon her devotees granting them their most cherished desires, or protecting them from their most dreaded fears. Although the Goddess may be honoured with as little as an empty-handed but sincere visit, devotees at temples generally perform some variation of the five-part devotional service (*pañcopacāra*) performed in home *pūjā*s. Worshippers may also make a pledge (*manauti*) in which they promise the Devī some loyal devotional activity in return for a favour granted. Regular temple visits, a pilgrimage and service at a temple, or rendering a particular offering such as a blood sacrifice (*bali*) or a child's first tonsure (*muṇḍana*) are common promises. In all cases, however, *darśana* embodies the conceptual notion of a profound and intimate perceptual interaction with the Devī.[8] In *darśana*'s ideal expression, the

---

[8] For the reciprocation of vision in *darśana*, see Eck 1981. For the exchange of sound in worship through *mantra*s, see Coward and Goa 1991. In Rodrigues 1993, I elaborate upon the suggestion that *pūjā* is an act of reintegration of all one's constituent elements (of which the senses are a part) with the Absolute. The

devotees' entire beings, their gross constituent elements, all their senses, including sight, and even their inner mental faculties are engulfed in a unifying "vision" of the Devī.

While I found that male *brāhmaṇa* pandits defined the typical five-part service as consisting of *gandha*, *puṣpa*, *dhūpa*, *dīpa*, and *naivedya*, worshippers described their offerings differently, mentioning instead the specific items they would use in Devī worship. These were *rorī/candana* (a fragrant red powder derived from flowers, and sandalwood powder), *karpūra* (camphor), *agarbattī* (incense sticks), *maulī/cunri* (a thread or cloth scarf), *ilāyacī dānā* (cardamom sweets), *nāriyala* (coconut), and *phūl kī mālā* (flower garland). One notes that the red powder (*rorī*), camphor, incense sticks, and cardamom sweets are less expensive forms of the fragrant paste derived from sandalwood (*candana*), the flame from a clarified butter (*ghī*) lamp, lavish incense (cone or powdered), or the food offerings prescribed by orthodox tradition. However, the choice of offerings is also noticibly adapted to the feminine nature of the Goddess. The feminine in Hindu thought is traditionally associated with blood, which is seen as the animating juice of life, the nourishment of life, and the reproductive complement of male semen (O'Flaherty 1980:33). Blood, or its symbols, are thus significant components in offerings to the Devī. The feminine is often conceived of as identical with the created cosmos and its natural component elements such as earth, water, fire, and air.[9] Although nature and blood are symbols of the profane creation and its processes, the Devī, who is the Divine Feminine, is associated with sacred qualities of purity and chastity. For this reason, in the items used in Goddess worship one finds a merging of the symbols of blood, purity, and nature.

The flame, paste, fragrant smoke, flowers, and food of the *pūjā* offerings symbolize the constituent elements of nature, as well as its nourishing qualities. The red powdered *rorī*, symbol of blood, is an important complement to sandalwood paste (*candana*), whose saffron yellow colour symbolizes the purity of renunciation. In goddess

---

reciprocation of sight and sound are the two most prominent features of *pūjā* which includes mutual touching, smelling, and tasting of devotee and deity.

[9] In classical Sāṃkhya philosophy, reality is composed of pure spirit or *puruṣa*, and pure matter, *prakṛti* (See Larson 1969, Aranya 1983, Eliade 1970). Over time, *puruṣa* came to be identified with the masculine principle and *prakṛti* with the feminine. The Devī is often identified with *prakṛti* (See, for example, *Durgā Saptaśatī* 1.78, 4.7, 5.9, and 11.4. Also see Kinsley (1986:135-136).

worship, offerings of garlands of red flowers, such as the hibiscus, are preferred to the yellow marigold blossoms more commonly offered to all deities. After being offered to the Devī, the red garland, when placed around a devotee's neck, evokes the image of blood oozing from the devotee's severed neck. The coconut, which is smashed when offered in order to release its contained fluid, also carries the symbolism of a sacrificial offering of the head and blood. In further contrast to the typical five-part offerings made to other deities, offerings to the Devī include the *maulī/cunri*. This offering is drawn from more elaborate ten or sixteen-part devotional services (*daśopacāra, ṣoḍaśopacāra*) which typically include an offering of clothing (*vastra*) to the deity. Since traditional Hindu thought envisions women as fond of clothing and ornamentation, the thread or scarf offering, which is made even in very simple acts of goddess worship, and which symbolizes the gift of a female garment (*sārī*), most likely is an acknowledgement of the Devī's femininity. The thread or scarf is generally dyed red with traces of yellow, reiterating the joint symbolism of blood and purity. When bound around the wrist after being offered, the thread evokes the symbol of a binding relationship of protection and service also found in such rituals as the Guru Pūjā and Rakṣā Bandhana.[10]

Both men and women visit temples for *darśana* of the Devī during the Navarātras, and both may worship in the ways described above. However, my observations in Banaras indicate that more women than men perform the "full" five-part devotional service. I noticed that men are far more likely to purchase a sole flower garland just before entering the temple for *darśana* while women often come to the temple with bags or plastic carrying cases crammed full of the necessary offerings for devotional worship. This observation was shared by a temple priest at the Devī Mahāmāyā Śītalā temple in Banāras who remarked that in general "men come for *darśana*, while women come for *pūjā*." The

[10] In the Guru Pūjā, students receive a wrist thread from their teachers (*guru*) as a symbol of the relationship which binds them to each other. In the Rakṣā Bandhana (Protective Knotting), sisters generally tie decorative strings around their brothers' wrists. The feminine power of sisters provides protection for their male siblings. The tradition originated in a similar gesture of protection, where members of the priestly class (*brāhmaṇas*) would tie a protective knot on the wrist of members of the warrior class (*kṣatriya*) symbolizing the latter's dependence on the protection of the former. Although the king and his soldiers are considered to be protectors of the earth and its subjects, the priesthood symbolically conferred divine protection upon them.

thrust of the priest's distinction between male and female modes of worship, I suggest, is less between the ultimate meanings and aims of *darśana* and *pūjā*, and more between the general activities suggested by the terms. According to him, men come primarily to see, women to do.

In temples in Banaras, I also noticed that women appeared to be far less restrained in their devotional fervour. Barriers are erected in the main porches of the most popular temples during the Navarātras in order to segregate the sexes as they approach the inner sanctum for *darśana*. This separation allows for clear observation of the differences between male and female activity. The men appeared more reserved and restrained when they entered the temple. They formed orderly lines which only gave way to a crush of bodies just before the doors to the inner sanctum. The women, in contrast, were far more lively, ringing the temple bells with abandon and enjoying the contact with the crowds despite the discomfort caused by the suffocating press of worshippers. The bodies on their side of the barricades often appeared to form a single mass which rhythmically surged like waves in the ocean. While women appeared to be far more comfortable with the physical contact with their own sex, the men appeared to maintain a certain territoriality around their persons for a much longer period of time and only surrendered this out of necessity to the crowd before the sanctum.[11]

C. *Pledged devotional activities (*manauti*)*

As mentioned above, devotees may pledge (*manauti*) to perform particular acts in return for a favour (*vara*) from the goddess. In my experience, women far exceed men in this type of pledging although both sexes do participate in barter with the Divine. Women often request from the Devī favorable marriages for themselves or their offspring, or the well-being of their spouses and children, or for the birth of children. Men seem to be concerned with success, economically or in work and school, the defeat of rivals, and the acquisition of personal power. It is quite common to see first tonsures (*muṇḍana*) of children performed at Devī temples. This is a highly visible, although not necessarily the most common, fulfilment of a *manauti*. Mothers (on

---

[11] In the case of both males and females, however, the attitude to public physical contact with members of the same sex is much more relaxed in India than in western cultures. For instance, it is quite common for male friends to embrace and walk hand in hand in public.

occasion with their spouses and often with other female family members) visit the temple of the Devī, where they had requested the birth of a child, in order to perform the child's first tonsure (*muṇḍana*). This ritual shaving of the head, removing the hair which accompanied the child at birth, marks a rite of passage (*saṃskāra*) from mother-dependent childhood towards independent personhood. When performed at a goddess shrine, the ritual suggests that the child is actually moving away from dependence on its earthly mother to a new state of empowered dependence on the Cosmic Mother.[12]

D. *Vowed devotional observances (*vrata*)*

Although resembling the pledged devotional activity (*manauti*), the vowed devotional observance (*vrata*) differs in nature. It is much more strongly associated with female religious practice.[13] Women perform *vrata*s throughout the year, often for the well-being of their marital relationships, their spouses, offspring, and other family members. Unlike *manautis*, which generally involve a "payback" of a pledge for a favour granted by the Devī, the *vrata* is performed before the granting of any boon. While a *manauti* may involve the offering of a child's hair, or a donation of a flag or bell to the temple of the Goddess, or even the sacrificial offering of a goat, *vrata*s always have an element of renunciation, personal asceticism, or austerity.[14] Thus *vrata*s may consist of

---

[12] A sacrificial interpretation of the tonsure ritual is found in Erndl 1987.

[13] An excellent study of the practice of *vrata*s among Hindu women in Banaras is found in Pearson 1992. For a detailed discussion of *vrata*s among women in the state of Maharashtra see McGee 1989, 1991. McGee (1991) points out that although there is an element of desire (*kāmya*) in the motives of women, the main reason for performing *vrata*s is a pressing sense of duty (*nitya*). According to her research, contractual rites (i.e., *manauti*, *navas* in Marathi) are generally motivated by desires (*kāmya*) (1991:81).

[14] My own research (based on a qualitative rather than quantitative assessment of devotees' motivations) suggests that *vratas* must be performed regularly in order to sustain the structures of the ritually created universe within which Hindus live. *Manautis* must be performed to restore the imbalance in the processes of the cosmos caused by divine intervention. People request special favours from deities when the karmic consequences they face in this round of worldly existence are unfavourable. The *manauti* is not merely the request, but the fulfilment of the devotee's side of the contract. While the request is desire-born (*kāmya*), the fulfilment carries an extremely strong and urgent sense of duty (*nitya*), since abrogating one's responsibility could lead to stern divine retribution. In this respect, *manautis* have a greater element of obligation (*nitya*) than *vratas*, which may occasionally be neglected without immediate dire consequences.

placing restrictions on the diet or complete fasting, restricting one's sleep, regularly visiting a temple, or performing some sort of pilgrimage.

During the Navarātras, a large percentage of both male and female goddess worshippers engage in *vrata*-like activities. It is quite common for devotees to restrict their diet to curd (*dadhi*) and fruit (*phala*). Many attempt to stay awake throughout the night. While an intense application of such austerities would be to sustain them for the entire nine days of the festival, devotees are much more likely to attempt such fasts or all-night vigils only on the first (*pratipadā*) and ninth (*navamī*) days, or on the last three days of the Navarātras. In Banaras, women engaged in Devī worship often modify their cooked food preparations throughout Navarātras. For instance, a preparation (*khiciṛi*) made of unprocessed rice (*kuṭu cāval*), green chili, and ginger is a staple cooked food during the Navarātras. Women also use flour (*āṭā*) made from a black skinned, leathery, horned water chestnut (*śṛṅgāra*) and flavour their food with a reddish rock salt (*sendhā namak*). The uncooked, unprocessed, or less-refined nature of these foods associates them more with renunciation and spiritual potency than with bodily nutrition.

E. *Pilgrimage*

Pilgrimage may be performed either as a *manauti* or as a *vrata*.[15] In return for such a favour as having her son married successfully (which often means his having a child not long after the marriage), a mother may perform a pilgrimage to the temple of the goddess from whom she had made such a request. Women who make such requests and perform such pilgrimages may spend anywhere from a few hours to a few days at the Devī temple. They often set up a domicile in some section of the temple's pilgrim shelters (*dharmaśālā*) and perform such services as worshipping the deity, cleaning the temple, and feeding the priests. Pilgrimage is often recommended as an ideal devotional activity for post-menopausal women, since they are free from the periodic pollutions which Hindu orthodoxy deems are caused by menstruation. Post-menopausal women are considered pure enough to prepare cooked food offerings for deities and for *brāhmaṇa* priests. Generally, the food

[15] Interesting studies of Hindu pilgrimages are found in Gold 1988 and Sax 1991, where the emphases and purposes are different from the type of local pilgrimage being discussed here.

eaten on pilgrimages is simple but delicious, such as deep fried whole wheat bread (*pūrī*), curried vegetables (*sabjī*), and a sweetened paste of wheat flour (*halvā*). Men may accompany the women on these excursions although they are less likely to engage actively in service (*sevā*) to the deity or the priests. They generally wander around the pilgrimage site, take *darśana* of the goddess, perform a little devotional worship (*pūjā*), chat with the priests and other pilgrims, and enjoy the food prepared by the women. After all, on such a visit, they are merely accompanying the women who are engaged in fulfilling their own *manauti*s.

Pilgrimages may also be performed by both men and women during the Navarātras out of either the ascetic spiritual practice (*sādhanā*) or *vrata* impulse. Pilgrimages such as the Nine Durgā Yātrā in Banaras require pilgrims to visit a different goddess temple on each of the nine nights of Navarātra. Since they return home after each temple visit, both women and men may engage in such a pilgrimage without having to leave their domicile for extended periods of time. On the other hand, pilgrimages to the temple of Vindhyavāsinī Devī, some ninety kilometers from Banaras or to the powerful pilgrimage sites located there (e.g., Kālī Kuam, Tārā Pīṭha, and Bhairava Kuṇḍa) may require more than a single day. I have met male pilgrims, both lay persons and members of ascetic orders (such as Aghoris), who might spend much of Navarātra at a single powerful site (*siddha pīṭha*) deeply engaged in spiritual practice (*sādhanā*). They cook and share their food with others at this time.

While the Nine Durgā Pilgrimage is prescribed for the Aśvina Navarātra, it is performed by large numbers of men and women during both Navarātras in Banaras. By comparison, the Nine Gaurī Pilgrimage, made to the pure, fair-skinned (*gaurī*) goddesses of the city, draws a very small number of pilgrims. The recommended time for the Nine Gaurī Pilgrimage is the Caitra Navarātra, but my observations showed that most pilgrims persist in performing the Nine Durgā Pilgrimage again during the spring festival. It suggests that both Navarātras are viewed as festivals to the Great Goddess, Durgā. It is noteworthy that while the Nine Durgā Pilgrimage attracts both male and female pilgrims, the Nine Gaurī Pilgrimage is performed almost exclusively by women, a point to which I will return later in this chapter.

F. *Spiritual practice (*sādhanā*)*

These observations bring us to significant points of difference between male and female religiosity concerning the Goddess during Navarātra. Men, more than women, are likely to engage in spiritual practice (*sādhanā*) during Navarātra. The ascetic mode of spiritual practice among women takes the form of the *vrata*. One of the salient distinctions between *sādhanā* and *vrata* is that while men perform *sādhanā* for themselves, women perform *vrata*s for others. Men therefore are often the lucky recipients of power, protection, or other benefits which derive from their own actions as well as the actions of women. The source of both power and protection is, of course, the Goddess. Through *vrata*s women intensify their identification with the purity and auspiciousness of the Devī. In this manner they embody in varying degrees that creative, nurturing, and nourishing power (*śakti*) which is virtually synonymous with the Goddess.[16] Through *sādhanā* men seek to tap into that power.

What further distinguishes the two activities is that male *sādhanā* involves ritual components which are generally forbidden to women. Men who are capable of reading Sanskrit often recite the *Durgā Saptaśatī (The Seven Hundred [Verses] to Durgā)*, the most popular devotional text of Goddess worship.[17] Orthodox tradition forbids women from reciting Sanskritic texts such as the *Durgā Saptaśatī*, and I have never observed women do so in public. Also, I have never observed women practice the recitation of sacred utterances of homage to the goddess (Devī *mantra*) while making fire oblations, alone. They do participate in such rituals, but in lesser numbers than men. Fire oblations (*havan*) are a widespread form of worship during Navarātra, especially on the final day (*navamī*).

Roles and images of women during goddess worship

A. *Priestess (*pujārī*)*

Hindu priests who perform the worship rituals for a deity in a public

---

[16] On the nature and worship of Śakti as the Goddess, see Bhattacharyya 1974, Coburn 1982, and Das 1934.

[17] It is also known as the *Devī-Māhātmya*. Excellent recent textual studies of the *Devī-Māhātmya* are by Coburn 1984, 1991. On the ritual recitation of the text in goddess temples, see Humes 1990.

temple, a patron's home shrine, or during a festival are called *pujārīs*.[18] *Pujārīs* are most often male, even in goddess temples and during goddess festivals. Since women, even from the *brāhmaṇa* classes, are far less likely to be trained in the recitation of Sanskrit prayers, they are rarely commissioned for such duties. However, there are no orthodox prohibitions against initiated women performing such functions. Although it is uncommon, I have seen women preside as priestesses at goddess temples throughout the year and during the Navarātras. Shanti Devi, for instance, ministers to the goddess at a small Kālī temple in Banaras. She took over the responsibilities after the death of her husband. Similarly, the daughters of the chief priest at the temple of Kātyāyanī Devī, the sixth of Banaras's Nine Durgās, minister to devotees during the Navarātras. I was also informed that a priestess, if qualified through special Śākta initiation (*dīkṣā*) may perform the extremely elaborate Durgā Pūjā ritual. Middle aged devotees told me that in their youth they had seen such female priestesses perform the Durgā Pūjā.

It is clear that men far outnumber women in the priestly function of goddess worship particularly in urban centres. Since goddess worship flourishes in villages and since it draws a substantial part of its character from non-Brahmanical sources, it is possible that there are larger percentages of women priestesses in rural worship centres where class concerns and Sanskrit liturgy are not of paramount importance.

B. *Spiritual healers (Hindi:* ojhā*)*

Spiritual healers (*ojhā*) often perform their work at the shrines of goddesses. To devout Śāktas, the Devī is perceived as the source of all power, and thus if properly propitiated may protect her devotees from the onslaught of afflictions. Afflictions may be both physical and psychological. They may include diseases caused by seasonal changes of climate, possession by some malicious spirit, or pernicious psychic attacks by one's enemies through the agency of sorcerers (*H: jādū karne vālā*). The causes of these afflictions are often personified as demons or minor feminine deities such as Śītalā, the goddess of smallpox or cholera, the Mothers (*mātṛkā*),

Yakṣīs, or Yoginīs. In some measure all these represent aspects or

[18] On the roles of priests in Goddess temples, see Fuller 1984.

subordinate forms of the Great Goddess, or beings who have derived their power from her. Her power is ultimately the source of destructive afflictions.

To devout Śāktas, however, the Devī is a compassionate and protective Cosmic Mother, who is immediately and intrinsically present whenever one is afflicted. The chills and fevers of disease reveal the battle between her protective and pernicious power. Healers are particularly adept at channelling the power of the Devī, both pernicious and protective. They may absorb a patient's disease into their own bodies, or serve as a medium through which the Devi's advice or power reaches the patient. Both men and women work as healers. At the renowned Durgā Kuṇḍ temple in Banāras, Sukhadevī, widow of the flamboyant healer Mithai Lal, currently ministers to his patients. Healers such as Sukhadevī are very likely to frequent sacred goddess sites reputed for their success at empowerment (*siddha pīṭha*). The Devī's power is particularly accessible during Navarātras.

C. *Artists*

It is because of the enhanced access to the Devī during the Navarātras that all those interested in tapping into her power, or attributes, visit or establish sites of Goddess worship. The Devī is highly accessible at her permanent temples but she may also be established in practically any material effigy.[19] Her presence virtually sprouts out of the soil and water, wherever a space is consecrated and an image installed, and it lingers there even after the images are discarded at the end of the festival.[20] Both male and female artists are among those who seek out the Devī's qualities.

Artistic inspiration is considered to emanate from the Devī's creative power. Sound, a grosser manifestation of the unstruck creative vibration (*anāhata nāda*) symbolizes and embodies all creative activity, including human conceptualizations. The Devī is considered to be the source and

---

[19] The Devī may be worshipped in a form as simple as a lump (*pia*) of earth or cowdung. More often the jar form is established, or more elaborate painted clay images are used for worship.

[20] The Devī's perennial presence in soil and water is mentioned in the *Durgā Saptaśatī* 11.4. The text (12.8) also states that the Devī will never abandon any place where she is established in a sanctuary through the recitation of the *Durgā Saptaśatī*. In the dismissal rituals at the end of the Durgā Pūjā, the priest entreats the Devī to remain in the earth, water, and home (See Appendix, Rodrigues 1993).

embodiment of all such vibrational creation (*nāda brahman*).[21] Poets, singers, musicians, and dancers visit Devī temples during the Navarātras and may even perform for the Goddess. These command performances naturally demand the highest expression of the artists' talents. While in the Devī's presence, or while performing for her, artists seek to acquire more of the Devī's creative power and thus enhance their artistry. Female artists are most often seen dancing or singing for the Goddess.

Singers and musicians may typically perform devotional folk songs (*bhajana*) or classical *rāga*s to the Devī with great passion. These may be short performances at temples or part of lengthy all-night vigils (*rātri jāgaraṇa*) where singing, music, and story-telling are part of the activities. During public Durgā Pūjā celebrations, women in Bengali communities sing about the coming (*āgamanī*) of the Goddess and her victory (*vijaya*) over the forces of chaos and darkness.[22] While Katthak is the classical dance form favoured in North Indian cities such as Banaras, and Bharata Nāṭyam is preferred in South India, I have seen women of all ages perform improvised folk dances before the Devī in both the north and the south.

D. *Nurturer and nourisher*

Just as female artists seek to embody the creative attributes of the Devī, and healers embody the Devī's protective and curative powers, women may also align themselves with the nurturing and nourishing dimension the Goddess's nature. An important epithet of the Goddess in Banaras is Annapūrṇā (She Who is Replete with Sustenance). The created world, the body cosmos of the Devī, is not merely imbued with life but serves as a source of nourishment for the lives it engenders. The food offerings (*naivedya*) made in the simplest of *pūjā*s attest to the nutritious dimension of the creation. The fruit (*phala*), itself part of the Devi's body, is offered back to her. Sanctified through her acceptance of it, it is eaten by the devotee as a blessing (*prasāda*).

In elaborate celebrations of Durgā Pūjās, particularly among those strongly influenced by the Bengali tradition, women play a very important role in the preparation of the food offered to the Devī. While some

---

[21] See Beck (1993:121-147).

[22] The so-called Maliya cassette contains a well-loved collection of these *gamani* songs interspersed between a dramatic and extremely popular recitation of excerpts of the *Durgā Saptaśatī* by Virendra Krishna Bhadra.

people may choose to fast during the Navarātras, for others Durgā Pūjā is a time of sumptuous feasting. The finest food is prepared and offered to the Devī and subsequently eaten by the devotees and guests. There are noteworthy restrictions in this extremely important ritual of feeding. Young virgin girls (under the age of twelve), who have not yet begun their menstrual cycle, are permitted to participate in the preparation of the uncooked food offerings. Once they have begun their menstruation, they are forbidden from preparing (or even touching) any of the food. Married women are generally permitted to touch and prepare the uncooked and cooked food offerings to minor deities. Durgā and Kālī, however, are major deities. During the Durgā Pūjā, pre-menopausal married women are generally restricted from any involvement with the food. Widows are restricted from all food preparations. Post-menopausal women are the most "pure" and may prepare the food (both cooked and uncooked) to minor deities. Only women who have taken a special Śākta initiation are permitted to prepare the food for the Goddess. Naturally, the women with the highest status in this hierarchy are post-menopausal initiated women.

I suggest that the raw food offerings are symbolic parallels of the young virgins in whom menstrual blood has not yet begun to flow. Both represent the pure, inactive, but highly potent fertility of the earth, the incipient creation, the integral Goddess herself. Menstruating but unmarried women represent an inauspicious state of blossoming but untapped fertility: a fertile field which has not been sown, a tree which does not bear fruit.[23] Similarly, widows embody the inauspicious nature of failed nurturing for they stand in contrast to the married mother in traditional Hindu thought who is supposed to sustain her spouse and her offspring through her fecund, nurturing, and nourishing power. The orthodox ideal would have women die happily married before their husbands. Post-menopausal women return to a state of virgin-like purity because their menstrual blood flow has ceased. They symbolize and embody the return to spiritual integrity from creative material diversification.

[23] Julia Leslie has discerningly pointed our how the state of 'womanhood' is considered inauspicious in orthodox Hindu thought. Orthodox tradition encourages women to move from the auspicious state of a virgin girl (*kanyā*) directly to that of a wife (*patnī*), particularly one utterly dedicated to her husband (*pativratā*). See Leslie (1991b:189-190).

E. *Goddess*

The most significant role played by women during the Navarātras is as the Goddess herself. This identification is explicit in the ritual worship of virgins (*kumārī pūjā*). The Kumārī Pūjā is generally performed on the ninth day of Navarātra, or on the conjunction period (*sandhi*) between the eighth and ninth lunar day (*tithi*). Although in certain traditions, such as the Bengali Durgā Pūjā, a male *pujārī* performs the ritual, in many other communities the Kumārī Pūjā is performed by married women for virgin girls. Typically, between one and nine girls under the age of twelve are invited to the home of the family that is conducting the ritual. The girls are treated as living forms of the Goddess. They may each be placed on a large brass platter where their feet are washed and decorated with red lacquer (*altā*). Following the ritual patterns observed when worshipping the Devī, the girls are given a seat (*āsana*), their hair rubbed with oil, and they are each given some decorative ornament.[24] They are fed with sweets, presented with an item of clothing, such as a scarf (*cunri*), and given some money (*dakṣiṇā*). Kumārīs, with whom I have conversed, generally said they found it a very pleasant experience.

An important symbolic component of this *pūjā* is revealed in the dietary patterns of the women involved in this ritual. In orthodox North Indian *brāhmaṇa* families, the married women maintain a fast, eating a diet of uncooked or unrefined food for the first eight days of Navarātra. "We think Durgā is also fasting like us," I was told by one of the women. On the ninth day, they feed the *kumārī*s cooked food such as deep fried bread (*pūrī*), curried vegetables (*sabjī*), and *halvā*, a sweet made from coarsely ground flour (*sūjī*), sugar, *ghī*, and dried fruits. At this point the married women, too, end their own fast. The raw or uncooked food, symbol of the virginal Goddess and *kumārī*, eaten throughout the Navarātra, is replaced at the end of the festival by the ripe and cooked food, symbol of the fertile Goddess. The collective fertile energy of the married females is harnessed through their fast. Furthermore, through the diet of uncooked food, they align themselves with their own pre-menstrual state and that of the virgin girls of the community. In the Kumārī Pūjā, through what appears to be an act of

---

[24] A simple token ornament may be stick-on decorative forehead dots (Hindi: *bindī*).

sympathetic magic, the married women transfer their fertile energy to the girls, encouraging or eliciting a maturation in them. The virginal Goddess has changed into the fertile Goddess, within whom flows menstrual blood, the vital substance capable of engendering life and nourishing it.[25]

Married women, too, are identified with the Devī during the Durgā Pūjā, although this is an implicit equation. In popular thought, the Devī Durgā is identified with Pārvatī, the wife of the ascetic god Śiva. Upon her marriage Durgā/Pārvatī left her parents' home to join her husband Śiva who dwells atop Mount Kailāsa in the Himālaya mountains. During the Navarātras, Durgā/Pārvatī is thought to return to the home of her parents, Himavat and Menā.[26] In a human parallel of this myth, married daughters who have left to live with their husbands, return to their parents' homes during the Navarātras. They are likened to the Goddess and treated specially during this time. They are encouraged to relax and not perform the chores of cooking and cleaning which they would normally do in their own homes (often under the watchful eye of their husband's mother). The animated atmosphere which is generated by the feminine presence of all the married daughters and their children, happily reunited in their parents' home, is seen as a palpable manifestation of the Goddess's presence in the household. Towards the end of the Bengali Durgā Pūjā, in an act which symbolizes their enjoyment in their parents' home, the women eat and feed each other sweets. These human manifestations of Durgā/Pārvatī are also being symbolically fattened up before their return to lives of austerity and hardship with their Śiva-like husbands.

Other explicit identifications of women with the Goddess may take place among left-hand Tantrics during their Navarātra rituals.[27] These rituals are often performed in secret, and may only be participated in by those who have received special initiations (*dīkṣa*). I was informed by self-professed male Tantrics that they engaged in a special five-element (*pañcatattva*) ritual on the confluence of the eighth and ninth solar days

---

[25] There are numerous other symbols of fertility in the Navarātra ritual. One of the most ubiquitous is an effigy considered to be an embodiment of the Goddess made of a water-filled earthen jar (*kalaśa*), topped with leaf-bearing twigs, and a coconut fruit. It is set on a low earthen altar which is sown with seeds.

[26] See, for instance, the *Śiva-Purāṇa*, Rudra-saṃhitā for a version of this myth.

[27] On Tantrism, consult Gupta, et al 1979, Goudriaan and Gupta 1981, Bharati 1965, and Brooks 1990.

of the Navarātras. This ritual worship, performed in the dead of night (*mahāniśā pūjā*), includes partaking in offerings of meat (*māṃsa*), liquor (*mada*), and sexual congress (*maithuna*). In the sexual act, the female partner is identified with the Goddess, envisioned as the dynamic energy (*Śakti*) which animates the cosmos. She unites with the male Tantric who embodies the static male principle (*Śiva*). If successfully performed, the integrative union with the Absolute, which transcends the duality inherent in the bipolar symbolism of male and female principles, is achieved. It is particularly significant that often in Tàntric rituals, women with the lowest status, such as women and prostitutes, are venerated as embodiments of the Goddess. Such identifications elevate the auspiciousness of womanhood in all its aspects.

Appraisal of the Activities, Roles, and Images of Women in Worship of the Great Goddess

It is clear from the foregoing descriptions that the Great Goddess is the object of devotion by both men and women in the Hindu tradition. In my qualitative judgement, equal numbers of men and women visit major Devī temples during the Navarātras and I would therefore suggest that the Goddess does not receive a markedly greater devotion from women than from men. However, I have drawn attention to what appear to be differences in the ritual worship patterns of the sexes. The motives behind men's devotional pledges (*manauti*) were self-centred, although I do not mean this in a pejorative way. Men generally seek to enhance their personal accomplishments (*siddhi*) and wealth (*artha*), through which they may benefit their wives, children, families and friends. In contrast, women generally seek the well-being of their marital relationships, place their husband and children's well-being first, and in so doing enjoy personal good fortune (*saubhāgya*).

The ascetic dimensions of spiritual practice, namely, male *sādhanā* and female *vrata*s appear to have the same differences in motivational purposes. However, they also differ partly in the types of practices engaged in by the respective sexes. Men may perform ritualized recitations of the *Durgā Saptaśatī* and independently offer sacred fire oblations. Women do not. However women may perform pilgrimages to particular goddesses, such as the Nine Gaurīs, who although they represent the Great Goddess during the Navarātras, do not function in this role for men. I suggest that this is because the Nine Gaurīs embody characteristics which specifically satisfy the desired goals of women, such as beauty, fertility, increasing their purity and auspiciousness, and obtaining successful marriages.[28] What is particularly noteworthy here is that not only do ritual practices vary, but that there are choice of images of the Mahādevī, too, which may differ between the sexes.

The most significant differences between male and female religiosity during the Navarātras is in the role and image of women during these festivals. Although men may overwhelmingly serve in the role of ritual specialists (*pujārī*), and although both sexes may function as healers or strive to procure the Devī's grace and power for artistic or other reasons, it is exclusively women who are identified with the Devī and her feminine attributes. This identification of women with the Goddess during the Navarātras is not isolated to select sects or cultural comities but is widespread throughout India. While it may seem natural for women to be identified with the Goddess, there are no comparable identifications of males with supreme gods during festivals. It is true that spiritually elevated males may be identified with the Absolute Brahman, however this principle of supreme reality is generally conceived of as transcending gender. Brahman is neither male nor female. At times, while engaged in the performance of certain rituals (e.g., *kuṇḍalinī yoga*) men may embody the supreme male principle of godhead (*paramaśiva*).[29] Alternatively, they may strive to emulate the qualities of such deities as Rāma, or Kṛṣṇa on a daily basis, but there is no widespread yearly festival or religious ritual during which ordinary men are unequivocally identified and worshipped as embodiments of a supreme male deity.[30]

It is worth pursuing the question why such a difference exists between the image of women and men in the Hindu tradition. I believe that clues to the answer lie in the institution of marriage

[28] See Rodrigues 1993 for a detailed speculative examination of the nature of the Nine Gaurīs. I have also suggested there that the Nine Durgās, in contrast, serve as a more comprehensive set of images of the Great Goddess since they are meaningful to both men and women.

[29] On Kuṇḍalinī Yoga, see Silburn 1988, Bharati 1965, and Brooks 1990.

[30] Anderson 1993 points out how the king might be identified with the god Kāma, or Śiva during the annual Spring festival. Such associations, which were not explicit, and which pertained to a certain powerful individual rather than all males, have all but disappeared.

(vivāha) where the images and roles of men and women in relationship to each other are defined. The traditional term for "husband" is *pati,* which means "lord" or "divine lord," (i.e., god).[31] A late medieval text, the *Strīdharmapaddhati* (Manual on the Duty of Women) reinforces the view that a woman should regard her husband as a deity, the highest object of her devotion.

> The good woman always regards her husband as a god...For the husband is god for women...There is no goal, no deity like the husband.[32]

Despite such precepts, women's actual attitudes to men vary from the orthodox position created and upheld by the *brāhmaṇa* male tradition. Nevertheless, I often heard women, even from non-*brāhmaṇa* classes, or widows who said they had experienced unhappy marriages, refer to their husbands as "divine lord" (*patideva*).[33] Clearly, the notion that the husband (alive or deceased) should be regarded by married women and widows as a god is pervasive in the Hindu tradition. This concept is passed on to girls and unmarried women through more subtle modes of cultural transmission than textual prescriptions. There are no festivals which promote the view since it is a cultural notion which is deeply embedded in Hindu society and thus taken for granted.

But what about women? It is clear that their influential role in the happiness of the home has always been recognized. The classic treatise on Hindu duty, the *Manusmṛti* states:

> The house in which female relations, not being honoured, pronounce a curse, perishes completely as if destroyed by magic. Hence men who seek happiness should always honour women on holidays and festivals with gifts of jewellery, clothes, and good food. In that family where the husband is pleased with his wife and the wife with her husband happiness will assuredly be lasting (*Manusmṛti,* III, 58f).

The husband is enjoined to honour his wife on all festivals and holidays. Furthermermore, the *Manusmṛti* (IX, 26) and texts such as

---

[31] For studies of Hindu marriage see Altekar 1973, Apte 1978, and Leslie 1991b. For the relationship between marriage and concepts of the Goddess, see Coburn 1982, Gatwood 1985, Harman 1989, Jacobson 1978, Leslie 1991a, Fruzetti 1982, and Shulman 1980.

[32] Leslie 1991a:108, quoting from *Strīdharmapaddhati* 32r.5-6, 32v.8-9.

[33] I wish to stress that orthodox tradition does not just expect a woman to worship her husband as "a god" but as "the god", the sole or supreme form of the Divine.

the *Mahābhārata* (13.11.10ff) do state that there is no difference between virtuous wives and the goddess of fortune (Śrī).[34] If this is so, should not women be worshipped by their husbands as goddesses throughout the year, just as men are to be always worshipped as gods by their wives? Or, just as a man may worship a male deity, such as Rāma or Kṛṣṇa whom he emulates, could not a woman worship, as her primary deity, the goddess whom she embodies? Julia Leslie (1991a:113) offers an answer to the second question. She points out how in Tryambakayajvan's *Strīdharmapaddhati*, an eighteenth century orthodox treatise on the duties of wom..., the goddess Śrī is upheld as a model deity for women to emulate, but not as a deity to be worshipped in lieu of their husbands. Thus orthodox prescriptions would have women model themselves after domestic goddesses, such as Śrī, Gaurī, or Sītā, provided these goddesses were lovingly and utterly devoted to their male spouses. So women may emulate the goddess Śrī. They may worship Śrī as long as the *devī* does not replace the exalted place of the husband in their lives.[35] Women may even be considered as embodiments of the goddess Śrī. And yet, if the latter identification is possible, why are men are not enjoined to worship their wives as embodiments of the divine such as the auspicious spouse goddess Śrī, at all times? Why is there this difference between the images of husbands, who are perpetually divine, and wives, who are not?

Perhaps the answer to this question lies in a particular dualism inherent in many schools of Hindu thought such as the ancient orthodox (*āstika*) system of Sāṃkhya and numerous philosophies influenced by it. In these schools, the principle of spirit (*puruṣa*) came to be equated with the male, and the principle of matter (*prakṛti*) with the female.[36]

---

[34] On the goddess Śrī, see Leslie 1991, Narayanan 1982, and Kinsley 1986.

[35] My own field research indicates that the qualities of domestic auspiciousness present in the goddess Śrī are fully encompassed by the Great Goddess of the Navarātras. However the Great Goddess also transcends spousal affiliations. She is independent and autonomous and not subject to the authority of any male deity. As such she serves as a deity who may be worshipped by males and by females since her subsidiary domestic aspects serve as models of fecundity, nurturing, and auspiciousness for female worshippers who align themselves with orthodoxy.

[36] This denotation of gender to the dual principles is present the grammatical form of the terms. Puruṣa is a masculine noun, which denotes a male being or man, while Prakṛti is a feminine noun. The *Sāṃkhya Kārikās* and commentaries pick up on this gender difference. In a particular simile, He (Puruṣa) is likened to a spectator who

While the male principle (*puruṣa*) is utterly transcendent and inactive, the created cosmos is perceived of as a movement from pure sublime integrity (*pradhāna prakṛti*) to impure diversification. While the male principle is never tainted, the female principle, by virtue of its creative nature spans the spectrum from the very pure to the most polluted. The transformations of Prakṛti are described through the concept of three qualities (*guṇa*) which are inherent in all of its diverse manifestations. In its most subtle manifestations, Prakṛti is filled with the quality of purity, the *sattva guṇa*, while its grossest manifestations are thick with the quality of darkness and pollution, the *tamas guṇa*. The *rajas guṇa*, whose symbol is blood, is the quality of activity or passion which characterizes the vital processes of material creation.

Although among devout Devī worshippers, the Great Goddess encompasses and transcends all dualisms, including notions such as Puruṣa and Prakṛti, a prevailing attitude is to equate the Devī with Prakṛti. Similarly, women, the human feminine, are also thought to embody the nature of Prakṛti. However, there is, I suggest, a crucial difference in Hindu thought between women and the Goddess, for while the Devī represents a fully pure, sacred, and transcendent Prakṛti, women are manifestations of a worldly Prakṛti. Through the ebb and flow of their menstrual cycles, which plunge them into periods of pollution, and through their association with child-bearing and nurturing, which link them with the cycles of rebirth and worldly existence (*saṃsāra*), women stand in opposition to the highest human goal (*puruṣārtha*) of liberation (*mokṣa*) from the vagaries of change, and the endless rounds of existence, death, and rebirth.[37]

Therefore, the nature of women in traditional Hindu thought is ambivalent. Negatively, women are often portrayed as fickle and unpredictable, like the forces of Nature.[38] Or they are seductively alluring, capable of shaking the resolute detachment of even the most capable world renouncers, enmeshing all in the cycle of worldly existence (*saṃsāra*).[39] However, women are also viewed, by men, as prized

---

eventually grows tired of Her (Prakṛti's) repeat dance performances. See *Sāṃkhya Kārikā* 2, 8, 18, 63, 67. On *Sāṃkhya* philosophy, see Aranya 1983, Eliade 1970, and Larson 1969.

[37] See O'Flaherty 1981, for an examination of attitudes to women in Purāṇic texts.

[38] For the ambivalent nature of goddesses, see Brubaker 1978, Harman 1989, and Shulman 1980.

[39] On the basis of a detailed study (1986) Julia Leslie concludes that the concept

possessions and faithful companions. Through women, human life is engendered, sustained, and empowered, and thus given the opportunity to enjoy worldly pleasures (*bhoga*) or gain liberation (*mokṣa*). Such a polar conception of womanhood further prohibits them from being perennially divine objects of constant devotion. It is not possible to venerate women during their periods of menstruation, a cycle which regularly plunges them into a state of pollution according to traditional Brahmanical standards. One cannot be simultaneously devoted to *saṃ sāra* and yet desire liberation from it.

This reasoning alone might serve to answer why women, in traditional Hindu thought, are not capable of being perpetually considered pure, auspicious, and thus continually divine. In fact, from many traditional points of view, women are often grouped with the lowest, or even classless members of society.[40] It is often stated in prescriptive texts that for male world renouncers (*sannyāsa*), firmly intent on liberation (*mokṣa*) from worldly existence (*saṃsāra*), any contact with women is detrimental. Thus women's association with periodic pollutions renders them constantly inauspicious in certain schools of Hindu thought. Were this attitude held by all male members of Hindu society, and its implications acted upon, there would be little interaction between the sexes. Clearly, the notion that women bear a persistent or continual impurity is not the cultural norm. There are cultural beliefs or ritual actions which enable women to discard their polluted status. Menstruation, for example, although it is deemed a polluted state, is sometimes viewed as a process through which women are purified and renewed. More often, women purify themselves through a post-menstruation ritual bath (*ṛtusnāna*). Even so, the regular entries into states of pollution, and the need for subsequent acts of purification, do not lend womanhood an elevated status on the scale of auspiciousness.[41]

Nevertheless, for the satisfactory functioning of society, to enable its structures to be maintained so that men and women may unite, produce

---

of "woman," or the inherent nature of women (*strīsvabhāva*) in Sanskrit religious law "is almost invariably negative" (Leslie 1991b:189). This view is nuanced and even opposed by the vision of the feminine found in some Śākta and Tantric literature.

[40] See, for instance, the *Bhagavad Gītā*. IX.32.

[41] Even those male *brāhmaṇa* priests who regularly work in polluting activities such as death rituals are considered low on the status scale of *brāhmaṇas* despite their purification rituals.

offspring, heirs, and so on, even those men who consider themselves to be extremely *sattvic* (i.e., pure), such as the highest caste *brāhmaṇa*s, should view women as adequately pure and auspicious marital partners. Said differently, although women are inauspicious due to their polluting associations, they need to be ritually elevated in status on the scale of auspiciousness to be suitable spouses for men who are thought to embody *sāttvic* purity. Thus the "feminine" in general, and womanhood and women in particular, must be collectively, regularly, and publicly sanctified through ritual action. This collective elevation in auspiciousness of the feminine does not free women from the need to periodically purify themselves after their polluting cycles, such as menstruation. Besides these regular rituals of purification, women may thereafter nurture and enhance their purity and auspiciousness (*saubhāgya*) through spiritual practices such as *vrata*s. In fact, such practices are probably deemed almost essential for a woman who wishes to elevate her auspiciousness further, or maintain it at levels deemed commensurate with her spouse. The divine precedent of such a process has already been articulated. Mythologically, even the supreme ascetic Śiva, the world-renouncer *par excellence*, was induced into fulfilling the demands of social *dharma* through his marriage to Gaurī, a supremely pure female spiritual practitioner, leading to the subsequent birth of their son, Skanda.[42]

I suggest that the Navarātras serve the important function of providing an overarching auspiciousness and sanctity to the "feminine" which is otherwise prone to the cadences of purity and pollution, auspiciousness and inauspiciousness. The festivals achieve this end through processes of reconstitution and rejuvenation of the body cosmos of the Devī, and through the simultaneous identification of women with the Goddess. The Great Goddess, although identified with Prakṛti, transcends its profane, mundane, inauspicious character. Because her image encompasses the nature of womanhood in all its stages and aspects, even those traditionally considered to be inauspicious or impure, the Devī confers on womanhood a sacred, purifying, and divine status. Although it is true that the Devī who is worshipped during the Durgā Pūjā of the Āśvina Navarātra is generally conceived of by worshippers as a virgin or a mother, both of which are auspicious states,

---

[42] See the *Śiva-purāṇa*, Rudra-saṃhitā 3-4.

she actually also embodies many states normally considered inauspicious for a woman. For instance, the Devī as portrayed in the *Durgā Saptaśatī*, who is worshipped during the Navarātras, is an alluring woman, attractive to the demons Mahiṣa, Śumbha, and Niśumbha as a potential spouse. Yet as an unattached woman, past puberty (attested to by her well-formed breasts), the Goddess is in a social and physical state which Brahmanical orthodoxy considers undesirable, and highly inauspicious for women. In the Durgā Pūjā ritual itself, women in that socio-physical state are prohibited from even touching any of the food offerings. This means that during the Navarātras, through the image of the Goddess, both male and female devotees are actually worshipping the "feminine," as the most sublime form of the Divine, not merely when the "feminine" is in an auspicious state, but in states which are traditionally perceived to be quite inauspicious.[43] Similarly, as Mātaṅgī, one of the forms and epithets of the Great Goddess worshipped during the Navarātras, the Devī's image is that of an uncouth, outcaste women.[44] As Kātyāyanī and Dhūmāvatī, she is worshipped as a widow, another inauspicious social condition.[45] It should be stressed that although the forms of the Devī which belong to such inauspicious social

[43] I even heard from a male Tantric practitioner that the Durgā Pūjā took place during the days of the Devī's menstruation. Almost no-one else shared this opinion, although I heard on more than one occasion, from men, that the Devī's colour (golden) corresponded to the colour of menstrual fluid, puzzling as that may sound. (The term *gaura*, from which the goddess Gaurī's name is derived, may signify the colour yellow or red). *Brāhmaṇa* pandits told me that the menstruation (*rajasvalā*) of the Devī (as the Earth) traditionally takes place during Ambuvācī, a three and a half day period in the month of Āṣāḍha. In the pool of the Devī cave temple at Kāmarūpa, Assam, the water turns reddish brown, and is collected by devotees for its auspicious power. While menstrual blood is normally considered inauspicious and polluting, the Devī's menstrual secretions are quite the reverse. Mary Douglas (1970) has discussed at length the dangerous power associated with what cultures deem to be polluting states and substances, such as menstruating women and menstrual blood. Although these human substances are often treated with great caution, when ritually manipulated and thus controlled, even they may become objects of worship due to their potency. Therefore, the menstruating Devī and her menstrual blood are embodiments of an awesome, but highly auspicious, dangerous power.

[44] For more on the nature of Mātaṅgī see Kinsley 1986:163, 207-208 and 1997: 209-222. Mātaṅgī is one of the epithets of Durgā praised in the *Durgā Cālisā* (Forty [Verses] to Durgā), a popular hymn to the Devī.

[45] On the nature of Kātyāyanī, see Rodrigues 1993. On Dhūmāvatī, see Kinsley 1986:163 and 1997: 176-192. Kātyāyanī is one of the Nine Durgās of the *Devī Kavaca*, an important appendage (*aṅga*) of the *Durgā Saptaśatī*. Durgā is also worshipped as Dhūmāvatī in the *Durgā Cālisā*.

classes and states are not central in the minds of worshippers, they are unmistakably present. As a result, when the "feminine" in all stages of life, from all segments of society, and in all social conditions is venerated during the Navarātras as the Divine Feminine, the Great Goddess, it is the human feminine, woman, that is collectively purified and rendered auspicious.

The Navarātras are periods during which the world, the body cosmos of the Devī, is literally recreated ritually, and thus rejuvenated and purified.[46] Thus the purification of the "feminine" is accomplished through the reconstitution of the Goddess, whose manifest body is essentially thought of as the creation. This ritual construction of the cosmos, which must be repeated at regular intervals, mirrors the cyclical patterns observable in nature, but more importantly, exercises an ordering influence on what might otherwise be an uncontrolled and chaotic creation. Although the Navarātra rituals are intended to shape and control every level and aspect of the cosmic manifestation, from its inception to its demise, the strongest influences are expected to be exerted at the plane of human existence, namely, on the world and human society.

Even the timing and mythological themes of the Navarātras are suggestive of rejuvenation and reestablishing order. The Āśvina and Caitra Navarātras coincide with the most pleasant times of the year, the autumn and spring, which offer relief from the searing heat of the summer, the humidity and disruptive floods caused by the monsoons, and the unpleasant cold of the winter season.[47] The Caitra Navarātra is a spring festival and the first to mark what is generally considered the New Year in Banaras (Eck 1982:258).[48] It stands as evidence for the ritual role played by the Navarātras in the rejuvenation of the cycles of time. Similarly, the month of Āśvina marks the end of the rainy season

---

[46] It is outside the scope of this chapter to discuss this ritual process of recreating and rejuvenating the body of the Devī. During the Durgā Pūjā ritual, the Devī is awakened in a localized, rudimentary form such as a wide-bodied jar (*ghaṭa*), composed of earth and water. She is then invoked into progressively more complex or expansive forms. These forms include trees, anthropomorphic clay images, cosmic diagrams, and living virgin girls. Readers are referred to Rodrigues 1993.

[47] The beginning of Āśvina is classically thought to coincide with the autumnal equinox, and the vernal equinox with the beginning of the month of Caitra. Astronomically this has changed (Klostermaier 1989:417).

[48] On the role of spring festivals in Hindu tradition see Anderson 1993.

and the time when kings traditionally waged war to expand their kingdoms. The Āśvina Navarātra is associated with kingship and warfare. Its first celebration by human beings is attributed to the prince Rāma. In the mythic tale of the divine hero Rāma's righteous war with the demon Rāvaṇa, in order to regain his abducted goddess-queen, Sītā, or in the myth of the goddess Durgā's victory over the buffalo demon Mahiṣa, and in the traditional territorial expansion of monarchs in accord with the dictates of *kṣatriya dharma* (the duty of warriors), one notices the theme of reconstituting space and society through righteous kingly control, and the reestablishment of good fortune and auspiciousness on the earth.[49]

In keeping with the intention to rejuvenate and revitalize the creation, the Navarātra rituals work to induce vivifying juice to flow within it. The sacrifices of blood (*balidāna*) spilled onto the soil in offerings to the Goddess, the sprouting of grains sowed in an earthen altar, and other such practices which are part of the Navarātra rituals suggest the themes of encouraging fertility and fecundity in the earth, in seeds, in plants, and in women. Although the Navarātras are periods in which the feminine in general, and womanhood in particular, is venerated in all its aspects and stages, one notices that three stages of womanhood are actually given primacy over others.[50] These are the pre-menstrual virgin, the married woman, and the post-menopausal mother. I understand this structuring of the developmental course of womanhood, through the encouragement of particular states within it, to be an attempt to orchestrate ritually the flow of creative juices (i.e., blood) through which the creative feminine (i.e., woman) develops. The creation (i.e., the feminine) cannot be allowed to unfold chaotically.

In the Kumārī Pūjā, we see the explicit worship of the young, pristine feminine, full of potential. The pre-menstrual virgin is the symbol of purity and rejuvenation. She is highly auspicious. Creative juices (i.e., menstrual blood) has not yet begun to flow within her. The married woman is venerated in the symbolism of the Durgā Pūjā image

---

[49] Sītā is identifed with the goddess of auspiciousness, Śrī Lakṣmī. The day following the Āśvina Navarātra, known as Vijayā Daśamī, is held in celebration of Victory, personified as the Devī. On the relationship between kings, power, and the Devī see Gupta and Gombrich 1986.

[50] For supporting evidence of this theme in the symbolism of the Nine Durgās and the Nine Gaurīs, see Rodrigues 1993.

cluster, where the Goddess is portrayed as a mother in the company of her children, Gaṇeśa, Kārtikeya, Sarasvatī, and Lakṣmī. It is not merely the fecundity of the feminine that is sought, but the regulated management of that fertility. For although the transition from *kumārī* to menstruating woman is sought and ritually encouraged, the unmarried menstruating female is thought to enter a liminal state of unpredictable energy, and ungoverned possibilities. Through marriage, child-bearing, and nurturing her spouse and offspring, the creative juice (*rasa*) of women is thought to be channeled productively. The pre-menstrual girl is under the social control of her parental family, symbolized by her father. The married woman is under the social control of her spouse's family, symbolized by her husband. In such a social construction, the widow is naturally an inauspicious state of womanhood for, like the menstruating unmarried daughter she represents the fertile feminine free from traditional social constraints. The post-menopausal mother is under the social constraints of her offspring's families, symbolized by her son.[51] She is beyond reproductive possibilities and thus no longer associated with the saṃsāric cycles of rebirth. Since the flow of menstrual blood within her has ceased, she enters a state of perennial purity, no longer subject to the periodic pollutions of menstruation. Her special status is confirmed through her sanction to prepare cooked food offerings for deities.

Conclusion

While the patterns of worship of the Goddess during the Navarātras differ between men and women in significant ways, as do their roles and images, both sexes participate in the ritual construction and maintenance of a universe within which the cycles of nature are rendered meaningful, and social structures and human actions are orderly and harmonious. Since the created cosmos is envisioned as the manifest body of the Goddess, the control of the cosmos involves the control of the Devī, the Divine Feminine. This is clearly a tall order, for the Goddess is generally conceived of as invincible, her power unsurmountable. Furthermore, she is the source of illusion and ensnares all the cycle of worldly existence. At best, the Devī's power may be partially

---

[51] For such orthodox prescriptions about keeping women under control, see *Manusmṛti* (*The Laws of Manu*) IX.2-16, or V.147-165.

appropriated through such spiritual practices as *sādhanā* and *vrata*s. Alternatively, she may be appeased (through *yātrā* and *sevā*), pleased (through *pūjā* and *darśana*), and supplicated (through *manauti*) for a variety of boons.

Although the Divine Feminine may be beyond the control of all but the most highly attained adepts (*siddha yogi*), at the microcosmic level of individuals and society, her form and nature is thought to be manifest in all women. Thus the ritual manipulation of woman is mandatory in attempts to manipulate the cosmos ritually. This perspective is of cardinal importance when trying to understand the constraints placed on women in traditional Hindu society. These are restrictions which emanate less from an entrenched misogyny than from a sort of cosmic gynophobia, a fear of an uncontrolled feminine creation. Perhaps this designation is extreme for there is not merely a fear of the power and unpredictability of Nature, the feminine, which may bring droughts, famine, disease, and destruction, but a reverence for and attraction to its beauty and bounty. Woman is the living microcosmic image of the macrocosm, the manifest body of the Great Goddess. During the Navarātras they are identified with each other.

I suggest that the veneration of the feminine at these festivals serves several functions. The rituals of the festivals elevate the feminine, in all its dimensions, to a high level of purity and auspiciousness through processes of reconstitution and rejuvenation. Even women in low status and inauspicious states, such as classless women, widows, and unmarried women are implicitly venerated during the Navarātra festivals, through the encompassing image of the Great Goddess. In his seminal study of the ritual process Victor Turner (1969:166-203) has discussed the role that festivals may play in status elevation. However, the Navarātras are festivals which neither induce a permanent status elevation for its participants (as in a rite of passage), nor permit a temporary status reversal (as in the Holī festival). Instead these festivals, I suggest, induce a temporary status elevation. Womanhood is transformed and purified, elevated in auspiciousness and venerated. However, certain states of womanhood are still given primacy over others. Thus the festivals serve to maintain orthodox values and social structures by giving particularly high status to virgins (through explicit worship), to married women (through implict veneration), and to post-menopausal mothers (through ritual sanction).[52] Unmarried women and widows, although superficially acknowledged and ritually elevated through the person of the Goddess, are still ranked low through ritual prohibitions (e.g., they are not permitted to touch food preparations or participate in the Kumārī Pūjā). Therefore, through ritually reconstructing the Devī's body during the Navarātras, through identifying women with her, and then orchestrating the feminine's development and actions, Hindu worshippers participate in a process designed to regenerate and vitalize a harmonious orderly creation in which their worst fears are dissolved and their greatest hopes are realized.

BIBLIOGRAPHY

Altekar, A. S. 1973 [1938]. *The Position of Women in Hindu Civilization, from Prehistoric Times to the Present Day.* Delhi: Motilal Banarsidass.

Anderson, Leona. 1993. *Vasantotsava: The Spring Festivals of India: Texts and Traditions.* New Delhi: D. K. Printworld (P) Ltd.

Apte, Usha M. 1978. *The Sacrament of Marriage in Hindu Society: From Vedic Period to Dharmaśāstras.* Delhi: Ajanta Publications.

Aranya, Svami Hariharananda. 1983. *Yoga Philosophy of Patañjali.* Translated by P. N. Mukerji. Albany, New York: State University of New York.

Bandyopadyay, Pranab. 1987. *Mother Goddess Durga.* Calcutta: Image India.

Beck, Guy. 1993. Sonic Theology: *Hinduism and Sacred Sound.* Columbia, South Carolina: University of South Carolina Press.

Bharati, Agehananda. 1965. *The Tantric Tradition.* London: Rider.

Bhattacharyya, Narendra Nath. 1974. *History of the Śākta Religion.* New Delhi: Munshiram Manoharlal Publishers.

_____. 1971. *Indian Mother Goddess.* Calcutta: Indian Studies Past and Present.

Brooks, Douglas Renfrew. 1990. *The Secret of the Three Cities: An Introduction to Hindu Śākta Tantrism.* Chicago: University of Chicago Press.

Brown, Cheever Mackenzie. 1990. *The Triumph of the Goddess: The Canonical Models and Theological Visions of the Devī-Bhāgavata Purāṇa.* Albany: State University of New York Press.

_____. 1974. *God as Mother: A Feminine Theology in India.* Hartford, Vt.: Claude Stark.

Brubaker, Richard L. 1978."The Ambivalent Mistress: A Study of South

---

[52] I am grateful to Patricia Dold for her helpful comments on an earlier draft of this paper and her discerning comments on status elevation and structure.

Indian Village Goddesses and Their Religious Meaning." Ph.D. diss., University of Chicago.

Coburn, Thomas B. 1982. "Consort of None, *Śakti* of All: The Vision of the *Devī–Māhātmya*." In John Stratton Hawley and Donna Marie Wulff, eds. *The Divine Consort: Rādhā and the Goddesses of India,* pp. 153-165. Berkeley, Calif.: Berkeley Religious Studies Series.

_____. 1988 [1984]. *Devī-Māhātmya: The Crystallization of the Goddess Tradition*. Delhi and Columbia, MO: Motilal Banarsidass and South Asia Books.

_____. 1991. *Encountering the Goddess: A Translation of the* Devī-Māhātmya *and a Study of Its Interpretation.* Albany: State University of New York Press.

Coward, Harold and David Goa. 1991. *Mantra: Hearing the Divine in India.* Chambersburg: Anima Books.

Das, Sudhendukumar. 1934. *Śakti or Divine Power.* Calcutta: University of Calcutta.

Divakaran, Odile. 1984. "Durgā the Great Goddess: Meanings and Forms in the Early Period." In *Discourses on Śiva: Proceedings of a Symposium on the Nature of Religious Imagery*, ed. Michael W. Meister, 271-288. Philadelphia: University of Pennsylvania Press.

Durgā-Saptaśatī. (Devī-Māhātmya). Mārkaṇḍeya Purāṇa. (1) *Śrī-durgā-saptaśatī.* n.d. Gorakhpur: Gītā Press. (2) *Durgā-saptaśatī saptaṭīkā-samvaliyāt.* 1984 [1916]. [The Durgā-Saptaśatī with seven commentaries, by Bhāskararāya, Caturdharī, Śāntanu, Nāgojibhaṭṭa (Nāgeśa), Jagaccandracandrikā, Daṃśoddhra, and Durgā-pradīpa. Edited by] Harikṛṣṇaśarma. Bombay: Veṅkaṭeśvara Press, 1916; reprint, Delhi and Baroda: Buṭālā Company, 1984.

Eck, Diana L. 1982. *Banaras, City of Light*. New York: Alfred A. Knopf.

_____. 1981. *Darśan: Seeing the Divine Image in India.* Chambersburg: Anima Books.

Eliade, Mircea. 1970 [1958]. *Yoga: Immortality and Freedom.* Translated by Williard R. Trask. Princeton, N.J.: Princeton University Press.

_____. 1963. *Patterns in Comparative Religion.* Cleveland: World Publishing Co.

_____. 1959 [1949]. *Cosmos and History: The Myth of the Eternal Return.* Translated by W. R. Trask. New York: Harper and Row.

Erndl, Kathleen M. 1987. "Victory to the Mother: The Goddess Cult of Northwest India." Ph.D. diss., University of Wisconsin-Madison.

Fruzetti, Lina. 1982. *The Gift of a Virgin.* New Brunswick, New Jersey: Rutgers University Press.

Fuller, C.J. 1984. *Servants of the Goddess: The Priests of a South Indian Temple.* Cambridge: Cambridge University Press.

Gatwood, Lynn E. 1985. *Devī and the Spouse Goddess: Women, Sexuality and Marriage in India*. Delhi: Manohar.

Ghosha, Pratpachandra. 1871. *Durgā Pūjā: With Notes and Illustrations.*

Calcutta: "Hindoo Patriot" Press.
Gold, Ann Grodzins. 1988. *Fruitful Journeys: The Ways of Rajasthani Pilgrimage*. Berkeley: University of California Press.
Goudriaan, Teun and Sanjukta Gupta. 1981. *Hindu Tantric and Śākta Literature*. Wiesbaden: Otto Harrassowitz.
Gupta, Sanjukta, Dirk Jan Hoens, and Teun Goudriaan. 1979. *Hindu Tantrism*. Leiden, Koln: E.J. Brill.
Gupta, S. and R. Gombrich. 1986. "Kings, Power and the Goddess." *South Asia Research* 6 #2:123-138.
Harman, William P. 1989. *The Sacred Marriage of a Hindu Goddess*. Bloomington: Indiana University Press.
Humes, Cynthia. 1991. "The Text and the Temple of the Great Goddess." Ph.D. dissertation. University of Iowa.
Jacobson, Doranne, and Susan S. Wadley. 1986 [1977]. *Women in India: Two Perspectives*. New Delhi: Manohar Publications.
Jacobson, Doranne. 1978. "The Chaste Wife." In *American Studies in the Anthropology of India* 95-138. Edited by Sylvia Vatuk. New Delhi: Manohar.
Kinsley, David. 1978. "The Portrait of the Goddess in the *Devī-māhātmya*." *Journal of the American Academy of Religion* 46, no. 4 (December):489-506.
_____. 1986. *Hindu Goddesses: Visions of the Divine Feminine in the Hindu Religious Tradition*. Berkeley, Los Angeles, London: University of California Press.
_____. 1997. *Tantric Visions of the Divine Feminine: The Ten Mahāvidyās*. Berkeley: University of California Press.
Klostermaier, Klaus. 1989. *A Survey of Hinduism*. Albany: State University of New York Press.
Kramrisch, Stella. 1975. "The Indian Great Goddess," *History of Religions* 14, no. 4 (May): 235-265.
Lakṣmī Tantra: A Pāñcarātra Text. 1972. Translated by Sanjukta Gupta. Leiden: E. J. Brill.
Larson, Gerald J. 1969. *Classical Sāṃkhya: An Interpretation of Its History and Meaning*. Delhi: Motilal Banarsidass.
Leslie, Julia. 1991a. "Śrī and Jyeṣṭhā." In *Roles and Rituals for Hindu Women*, pp. 107-129. Edited by Julia Leslie. Rutherford: Fairleigh Dickinson University Press.
_____. 1991b. "Suttee or Sātī." In *Roles and Rituals for Hindu Women*, 175-191. Edited by Julia Leslie. Rutherford: Fairleigh Dickinson University Press.
_____. 1989. *The Perfect Wife: The Orthodox Hindu Woman according to the Strīdharmapaddhati of Tryambakayajvan*. Oxford University South Asian Series. Delhi: Oxford University Press.
Mahābhārata. 1933-59. Edited by Vishnu S. Sukthankar (and others). 19 vols. Poona: Bhandarkar Oriental Research Institute.

McGee, Mary. 1991. "Desired Fruits." In Roles and Rituals for Hindu Women, pp. 71-88. Edited by Julia Leslie. Rutherford: Fairleigh Dickinson University Press.

_____. 1989. *Feasting and Fasting: The Vrata Tradition and its Significance for Hindu Women.* (Th.D. dissertation, Harvard University, 1987.) Ann Arbor, Mich.: University Microfilms.

Narayanan, Vasudha. 1982. " The Goddess Śrī: The Blossoming Lotus and Breast Jewel of Viṣṇu." In John Stratton Hawley and Donna Marie Wulff, eds., *The Divine Consort: Rādhā and the Goddesses of India*, pp. 224-237. Berkeley: Berkeley Religious Studies Series.

O'Flaherty, Wendy Doniger. 1981. *Śiva, the Erotic Ascetic.* New York: Oxford University Press. Reprint of *Asceticism and Eroticism in the Mythology of Śiva.* London, New York, Toronto: Oxford University Press, 1973.

_____. 1980. *Women, Androgynes, and Other Mythical Beasts.* Chicago: University of Chicago Press.

Östör, Ákos. 1980. *The Play of the Gods: Locality, Ideology, Structure, and Time in the Festivals of a Bengali Town.* Chicago: University of Chicago Press.

Pearson, Anne. 1993. "'Because it Gives Me Peace of Mind: Functions and Meanings of *Vrat*s in the Religious Lives of Hindu Women in Banāras," Ph.D. dissertation. McMaster University.

Purohita-darpaṇa. Bhattacharya, Surendramohana, ed. 1973-74. 37th ed. Revised by Yogendracandra Vyākaraṇatīrtha Vidyāratha. Calcutta: Satyanārāyaṇa Library.

Rodrigues, Hillary. 1993. "The Image of the Goddess Durgā and her Worship in Banāras." Ph.D. dissertation. McMaster University.

Sax, William. 1991. *Mountain Goddess: Gender and Politics in a Himalayan Pilgrimage.* New York: Oxford University Press.

Shulman, David D. 1980. *Tamil Temple Myths: Sacrifice and Divine Marriage in the South Indian Śaiva Tradition.* Princeton: Princeton University Press.

Silburn, Lilian. 1988. *Kuṇḍalinī: Energy of the Depths.* Albany: State University of New York Press.

Śiva Purāṇa. 1970. Translated by a Board of Scholars. 4 vols. Delhi: Motilal Banarsidass.

The Laws of Manu. 1975. Trans. by G. Buhler. Delhi: Motilal Banarsidass.

Turner, Victor. 1977. [1966]. *The Ritual Process: Structure and Anti-structure.* Ithaca, N.Y.: Cornell University Press.

Van Kooij, K. R., trans. 1982. *Worship of the Goddess According to the Kālikā Purāṇa.* Leiden: E. J. Brill.

CHAPTER FIVE

BETWEEN PESTLE AND MORTAR: WOMEN IN THE MARATHI SANT TRADITION*

VIDYUT AKLUJKAR

Introduction

The Sant tradition of Maharashtra (circa 13th to 17th c. CE) records women's contribution on many levels. Some women were Sants in their own right and even today these are fondly remembered and venerated for their steadfast *bhakti* and beautiful poetry. Two main females who are celebrated as Sants are Janābāī (circa 13th century) who was an orphan maidservant in Sant Nāmdev's house, and Bahiṇābāī (1628-1700), who was a brahmin housewife, and the first female to have written an account in verse of her entire life. Other females such as Muktābāī, or Kānhopātrā have some *abhaṅgas* recorded on their names and occupy a place in the larger circle of Sants. On the other hand, there are the other women, i.e. women in a male Sant's life, his mother, sister, wife or daughter, who are remembered mainly for their nuisance value to the Sant, or as his stepping stones towards his world-weariness. In addition to the portrayals of these women that appear in the Sant's lives, there are stories and anecdotes of women that appear in the poems of the Sants. And finally, there are some types of women which are used by the Sants as paradigm of a virtue or a vice. To my knowledge there is no attempt anywhere, either in English or Marathi, to take in to account all side of the female representation in the Sant tradition of Maharashtra. There are studies of a particular female Sant, but not a comprehensive

---

* An earlier draft of this paper was read in July 1994 at the Sixth International Conference on Early Literature in New Indo-Aryan Languages, and the University of Washington, Seattle, U.S.A.

study of the female contingent. In order to get a comprehensive vision of the female collective consciousness, we need to look at all these pictures and caricatures of women in the Sant literature of Maharashtra. Although an exhaustive account of each and every female is an impossibility given the space limitations of this paper, I propose to survey and analyse in the first part of this paper, the portrayals of women on either side of the *bhakti* fence in the Marathi Sant tradition, with special reference to the lives of women related to or associated with Nāmdev (1270-1350 CE) and Tukārām (1598-1649 CE). The latter part of this paper will survey the literary representations of various types of females, through stories and anecdotes preserved by the Sant tradition.

My choice of the above two Sants is influenced by practical considerations. These two are chronologically as well as influentially central figures in the extensive Sant tradition of Maharashtra. Nāmdev's influence was felt all the way up to Punjab, and for centuries, Tukārām's proverbial *abhaṅgas* have become the most used coinage in everyday Marathi of both the masses and the elite alike. On the names of both Nāmdev and Tukārām appear exquisitely preserved records of women in their lives who troubled them in their path of *bhakti*. At the same time, both these male Sants have been associated in popular tradition with kindred spirits who were women Sants, i.e. Nāmdev with Janābāī, and Tukārām with Bahiṇābāī. In short, they offer us the most colourful examples of male Sants associated, on the one hand, with female Sants and on the other hand, with other females. In addition, they furnish us with many stories and anecdotes of women that they use as stock examples of virtue or vice. Hence, although I will occasionally draw upon the other Sants, I propose to concentrate mainly on the cluster of women around Nāmdev and Tukārām for the present study.

Sources

My sources of information for this study are the five volume compilation of the Sants' verses or *abhaṅga-gāthās*, which is based on the *vārkarī* sect's traditional canon. There are no critical editions of the works of Janābāī or of Bahiṇābāī. And the information about the other females comes to us mainly through some *abhaṅgas* on their names incorporated in the male *abhaṅga* collections, or through *abhaṅgas* about these females by the male Sants. Therefore in order to study all these females the only choice is to look at the traditional canonical collection of all Sants' poems. For a detailed discussion of the various manuscripts, partial editions, and an attempt at a critical edition of Tukārām's works, I refer the reader to the 1950 edition published by the Government Central Press, in Bombay under the editorship of Purushottem Mangesh Laad. I have used his edition only to compare it with the standard canonical edition of the works of all Sants which is the five volume text of the *Sakala Santa Gāthā*, (henceforth SSG, for short,) edited in 1983 by R.C. Dhere. Apart from the SSG, which is essentially based on the 1908 edition of the canonical *Sant-gāthā* text of Nānā Mahārāj Sākhare, I use the occasional hagiographical accounts as they appear in the extensive Sant literature. Often, in the *abhaṅgas* on the names of minor Sants or the wife, the sons or the daughter of a Sant, we find accounts of the incidents in a major Sant's life that are essentially hagiographical accounts. I have used these as well as the standard hagiographical works such as Mahīpati's (1715-1790) *Bhakta-vijaya*, written in 1762. For that text of Bahiṇābāī's verses, which were not included in the above canonical text, I use *Bahiṇābāīcā Gāthā* (second edition, 1956) published by the Chitrashālā Press, Pune. All translations in this paper are mine.

Part one

As mentioned above, Janābāī of Nāmdev's house, and Tukārām's disciple Bahiṇābāī are the two female Sants whose works we shall examine in this paper. Who are the women we consider as being on the other side of the *bhakti* fence? They are mother Goṇāī and wife Rājāī from Nāmdev's house and Āvalī, the second wife from Tukārām's. A brief introduction is in order here. Sant Nāmdev was the only son of Goṇāī and Dāmājī who were tailors by caste and profession and lived in Paṇḍharpur. His mother Goṇāī and his wife Rājāī, are the two women who figure in the story of Nāmdev's early conflicts with the mundane. There are *abhaṅgas* on the name of these two women, and they get mentioned in the *abhaṅgas* of the other members of Nāmdev's family as well as in the verse-stories of the later hagiographer Mahīpati Taherabadkar. Sant Tukārām, a merchant of Dehu, mentions his mother, first wife and daughter occasionally to talk of the bonds of worry, desire and delusion that he has severed (*bāīla melī, mukta jhālī / deveṁ māyā soḍavilī // poreṁ melīṁ, bareṁ jhāleṁ / deveṁ māyāvirahita keleṁ //* SSG 4:65), but his second wife Āvalī was his major adversary. Her trials and tribulations in her marriage to Tukārām have been immortalised in many of the *abhaṅgas* on Tukārām's name. The oral tradition in Maharashtra remembers her name as Āvalī, or sometimes as Jijāī. However, in Tukārām's verses, she is mentioned only as *strī* or "woman," unless he is calling her names such as *pisī*, *lānsī*, or *rāṇḍa*, i.e., "a madwoman, a slut, or a bitch." Even in Mahīpati's *Bhakta-vijaya*, other Sant's wives or mothers are mentioned by names, but Tukārām's harassed wife remains a nameless woman, a *strī*. This is surprising in view of the facts that Mahīpati claims to be a disciple of Tukārām, devotes three and a half chapters of his *Bhakta-vijaya* (chapter 48, 49, 50, and part of 51) to Tukārām's life and in chapter 49, he chooses to gloss at length on the eleven verses of Tukārām's in which Tukārām instructs his contrary wife on the significance of his lifestyle steeped in *bhakti*. In short, although Tukārām's domestic life and its strife remains of central importance to his major hagiographer, the main thrust in Mahīpati's account is to exalt Tukārām, and true to that spirit, the Sant's wife remains nameless. I shall start by examining the roles of these lesser known women in the lives of the two Sants in their chronological order, and later deal with the more famous women Sants associated with them.

At the beginning of the *Abhaṅga Gāthā* of Nāmdev, there is a prologue of his biography in verse, and in it are several sections where conversations are recorded between Goṇāī and Nāmdev, Goṇāī and God, God and Nāmdev, and all three together. I am not concerned here with the issue of authorship of these *abhaṅgas*, since to me, it is enough that these *abhaṅgas* record the popular tradition of conflict between Nāmdev and his family. There seems to be little doubt that there was a conflict between the Sant's uncompromising worship and the household duties he failed to perform. Many of the incidents here find mention again in the *abhaṅgas* on the name of Nāmdev's sons, some in Janābāī's, and some are mentioned as well in chapter 4 of Mahīpati's *Bhakta-vijaya*. My discussion essentially follows the accounts as they appear in the *abhaṅgas* attributed to Nāmdev. In these *abhaṅgas* there is a lot of repetition and many time the same thought is expressed in slightly different words, in a manner consistent with recording multiple versions of an oral tradition. But the human drama emerging from these story-poems is fascinating.

Nāmdev was the child-Sant, and according to traditional accounts, he had experienced the grace of God early in his life. God used to eat off his hands, and Nāmdev would share food in God's house. Naturally, as he grew up, Nāmdev became thoroughly immersed in God, and started to live in the temple singing and dancing in ecstasy instead of minded his tailoring shop. His parents had brought home a daughter-in-law, Rājāī, hoping to cure Nāmdev's excessive addiction to God, but to no avail. Finally, his mother confronted him and poured out her heart in an effort to make him see the light.

Goṇāī is a concerned mother, and although she is herself worshipful of the God, she has her feet firm on the ground, and believes in fulfilling her daily duties to the best of her abilities before she can immerse herself in worship. Her arguments stem from her well-defined sense of duty and are quite consistent with her place in this world as understood by herself and her society. At first, she praises her son. She tries to remind Nāmdev of her bond to him ever since she carried him in her womb, and of her pride in him when he was blessed by the God as a child (*upajalāsī taiṁ jālā santoṣa / ānanda ullāsa vāṭe jīvā // gaṇa gotā mājī kele bāre nāva / paṇḍharīcā deva prasanna kelā //* SSG 2:37). "When you were born, I was so happy. My heart was full of joy, full of delight. You earned a good name among our family and relations. The God and Paṇḍharī was pleased with you." She is not averse to worship, but she avoided. She praises his intelligence and uses his peers as examples. She says, "Nāmyā, you are no longer a child (*are nāmadevā navhesī lekarū /* SSG 2:31). Look at the other people's sons, they may not be as bright as you are, but they look after their parents (*tujahūna loka āhetī ājñāna / na visaṁbatī kṣaṇa māyabāpā //* SSG 2:30). They do something worthwhile with their lives. Look at you on the other hand. Why, you don't even glance at the house, let alone the shop, you are at the feet of this God all day long, singing, dancing, and forgetting yourself altogether. We have seen plenty of devotees, but you are totally mindless of your own good. What kind of other-worldly worship is this? Nāmyā, it has burnt your family to ashes (*kaisī tujhī bhaktī laukikāvagaḷī / saṃsārācī hoḷī kelī nāmyā //* SSG 2:29). Cure this addiction to God; why are you bent on total destruction (lit. drowning) of home (*sāṇḍī devāpiseṁ karū nako aiseṁ / baḷeṁ ghara kaiseṁ budavīsī* // SSG 2:28)?"

To this, Nāmdev simply confesses that he is fed up with the world which is nothing but poison and that therefore, his only hope is God. He advises Goṇāī to join him, stay there in God's Paṇḍharī, rather than leaving for that strange place she calls home. Of course, the battle of wits is unresolved and she answers by expressing her firm resolve to succeed in her mission, and take him home instead. Now she turns to address God, and demands that He give her back her son. In this appeal to God in fourteen *abhaṅgas*, she uses request, accusations, provocations, threats, and finally, out of exasperation, total submission (SSG 2:39, 40, 42, 44, 45, 46, 47, 48, 49, 51, 52, 55, 57, 58). God tries to tell her in many words why the matter is no longer in His hands (SSG 2:41, 43, 50, 53, 54). He describes Nāmdev's God-centered attitude, acquired as a result of deeds in many births, his utter distaste for the world, his firm resolve not to leave God, and his true devotion which makes him realise all his worldly relations in God. This is no news to Goṇāī. That is what she is fighting at the moment, and with a woman's logic, when her son leaves her side for God, she tries to make God her ally. She asks God, "You are the Lord in possession of the whole universe, what do You lack (*tuja kāya uṇeṃ barhmāṇḍa nāyakā / navhesī maja sārikhā ekadesī* // SSG 2:48)? Why must You snatch away the one and only son that I have? Are You tired of being the One and Only? If You are thirsty for company, must You take away the only son of a poor tailor? Have You forgotten who called You here in Paṇḍharī in the first place, and for ages to come, who made You stand steady on this brick? It was Puṇḍalik, the devotee who was so good to his old parents that even when You came to his door, he would not get up from the service of his old father, and threw You a brick to stand upon while You were waiting for him (SSG 2:51). God, why don't You smarten up? Why do You hanker after someone else's wealth (*goṇāī mhaṇe devā hoī kāṁ śahāṇā / vāṁyāṁ kāṁ paradhanā dharisī lobha* // SSG 2:38)? Why should You lure away other people's children? Now remember Your reputation as a merciful God, and unite me with my stray calf (SSG 2:42)." If God does not comply, she threatens to sit at His door and go on a hunger strike (*tujhe dvārī baisonī upavāsa karīna / nāmā gheuna jāīna guṇa rāśī* // SSG 2:62). God showers her with praise and congratulations for giving birth to a great devotee (SSG 2:54), but she is not flattered. At last the God asks Goṇāī, "How can He abandon the devotee who has come to Him in good faith? Who will then believe in Truth?" (SSF 2:54). When she fails to bring God to her side, Goṇāī begs the other Sants to put some sense in Nāmdev, but they too, echo God and praise her for her fortune instead. Her resolve to go home with Nāmdev or stay there indefinitely and reason with God is undiminished. Finally God cannot take it any more, and He says to Nāmdev, "Your mother has set her heart on you, go back to her. After all, she has raised you on her own milk, you should not abandon her." Nāmdev answers that God is not being fair. Nāmdev had turned to God in the first place out of fear of his mother, so how can God send him back to her (*nāmā mhaṇe śaraṇa āloṁ jicyā bheṇeṁ / tice hātī deṇe ucita navhe //* SSG 2:68)? When neither the headstrong mother nor her stubborn son listens to God, He resorts to a miracle. He tells Goṇāī to take back Nāmdev, and when she gladly does so and starts to walk away, she finds God in her hands instead. God and Nāmdev have become one and the same. This miracle is supposed to have enlightened her; but accordin to another version, Goṇāī remains a worldly woman to the core, and resists "enlightenment" based on a miracle with characteristic wit (SSG 2:69). This is how the incident is related: I offer a full translation of the *abhaṅga*:

"God became Nāmā and Nāmā became God in order to test the attitude of Goṇāī. (God said,) 'Here, take back your Nāmā, who cares for him?' She was ecstatic with love. She took him with her by the hand, and as she turned to look, there was God in her hand. She flipped. 'Oh my Father, who wants You? What would I, frail as I am, do with You? All those sixteen thousand women of Yours, with the eight superior ones, all of those would come running to finish me off. By the way, You have given Your work to Puṇḍalik once, remember, You can't come with me You rascal!'" [She refers here to the traditional belief that God promised to remain for ever in Paṇḍharpur, standing still on a brick thrown to him by his earlier devotee, Puṇḍalik.]

We do not know whether or not Goṇāī gave up her mission to try and tame Nāmdev's *bhakti*. There are contradictory accounts recorded in the tradition (SSG 2:69, 70; SSG 2: Janābāī 138). It is more than likely that she had to give up and that Nāmdev's all-encompassing *bhakti* went on without regard to his householder's duties. There is amply evidence to believe that Nāmdev was unaffected by his mother's arguments. So, on to the next chapter in the war of weltanschaungs. When the mother fails to bring back her son, the wife takes over (SSG 2:84-97; also in SSG 2: Nāmdev's son Gonda's *abhaṅgas* 9-14). Rājāī has been a dutiful wife to Nāmdev, and has already given him four sons and two daughters. But Nāmdev is no longer there. He is lost in his *bhakti*. At first, Rājāī tries to reason with her husband, and tells him to listen to his mother. She tries to convey to him her worries, her loneliness, and her sense of having failed to older generation, and when he turns a deaf ear to her, she resorts to something quite logical. Mother Goṇāī, as we saw earlier, had directly appealed to the God, the cause of her son's obsession. There is a rationale behind Goṇāī's choice. Nāmdev, as a child-Sant, often indulges in calling God Viṭhobā in the feminine gender as his mother Viṭhāī. In keeping with Nāmdev's attitude, as a mother to Mother, Goṇāī tries to reason with the God in broad daylight. Rājāī is Nāmdev's wife, she has no such leverage, as she remains on a lower rung of the household-hierarchical ladder. She is clever though, and more subtle than her mother-in-law in choosing the time and the person for her message. Therefore, in the darkness of midnight, she seeks out the better half of God. Her message to Viṭhobā, given to Goddess Rakhumāī to deliver, is recorded in five *abhaṅgas* on her name. In what follows, I offer a partial translation, enough to set the tone.

"O Rakhumābāī, ask your husband, why has He fooled my husband? He has no clothes, no pot, nothing to eat, but he goes on dancing day and night like a shameless man. I have got fourteen mouths to feed (this fact corroborated by Janābāī in one of her *abhaṅgas* SSG 2: Janābāī 137) in my house, and I have to go from door to door in order to feed them. You better realise this and convince Him to find a better way, or else, this Rājāī of Nāmā won't remain good any more (SSG 2:85)."

"How can I describe the ways of these fools? They all become crazy at the feet of God. All become charmed and dance like ghosts in bliss. They are all useless in the world, they bow at each other's feet, and sway in their joy of Brahman."

"Look! My poor naive mother-in-law gave birth to a bright gem. And he has joined hands with the God who reclines over the serpent Śeṣa. What is poor Rājāī to do?" (SSG 2:86).

"Listen Rukmābāī, you sit in these fine silks, but poverty does not leave me, what am I to do? The fortunate women wear jewellery, I am the unloved one, what can I do? Some get to wear divine robes, and all I have are these worn out rags. It seems that poverty has come to rest forever with us, Mother, who will listen to my complaints? The hut is broken, the wind howls from all side, I have a lot to suffer, Mother, whom shall I tell? Let alone a bed of flowers, let alone a mattress, all I have for a bed is a torn quilt. My son and my daughter are ready for marriage, but my husband never comes home. All the neighbours are laughing at us, they say Nāmāī is gone crazy (SSG 2:88)."

"Please ask your husband, why does He make us poor ones suffer so much? What are we to do, Mother, under whose roof shall we sit? He has lured my husband away from me; He does not let him go even for a moment. We are poorer by contact with you; how can you not feel for us? I cannot fathom the entire misery of this world, you better do whatever is to be done (SSG 2:89)."

The heartfelt agony of a dutiful wife at her wit's end in these *abhaṅgas* is hard to miss, but her message falls on deaf ears. Nāmdev does not change his ways. Her gentler efforts in vain, Rājāī becomes desperate and resorts to the only course available to her. With her son Viṭhā in her hand, and another son Nārā on her hips, she goes to the river Bhivarā at Paṇḍharpur, and tying her children to herself, she jumps in the river, and gets drowned in a whirlpool. Nāmdev still does not heed, but now God takes action. God wakes up from his yogic trance, and uplifts all three of them and brings them to meet Nāmdev who is still at his temple. Nārā calls out to his father Nāmdev, but Nāmdev tells his son to go back home, and Rājāī, in total disgust once again attempts suicide. This time she finds a dead serpent, cuts it in pieces, cooks it in its own poison, and starts to eat and feed her children. But when she lifts the lid, the pot is full of gold. According to one account, this miracle enlightens Rājāī (SSG 2:90).

There are a couple more accounts of Rājāī's miseries, her attempts to resist, or confront the situation, and although the details of her difficulties may differ, it is noteworthy that the resolution of the conflict always enlists the help of a miracle. Another account (SSG 2:92-97) in five *abhaṅgas* on Nāmdev's name lists Nāmdev's inadvertent mistreatment of Rājāī's brothers as the cause of Rājāī's sorrow. Here is how the story goes. Rājāī's brother come to visit their sister. When Nāmdev appears, they get up to pay respects, but

Nāmdev is so engrossed in his God, that he fails to acknowledge their presence, and this upsets Rājāī. Like a good wife, she somehow swallows that and asks Nāmdev to arrange for a feast for the brothers, but Nāmdev reminds her, that it is the tenth of the month, which is designated as a half day fast for all Vaiṣṇavas, and that the day after is the eleventh, another day-long fast. The brothers had got up early in the morning and had walked quite a distance to visit their sister. They are worried and cannot sleep due to hunger. After reminding her of her religious duties, Nāmdev retires to the temple. With the prospect of spending that day and the next in *harikathā* and *bhajan* on an empty stomach, and not being able to entertain her brothers at her house, Rājāī is very sad at heart. She wonders, "Why did my father give me in marriage to such a man? No meals, no snacks, no jewels, no clothes. The only thing I am chosen to enjoy in this life is misery."

Now God sees that the beloved of his *bhakta* is worried and comes in disguise to drive away her misery. He comes as a merchant, in the absence of Nāmdev, and delivers a sack full of gold coins and leaves. Nāmdev comes and learns that a merchant called Keśavarāj has come and delivered this sack full of wealth, and he recognises the deed of God for what it is. Nāmdev goes out, brings back some needy brahmins, and distributes the wealth brought home by God. Suspecting Nāmdev's sweeping generosity, Rājāī hides some coins from him but when she recovers them, she finds them to charcoals. She then confesses her sin to Nāmdev, and as he glances at the charcoals, they turn back to gold coins, and Nāmdev again gives them away to the needy brahmins. This triple miracle is the occasion for Rājāī's enlightenment and conversion to *bhakti* in some accounts.

In the *abhaṅgas* on the name of one of the four sons of Nāmdev, there is a similar account of the incident with Goṇāī and Rājāī. However, there Goṇāī is convinced of the greatness of the Sant by his childhood exploits with the God, and the two stories of Rājāī's plight are mixed there, so that it is the gold coins in the pot of the serpent she cooks that Nāmdev takes out and distributes among the needy brahmins at which Rājāī scolds him and curses her fate so as to make God appear before her in disguise once again offer her some wealth. This tale also culminates in God's triple miracle and Rājāī's enlightenment. In Mahīpati's *Bhakta-vijaya*, chapter 18, another account appears of the conflict between Rājāī's attempts at fighting poverty and Nāmdev's resistance. Rājāī borrows a philosopher's stone, a *parisa*, from the wife of a neighbour Parisā Bhāgvat, who has been granted the stone as a boon by Rukminī, the consort of Viṭhobā. Rājāī hopes to put an end to her poverty by using the stone, but Nāmdev discovers her plans which he deems unsuitable to a *bhakta's* wife, he takes the stone and throws it into the river. Both Rājāī and Parisā's wife, Kamaḷjā, are heartbroken, and start to cry. Parisā Bhāgvat, when he learns of this incident from his wife, demands the stone back. Nāmdev simply takes a handful of pebbles from the river-bed, and claims that all of them are philosopher's stones. The villagers test this claim, find it to be true, which enlightens Parisā Bhāgvat to accept Nāmdev's greatness, and shun the worldly wealth. Mahīpati does not mention whether the wives were convinced or not.

Even if we discount the account of these miracles leading to the women's conversion as a standard motif found in any Sant's hagiography, we cannot miss the sincerity in Goṇāī and Rājāī's earlier appeals to Nāmdev and to God. Unlike the women in other Sant's life-accounts (such as the two wives of Gorā the potter, in *Bhakta-vijaya*, ch. 17), these two are not just nameless women serving as bonds of *māyā* making the Sant's lot difficult. Nor do they resemble the typical wailing women of renouncer husband in North Indian folktales such as *rājā* Bhartṛhari, or king Gopīchand (Gold, 1992). They have no intention of either making the Sant give up his worship completely, or joining him in his total disregard for the family. We see them taking their social roles of a mother and a wife very seriously and wholeheartedly. Between the two of them, they have used practically all the arguments to make the Sant assume his share of the household responsibility. As coming from good, intelligent, god-worshipping, strong women, their own arguments are impeccable and hard to refute by reason alone. Therefore, the dispute between the divine and the domestic remains unresolved at the rational and social level. I think it significant that nothing short of a miracle converts them to the path of total abandonment in Nāmdev's style of *bhakti*. Even then, as we shall see in part two of this paper, they are seen as impediments to the Sant's progress in the self-sacrificing path of *bhakti*.

Both these women pale in comparison to Tukārām's second wife who is portrayed by Tukārām as a sharp-tongued nag. She a lot more to complain about. Tukārām himself describes why he chose to become a renunciate. He was unhappy with his low caste, and his profession as a shop-keeper. His mind was not in his shop. He was troubled by a pseudo-righteous Brahmin, Sālomālo, who used to plagiarise Tukārām's *abhaṅgas*, and instigate Brahmins against the low-born Tukārām. Due to Sālomālo's malice, in addition to some natural disasters such as famine, Tukārām suffered many a loss in his life. The notebooks of his *abhaṅgas* were thrown into the river by his rivals. Moreover, he went bankrupt, lost his shop, and lost his parents, first wife, and his children in a famine. This loss turned him wholeheartedly towards God. He gave away whatever he had to the needy, and went on singing and dancing in God's name. Of course, the second wife was at home left to her own resources without the husband's support and naturally, she started to complain, curse, and finally resorted to abuse and violence. Tukārām gives a running commentary on her in eight *abhaṅgas* has she talks (SSG 4:3766-3773). He also relates in eleven *abhaṅgas* how he advised her to change her perspective, put her burden on the God, stop worrying and live in the total abandonment of *bhakti* (SSG 4:3774-3784). We find a clear mention and a gloss to these eleven *abhaṅgas* of Tukārām's in Mahīpati's *Bhakta-vijaya* (chapter 49: verses 57-116), written in 1762, which indicates that the tradition of a conflict between Tukārām and his wife was well-known as early as in Mahīpati's times. The earlier eight *abhaṅgas* in Tukārām's *gāthā* are full of emotion and real-life drama. It is as if a candid camera is recording the confrontation scene as it happens. The wife is presented to us through her accusations, curses, and her hysterics as related by her husband, who is at once the cause of her misery, the witness of her outburst, the reporter and the record-keeper of the incident. However, the *abhaṅgas* are also like a three-way-mirror reflecting the scene from many angles. In the speeches attributed by Tukārām to his wife, we get a vivid picture of the Sant himself from his wife's angle, and come to know of her trials. In the remarks at the end of these verses we hear Tukārām the Sant respondent to his wife, the householder, and aggravating her misery by his calm and quiet demeanour. To my knowledge, these *abhaṅgas* are unparalleled in the entire Sant tradition for their most life-like presentation of the tensions between the domestic and the divine. Every *abhaṅga* below starts with the woman's speech, and end with a comment of Tukārām. My partial translations retain this format.

"'How long can I pull on being a wife? How many more calamities must I endure? Shall I offer my body to these children to tear into morsels? They would be better off dead. My husband does not let me save anything in this house, he robs me outright, I don't even have dung to sweep my floors with.' Tukā says, 'the bitch does not think, she carries a burden on her shoulders and whines'" (SSG 4:3766).

"'Who knows? He must have been my mortal enemy of a past life, that is why he has become my husband in this life. How am I to endure this misery all the time? How many people an I to beg? What good has the mother-fucker God ever done for anyone in this world?' Tukā says, 'the wife is breaking down with hysteric seizures. She cries, she laughs, she sobs and rants on and on'" (SSG 4:3767).

"'The sack (of grains) has arrived (at our) home and still he won't let my children eat the grains. He has to fill other people's bellies. Damn the rogue the robber and the sucker.' 'The madwoman is outraged and drags me by my arms like a witch,' Tukā says, 'the bitch is bankrupt in her merit from the past'" (SSG 4;3768).

"What will you eat now, my son? The husband is mad after that God. He claps his head and wears those garlands, and has given up his business altogether. He does not fill his own belly nor does he worry about ours. *Ṭāḷ* in hand and mouth opened wide, he sings in the temple of that God. What are we to do now? Leave home, go to the forest?' Tukā says, 'Have patience, nothing has happened yet'" (SSG 4:3769).

"He can't work. Why would he? He gets to eat without lifting a finger. As soon as he gets up, he starts to clammer with the *Ṭāḷ*. He doesn't let anyone sleep. From dawn to dusk, it is *chini chini chini*. He makes a racket all the time. He is a living corpse. It is as if he has percolated all shame, and drunk it. He does not even bother glancing at his family. His widow is in pain here, she is throwing stones at the mention of his very name.' Tukā says, 'Here, woman, I wrote it all down'" (SSG 4:3771-3772).

We witness here an outburst of a cornered woman whose situation is similar to the women in Nāmdev's house, but whose spirit and language are quite different from theirs. The story of Tukārām's wife remains essentially different from the cluster of stories about the women in

Nāmdev's house. Unlikely in the story of Nāmdev, no miracle takes place here to convince Āvalī of her husband's greatness. Unlike the two in Nāmdev's house Tukārām's wife has no direct dialogue with God. Later on, Mahīpati narrates in chapter 49 of his *Bhakta-vijaya* an incident in which she runs with a stone in her hand which she intends to hurl at the divine Feet of God at the Temple, where Rukmiṇī listens to her complaint against the Sant and grants her wealth, which, of course, Tukārām does not allow her to enjoy. But other than that, in Tukārām's *abhaṅgas*, and elsewhere too, she deals directly with her husband, and not with the God. She comes across as a disenchanted, bitter, and essentially helpless woman, faced with an unsympathetic, unproviding, and adamant husband, who is obsessed by a God that she does not understand or care for. All we have is this record of her passionate breakdown reported candidly by Tukārām. Unlike Nāmdev's mother and wife, we do not get any *abhaṅgas* on her name of praises to God. Even Mahīpati portrays her as a cantankerous wife who does not understand the magnanimity of her Sant husband, and does not flinch in cursing, foulmouthing, and once even hitting Tukārām with a sugarcane. Up to Mahīpati's times we do not even get to know her name. He too, following Tukārām, mentions her only as *strī*, or a woman. All of this coupled with the fact that these *abhaṅgas* of the conflict between the Sant and his woman are found in all the oldest manuscripts from Dehu, Paṇḍharpur, and Talegao traditions, and have been preserved in the critical edition of P.M. Lad, provides us with strong reasons to believe in the authenticity of the incident. Tukārām later tries to persuade his wife of the futility of her short-sighted expectations, and ties to instruct her in his path. We do not know whether she changed her outlook or not. There is no indication in the *gāthā* of Tukārām that she did. Even if she did, it was probably because she had no other choice, short of giving up the ghost. Her outrage and her desperation at the total lack of sympathy from her husband are what haunt us in her most life-like description at the hands of her husband.

Of course, elsewhere we hear more unkind works about her short-tempered nature from her husband, the Sant. Tukārām thanks God many times for giving him all the miseries in life, since like Kuntī, he believes, that the sorrows and miseries of this world constantly remind him of God, and anchor him firmly in Bhakti (cf. *vipadaḥ santu naḥ śaśvat tatra tatra jagadguro / bhavato darśanam yatsyād apunarbhava-*

darśanam // Kuntī's speech in the *Bhāgavata Purāṇa* 1:8-25). His wife gets an honourable mention among his miseries. "God, it's good that You made me a peasant. Or else the false pride would have killed me" (SSG 4:63). "God, it's a good thing that I went bankrupt in this famine. That is what nauseated me towards this world, and reminded me of You. I'm glad that my wife is a shrill nag, and that she embarrasses me in public. I'm glad that I'm humiliated in this world. It's a good thing that I lost all my wealth, all cattle, and all shame. That is what made me come to you for help" (SSG 4:3763). We know, that in the eyes of Tukārām, his wife is useful to him only as a painful reminder of worldly misery.

Rājāī, Goṇāī, and Āvalī. Typical examples of disempowered women. These women are seen as trapped in a society which assigns them only the role of nurturing their family, but offers no protection against a husband who refuses to share the load. When they try to assume their assigned traditional roles, they are accused of being obstacles in the path of worship by their *bhakta* husbands. A woman's natural concern for her husband, her children, and her family is criticised and ridiculed by her God-centered husband. She is mostly ignored, and sometimes rebuked and belittled by her Sant husband who preaches equality for all beings. Is the condition any different when a woman abandons tradition and wants to become and *bhakta* herself? Hardly. If she herself wants to follow the path of *bhakti*, but her husband is a worldling, then she is opposed by the husband, scorned by the family as a loose woman, and often abandoned or abused by society. The predicament of a female Sant has been mentioned several times so far, so I will not belabour it. Suffice it to look at only two examples of women Sants, Janābāī and Bahiṇābāī, separated from each other by more than three centuries. They differ in every respect: their families, their status, their attitude towards God and towards the society in which they live, and their poetry. The only thing they have in common is their maltreatment by society. Mahīpati devotes a chapter of his *Bhakta-vijaya* to Janābāī whereas he devotes five—six full chapters and portions of a few more—to Nāmdev's stories. Mahīpati has no story to tell of Bahiṇābāī who was the closest to him in time, and only mentions Bahiṇābāī in passing in the summary verses of the epilogue of his *Bhakta-vijaya*.

Sant Janābāī was an orphan maidservant living in Nāmdev's house. She was a sensitive and imaginative poet in her own right, and so she managed to surpass the habitual neglect coupled with hard physical labour that was her lot as an orphan servant in her master's family. The fact that Janābāī often speaks of herself as "Namadev's Janābāī" and mentions Nāmdev's family, whereas in Nāmdev's verses we find not a single mention of Janābāī, may indicate her lowly position in her master's family. Very modestly, she gives credit of her good fortune to her association with her master, Sant Nāmdev. She says, "Along with the bride, the guests also get to eat delicacies at the wedding. Similarly, since Janābāī is a servant of Nāmyā, she too has been able to join with Viṭhobā" (SSG 2: Janābāī 31). She does record, however, her harassment at the hands of the priestly establishment of the temple. The reason for this harassment is precisely Janābāī's choice of the path of *bhakti*. As a person immersed in passionate worship of Viṭhobā, she has overcome her place and conveyed through her poems her exalted status as the beloved friend of God. For example, at one place she says,

"'My mother and my father are both dead, now You have to take care of me, Viṭṭhala! Hari, I have no one, and my head is itching.' Viṭṭhala said to His consort Rukmiṇī, 'Poor Janī of mine, she has no one,' and so He grabbed some oil and a comb in hand, and He combed my hair, and braided it. When He tied a knot at the end of my braid, Janī said to Him, 'Now how about a back-rub?' Janī said, 'O Gopāla, You will celebrate with a weakling like me'" (SSG 2: Janābāī 133).

At other places, she relates how God, her buddy, alleviates all her takes by giving her a hand (SSG 2: Janābāī 83, 84, 86, 87, 88, 89, 90, etc.). When she has a washload to finish on an empty stomach, God comes running behind her and uses all four of his hands to finish her task (SSG 2: Janābāī 129, 135). When she goes to the woods to collect dung, God goes with her and not only collects dung, but helps her make patties and ties them in a bundle, and lifts it to his head while Janī has only to walk behind (SSG 2: Janābāī 130). When she has mountains of grains to grind at a grindstone, God sits opposite from her and makes light work of her formidable task (SSG 2: Janābāī 125, 126, 128, 135). Janābāī does not limit herself to these descriptions of God as her associate, her helper, and her buddy. Her devotion to God sums up all her emotions, all her passions, and gets a forceful expression such as in the following verse: "I eat God, I drink God, I sleep on God, I give God, I take God, I deal with God. Here God, there God, there is no place empty of God." Janī says, "Viṭṭābāī has filled everything inside and out, and has remained besides" (SSG 2: Janābāī 198).

All such descriptions of her mystic experiences are interpreted as boasts by the temple priests and they find a way to humiliate her. They try to accuse her of stealing the ornaments of the God's idol, convict her and prepare to impale her at a stake (SSG 2: Janābāī 154; Mahīpati's *Bhakta-vijaya*, chapter 21). She wonders whether God is dead, but is saved from her fate by divine intervention as the *sūl* or the stake turns to water.

Finally she flips, and in defiance of the society which does not allow her to swim against the current, she proudly proclaims her liberated ways as tantamount to those of a prostitute (SSG 2: Janābāī 232). "Instead of covering my head with modesty, the end of my *sārī* has fallen off my shoulders. I am preparing to enter the market as I am. Who can obstruct me now?" Janī says, "God, I have become a whore, I have opened a shop in this marketplace and Paṇḍharī. You can pour oil on my wrist (and I will howl Your name). I have come to You house now."

Bahiṇābāī (1628-1700) is another example of a woman who wanted to embrace the path of *bhakti* and suffered for it. We have more details available to us of her life, thanks to her own feat of recording them in verse. Although Janābāī is more celebrated in the Sant tradition than Bahiṇābāī, specific dates cannot be ascribed to Janābāī, all we know is that she is said to be a contemporary of Sant Nāmdev. Mahīpati devotes a chapter of his *Bhakta-vijaya* to Janābāī whereas he devotes six full chapters and portions of a few more to Nāmdev's stories, and a similar number to sing Tukārām's glories. But Mahīpati has no story to tell of Bahiṇābāī who was the closest to him in time and only mentions Bahiṇābāī in passing in the summary verses of the epilogue of his *Bhakta-vijaya*. Bahiṇābāī was perhaps the first woman Sant who has narrated her own life in detail in 78 *abhaṅgas*, and has given us the exact date of her birth, etc. She was a child bride of 3 years, married off to a thirty year old brahmin widower. She was subjected to demands of married life from the age of eleven years onwards, but her heart was not in it. Sant Tukārām's appearance in her dream guided her to the path of *bhakti* and to chanting the name of Viṭhobā. Of course, her husband tried to argue her out of it, by saying that "we are brahmins who chant the Vedas all the time, why do you need this lower caste Tukārām to come in your dream and instruct you?" (*Bahiṇābāī Gāthā* 32). Bahiṇābāī tried to reconcile to the demands of her husband and find pleasure in being a dutiful housewife, but succeeded in neither draining herself of her powerful emotion of *bhakti* nor in pleasing her hard-to-please, hot-tempered husband. So she tried to engage in her pursuits of *bhakti*, while remaining a dutiful wife to her husband. Soon her game began to spread and the husband began to be upset. At one point in Bahiṇābāī's *abhaṅgas*, we find that she reads accurately the thoughts of her husband who was in all likelihood just jealous of the attention and the fame she was getting. "They will now all some and bow at her feet, and she will treat me as a straw. All these people come to consult with her, and here I am a brahmin tuned a fool. They all quote her name as the Gosāvīṇ, and no one remembers me while she is around" (*Bahiṇābāī Gāthā* 33). He is said to have abused, beaten, and confined her to their cattle-shed. When neither words nor physical abuse won her back, he prepared to leave her, but suffered a sensation of burning limbs for a whole month, and finally he was convinced of her sincerity in her chosen path.

Even after this, until she died at the age of 72, Bahiṇābāī lived a split life, torn between the cruel demands placed on her woman's body by her mismatched marriage, and her own urge towards renunciation and *bhakti*. Her mental torment find a powerful expression as follows: "The Vedas call out, the Purāṇas roar: 'There is no merit in company of a woman.' I was born with a woman's body. So how do I arrange for a better life, for *paramārtha*? Idiocy, possessiveness, temptation, and illusion, all these make a woman's company disastrous." Bahiṇī says, "thus is a woman's body deemed treacherous. How on earth can I aspire for a better goal?" (*Bahiṇābāī Gāthā* 63). Bahiṇābāī is all the more tormented since she does not want to follow a path of *bhakti* in place of her social duties. She wants to have her cake and eat it too. She chooses not to abandon her husband, nor her family as many women Sants before her were forced to do. She calls out to God for help in this enterprise, and says, "Hari, You alone are my friend, my brother. You are Pāṇḍhuraṅga, the resort of the weak. Arrange it so I can worship You and fulfil my duty as a good wife" (*Bahiṇābāī Gāthā* 68). But even with God's help, it is not easy, and we find her recording her trials as an aspiring soul trapped in a woman's body. "What sins have I committed in my past lives that I was abandoned by the Best Man, by God? I acquired birth as a human being, but with this female body. My untold sins must have ripened. I am not entitled to listen to the meaning of the Vedas, and the brahmins have hidden the *gāyatrī mantra* as well. I may not utter the sound of *praṇava*. I may not listen to the utterance of a *bīja mantra*. I may not talk with another man, since my husband is hot-tempered as Jamadagnī incarnate." Bahiṇī says, "my life is torture, but God takes no pity over me" (*Bahiṇābāī Gāthā* 64). Finally she reconciles to her lot as a woman by embracing the doctrine of Karma and *prārabdha*. She says, "Many miseries have I endured, my friend, I have been humiliated to the core. This misery is my lot, I had started it earlier, this is how I tried to console my mind. Even Brahmā and the others could not escape suffering their sorrows, so the rest are nobodies compared to them." Bahiṇī says, "such is the fate of my body, begun by me, so what can God do about it?" (*Bahiṇābāī Gāthā* 70).

We see in the above examples that a woman in the Marathi Sant tradition is at fault no matter which way she turns. Whether she defies the tradition or follow it faithfully, a woman is not free of blame. Why is this so? The answer lies is society's denial of free-will to a woman. A woman, married or unmarried, is to follow only the path her mentor dictates. If she has no husband, and is an orphan like Janābāī, she may take to *bhakti* inspired by her master, but even her choice is not entirely free of obstacles. Not only does the society accuse her and abuse her, but she senses partiality even in God's graces. She feels that God has accepted Rājāī and Goṇāī quite wholeheartedly, but He is not so generous with herself. She accuses God, "Rājāī and Goṇāī get to stay always at Your feet, but You treat me as a lowly person and therefore keep me only at the door" (SSG 2: Janābāī 70). Perhaps it is in response to this complaint of Janābāī's that Mahīpati's *Bhakta-vijaya* 21 narrates a story in which God comes to her hut in secret and compensates for his lack of consideration that she accuses him of. Nevertheless, an orphan like Janābāī somehow finds solace in God's *bhakti* and gets over her handicap of being born a woman. We find her advocating, "One should not get despondent of this birth as a woman, the Sants have showed a way out. I am a servant branded as one of the house of the Sants, so Viṭhobā has granted me an aspect of His love" (SSG 2: Janābāī 81). But if married, a woman has no other choice than that of following her husband. She is to follow only the path that he chooses for her. If he is a Sant, then she is not free to be a traditional housewife, as we saw in the cases of Rājāī and Āvalī, and if he is a traditional husband, and she chooses to be a Sant, as Bahiṇābāī did, then heaven help her.

Part two

When we turn from the portraits of these individual women to the sketches and caricatures of women in the Sants' poems, a similar fragmented pattern emerges. In general, the Sants praise woman in the form of the mother, and revile her in the form of a temptress. Nāmdev offer a very simplistic bilateral division of all women based on the virtue or vice of their physical beauty. He says,

"The beautiful woman, the pretty woman, the desirable woman should be recognised as the sinner. When one sees her, the desire to be with her is strong, and that destroys the merit of chanting of the *bhakta*. Nāmā says, one should not glance at her face, since such a bitch is a sinner, and she destroys a man as well."

"The ugly woman, of inferior body, is a woman to be congratulated as the mother. No one ever can be attracted to her, and thus she is no threat to one's worship. Such a matron is in fact kind, and beneficial to a man, as she does not destroy his *bhajan*. Nāmā says, one should look at her face as a mother, and should bow at her feet" (SSG 2:1943, 1944).

Even though we understand that it is his urge to worship without distractions which prompts him to categorise women into such a sweeping division, it is difficult to accept his convoluted reasoning which transfers the blame for a wavering mind of the weak aspirant to the beauty of the woman he beholds. In the manner of reasoning, the physical attributes of ugliness or beauty are somehow transformed into moral attributes of virtue and vice, or in even stronger terms, merit and sin. This fateful division of women based on the effect of their existence on men permeates through the psyche of the whole society, which then finds it easy to blame a woman for all the evils in the minds of men.

The temptress/nurturer dichotomy prevails throughout the Sant literature, with many variations on the theme. Although Nāmdev, the child-Sant, brands all beautiful women as sinners and therefore deems them disastrous to the worship of a *bhakta*, Tukārām shows a mature Sant's response to the tempting beauty of women. Even the temptress can sometimes be transformed into a mother, and then she ceases to be a temptress. The *gāthā* of Sant Tukārām records the story of a woman who approaches Tukārām in order to seduce him. Tukārām addresses her as "mother" and thus distances her effectively. This is what he says to her: "Any other woman is like the Goddess Rakhumāī to me. This is the eternal rule I follow. Go away, dear mother, do not exert yourself; we, the servants of Viṣṇu are not of that type. I cannot bear to see your fall. Please don't say the wicked words." Tukā says, "If you want a mate, is there a lack of other men?" The formula practised by the Sants at all times and prescribed to those who want to follow the path of *bhakti* is: "Treat women belonging to others as your mothers" (SSG 2:1941, 4:3784-3786).

When is a woman regarded as a temptress? She does not have to be "the other woman" or a prostitute for that; even a dutiful housewife, or a concerned mother can be seen as a temptress by a Sant, because, as we say in the life-story of Nāmdev, insofar as she cares for the Sant, and ties him with the worldly love, she proceeds to be an impediment in his path of unconditional worship. Here we notice the duality in the Sants' treatment of women. Although Nāmdev worships the God in the form of the mother, and in general upholds the mother's love as the ultimate selfless love, he deserts his own mother in favour of God. Any woman can be regarded as a temptress and no woman is as motherly as the God. Tukārām praises the selfless love of a mother (SSG 4:2180), and sees both the Sants and the God as mothers (SSG 4:1994, 2058, 2180-2181, 2183-2185, 2197-2198). In fact, the Sants are sometimes said to be better than the mundane mother, since the mother brings you into this world, whereas the Sants show you a way to be rid of this world. When parents praise a child, they have a vested interest in him. God is always better than parents, since God's love for a devotee has no strings attached (*māyābāpeṁ sāṁbhāḷitī / lobhākāraṇeṁ pāḷitī / taisā navhe devarāva / yācā kṛpāḷū svabhāva //* SSG 4:3007).

Further subdivisions are introduced to the above two-fold division. When the Sants consider woman in the form of a wife, they see her role typified either as a devoted wife, a *pativratā*, or a deceitful wife, *sindaḷī*, or *vyabicāriṇī*. It is no surprise to find the Sants sympathetic to the devoted wife. On the whole, a deceitful woman, a *vyabicāriṇī* is censured and cursed to an after-life in hell (SSG 4:2336). She is said to destroy due to her misconduct both her father's family and the one into which she is married (SSG 4:2338). The Sants have further used these two types of women as analogies for themselves and for the householders. At one point, Nāmdev has effectively used the *vyabhicārī nārī* as a prescriptive model for the householders. He says, if you are engaged in mundane affairs, you still must concentrate on the Lord just as an adulteress behaves in her own household, all the while keeping the other man in her mind (SSG 2:1848). As steadfast *bhaktas* of God, the Sants regard themselves as *pativratās*, or faithful women. When some deceitful householders dislike Tukārām for his outspokenness, he remarks, "When an adulteress hears praise for a faithful woman, she get a headache. Our comments on the world are spontaneous. We do not take permission of other to say what we do" (SSG 4:2353).

Here one curious point need notice. When the Sants preach the householders general norms of morality, they unequivocally curse a women who cheats on her husband. However, the prostitute (*gaṇikā* or *kuṇṭaṇī*) is given a differential treatment in real life as well as in the literature of the Sants. Within the realm of *bhakti*, the Sants were supportive of all outcastes, and anybody, however low his status in the society was welcome in their fold as long as he or she chose to embrace the path of true *bhakti*. Consistent with this spirit, Sant Kānhopātrā, a prostitute who lived near Mangaḷveḍhe, is included in the list of Marathi Sants without hesitation (Mahīpati's *Bhakta-vijaya* allots her an entire chapter, 39). Perhaps, because the Sants recognise the helplessness of a prostitute in the male-dominated societal order, or perhaps, because they were using the inherited stock of traditional Vaiṣṇava stories, they cite the prostitute as an example of the real downtrodden and deserving persons that are saved by the merciful God (SSG 2:1218, 1220, 1228, 1316, 1317, 1323, etc.; SSG 4:306, 1812, 1813, 1826, 1871, etc.).

It is no wonder that the Sants praise the devoted wife as the paradigm of virtue, and often use her as an analogy for the *bhakta's* concentration of mind on the Almighty Lord (SSG 3:415; *pativrate jaisā bhratāra pramāṇa āmhāṁ nārāyaṇa taiśā parī* // SSG 3:416). However, even a wife who does not hanker after another man may prove to be detrimental to her husband by her excessive demands on him. Tukārām presents many pictures of such women and warns people against them (SSG 4:2327-2332). A wilful woman who makes her husband dance to her tune is despised by the Sants. She is caricatured as the worst kind of temptress. Her fault seems to lie in the fact that she not only severs a man from his own family, but she also makes him worship her rather than the God, and thus deprives him of a chance to be enlightened.

Correspondingly, the man who is under the thumb of his woman is ridiculed over and over again (SSG 4:2327, 2328). He is like an insipid dog who eats without discretion, like a monkey on the rope of a street-player, he is a jackass while he lives and he goes to hell after he dies. These pictures are all quite consistent with the overall norm of the society which denies free-will to women and considers a man as the prime candidate for enlightenment.

Compared to Nāmdev, who places the blame of a wavering aspirant squarely on the shoulders of women, Tukārām is usually fair to both sexes within the constraints of his society, and his *bhakti*. Whether it is a man or a woman, if they worship God, then they are like God to him (*ho kaṁ nara athavā nārā / jyāñcā āvaḍatā harī // te maja viṭhobā samāna* / SSG 4:2129). He ridicules both men and women who are deluded by *māyā*, and are misbehaving (SSG 4:2343, 2344). Somehow, his pictures of such misguided women rather than those of such men are more vivid and full of humorous details, and hence are quoted and remembered by generations after him. Here is, for instance, a well-known sketch of a woman about to go to Paṇḍharpur on a pilgrimage. This has become so famous in Maharashtra, that one of its lines, i.e. *avā nighālī paṇḍharapurā*, is used as a proverb in Marathi to describe any person who cannot make up his mind about what is good for him. I offer a full translation of the *abhaṅga*.

"'Listen, daughter-in-law, don't waste milk, or curds.' Āvā started to go to Paṇḍharpur, but she turned back from the town's boundary, and came home again. 'Daughter, pay attention to what I say. Look after the chipped half of the grinding stone. The *kalavaḍu* (a drinking pot) that I always use; don't break it in my absence. The curd is set solid, don't break it without me. This mortar, this pestle, this grinding stone, this is where my mind hovers. When the beggars come the door, tell them that I am gone to Paṇḍharpur. Eat in moderation, don't waste in excess.' The daughter-in-law said, 'Very well, you proceed to your pilgrimage and be happy. Mother, you look after your own merit, and leave all such desires behind.' As she heard this speech of her daughter-in-law, the mother-in-law was doubtful. She thought, 'The witch is putting on an act. She wants me to vanish. Why should I go on a pilgrimage? What will I see there? Children, grandchildren, the home and the yard: this is where lies my Paṇḍharpur.' Tukā says, 'Thus are the people engulfed in Māyā'" (SSG 4:2343).

Tukārām was a great social commentator. He is extremely critical of anyone who sells his daughters, his cows, or his *kathā*, which is God's praise in the form of a story (SSG 4:2316). The nouns he uses for all these, *kanyā*, *go*, and *kathā*, are feminine in Marathi. He does not condone a man with two wives, although the practice was there is his society, and many Sants such as Tukārām himself and Gorā Kuṃbhār are said to have had two wives (SSG 4:2333). This discrepancy in preaching and practice may not be an indication of hypocrisy on the part of Tukārām, as it may seem superficially, but more a criticism of a evil in the society to which he himself had fallen victim at the wishes of his elders. All kinds of mismatched couples are described by Tukārām with equal criticism. Just as he notices the helplessness of a man whose wife is infertile, he takes about the plight of a woman who is married to an impotent man (SSG 4:2782). He has no sympathy, however, for the infertile woman who wraps rags around her belly and pretends to be pregnant. That is hypocrisy, pure and simple, according to him. Tukārām depicts the miseries of a man sandwiched between two wives (SSG 4:2333), and he shows awareness of women's miseries resulting out of cruel marriage practices prevalent in his society. Since the girls were married off by their elders, sometimes even before they were born, and other times to over-ripe husbands twice their age, women were subjected to mismatches of all types. Here are two such sorry friends as seen by Tukārām.

"Two friends. One has a boyish husband, the other is married to a widower. It is the perpetual take of this world. 'My husband is so you, he constantly runs away to play with the kids. All evening long he spends in playing, and stays outside the house while I wait for him on the bed. I don't have enough merit accumulated in my past lives. How can I describe my sorrow?'

'Friend, you want to listen to my misery? The old man coughs all the time. If I take the initiative and go near him, he won't let me touch him, he is too tired.' Tukā says, 'women, this is how your karma rewards you. Why do you blame the God?'" (SSG 4:4405).

Of course, since Tukārām concludes that the women have themselves to blame for their misfortune in this life, he does not feel the need to challenge the society on their behalf. His answer to all such miseries of this life would be to discard the passion which ties one to this miserable world and immerse the mind in *bhakti* of God (*prapañcācā chanda ṭākūniyāṁ govā / dharāveṁ keśavā hṛdayāñta* // SSG 4:2349). That is what he did when he was troubled with the miseries of this world. But we saw earlier how that choice was not open to all married women unless their husbands also become *bhaktas* with them and abandoned everything in this world. Therefore, all these miserable women that we witness in the Sants' poems and in their lives remain rooted in their respective miseries.

Conclusion

The condition of women in the Marathi Sant tradition, can be summed up in the words of Bahiṇābāī. As a disciple of Sant Tukārām, she too believed that her lot in this life as a woman was a result of her sins in her past lives, her *prārabdha*, and that she had to endure all her trials patiently. However, as his true disciple, she also wanted to follow the path of *bhakti* as he did. As we saw above, that was not easy. Tukārām's advice to his own wife was to follow the path of *bhakti* became celebrated in the tradition, and was quoted by other life Mahīpati as exemplary, whereas Bahiṇābāī could not advise her own husband and be accepted wholeheartedly let alone be praised by him or others in her lifetime and, as a result, had to endure her split personality all her life. She has crystallised her hard-earned life-long wisdom in the following two lines: "A woman's body is a body controlled by someone else. Therefore, the path of renunciation is not open to her" (*striyece śarīra parādhīna deha / ne cāle ūpāva viraktīcā // Bahiṇābāī Gāthā* 60). I submit that as we look at the various lives of individual and typified women, married, unmarried, widowed, or orphaned, in the long Sant tradition, the only truth that emerges is that "Awoman's body was a body controlled by someone else, and therefore, no path was open to her without the permission of the other."

BIBLIOGRAPHY

Bahiṇābāī. *Bahiṇābāī Gāthā.* Pune: Chitrashala Prakashan, second edition, 1956.

Bhāgavata Purāṇa. Bombay: Nirnayasagara Press, ninth edition, 1950.

Dhere, R.C., ed. *Sakala Santa Gāth (Gāthā Paṭcaka).* [SSG for short]. A compendium of major Marathi Sants' works based on the Sakhare tradition of manuscripts. Volumes 1-5. Pune: Varadā Prakashan, [first edition, 1908] latest edition, 1985.

Gold, Ann Grodzins. *A Carnival of Parting: The Tales of King Bharthari and King Gopi Chand as Sung and Told by Madhu Natisar Nath of Ghadiyali, Rahasthan.* Berkeley: University of California Press, 1992.

Inamdar, Hemant Vishnu. *Santa Nāmadeva* (Nāmdev: The Saint-Poet o Maharashtra). Pune: Kesari Prakashan, 1970.

Mahīpati. *Bhakta-vijaya.* Ed. S.R. Devale. Pune: Sharada Prakashan, 1989.

Schomer, Karine and W.H. McLeod, eds. *The Sants: Studies in a Devotional Tradition in India.* New Delhi: Motilal Banarsidass, 1987.

Sheorye, Indumati. *Santa Kavayitrī.* Bombay: Tata Institute of Social Sciences, distributed by Popular Prakashan, 1989.

Tukārām: Śrī Tukarāma Bāvāncyā Abangāñcī Gāthā. Ed. P.M. Lad. Bombay: Government Central Press, [first edition, 1950] second edition, 1955.

Zelliot, Eleanor and Maxine Berntsen, eds. *The Experience of Hinduism: Essays on Religion in Maharashtra.* Albany: State University of New York Press, 1988.

CHAPTER SIX

ŚAṄKARA ON THE SALVATION OF WOMEN AND ŚŪDRAS

KATHERINE K. YOUNG

The Advaita-vedānta view that women and members of the lowest caste called *śūdra*s cannot attain liberation (*mokṣa*) is usually attributed to the great eighth-century philosopher Śaṅkara himself.[1] It is based on the argument that the path of knowledge (*jñāna-yoga*) involves both knowledge of the Vedas and renunciation. Because women and *śūdra*s were without knowledge of the Vedas (*avaidika*) in the sense that they either did not have, or were prohibited from having it, and were not able to take renunciation (*sannyāsa*) on account of the injunction to serve and follow their masters, they could not pursue the path of knowledge and attain liberation. A close reading of Śaṅkara's works suggests, however, that he did not hold this position himself; rather, later thinkers ascribed it to him.

The task at hand, then, is to examine Śaṅkara's writings—specifically, passages in the *Bhagavad-gītā* (3:20: 9:29-34; 18:44-55 and 18:66); *Bṛhadāraṇyaka-upaniṣad* (3:5:1; 4:5:15; 2:4:1-14; 4:2:1-4; 6:4:17); *Muṇḍaka-upaniṣad* (1:2:12); and *Vedānta-sūtra*s (=*Brahma-sūtra*s) (1:1:2; 1:1:4; 1:3:34-38; 3:4:26-27; 3:4:36-40; and 4:4:22) with the following questions in mind. Are there any explicit

---

[1] The traditional date of Śaṅkara is 788-820 CE; Paul Hacker thought that he more likely lived around 700 (see Halbfass 1995, 100 note 44). For a discussion on the authorship of the works attributed to Śaṅkara and his disciples, see Hacker's analysis presented in the chapter "Śaṅkara the Yogin and Śaṅkara the Advaitin: Some Observations" in Halbfass 1995, 101-134: "it appears that all his independent works are collected in the 22 Prakaraṇas going under the name of *Upadeśasāhasrī*, all the rest being spurious. The authentic commentaries are those on the *Brahmasūtras*, on the *Bhagavadgītā*, on the Adhyātmapaṭala of the *Āpastamba-Dharmasūtra*, and on 10 Upaniṣads ...." (p. 128).

prohibitions against women and *śūdra*s taking *sannyāsa* and attaining salvation? Is knowledge of the Vedas a prerequisite? Are there examples of women and *śūdra*s attaining salvation in the scriptures? In his commentaries, does Śaṅkara hold to the literal meaning of those passages that seem to accept the renụnciation and salvation of women and *śūdra*s? Can women and *śūdras* attain salvation in this life or must they await rebirth as brahmin (*brāhmaṇa)* or twice-born (*dvija*) men? If women and *śūdra*s can attain salvation in this life, then what is meant by the idea that *brāhmaṇa*s and royal sages (who are *dvija*s) attain the supreme goal more quickly? And how are we to interpret passages that seem to suggest that only *brāhmaṇa* men can take *sannyāsa*? Is *sannyāsa* the only means for attaining salvation according to Śaṅkara? Does Śaṅkara use the same language when referring to the goal for women and *śūdra*s as he uses for *brāhmaṇa*s or *dvija*s?

The final section of this analysis will suggest who introduced the idea that Śaṅkara was against the liberation of women and *śūdra*s. It will also place the discussion in the larger context of historical vicissitudes: a new brahmanical universalism to compete with the heterodox religions and to come to terms with social change but also a reinforcement of brahmanical exclusivity to stem the tide of change and regroup under the banner of the duties of caste and stages of life (*varṇa-āśrama-dharma*). Śaṅkara's hermeneutical skill can be seen in his reconciliation of these seemingly contradictory goals.

Text, Context, and Interpretation

Is salvation promised to everyone? Perhaps the strongest statement of universal salvation is found in *Gītā* 9:29-34.

> I am the same to all beings; there is no one who is hateful or dear to Me. But those who worship me with devotion, they are in Me and I am also in them.
>
> samo 'haṃ sarvabhūteṣu na me dveṣyo 'sti na priyaḥ |
> ye bhajanti tu māṃ bhaktyā mayi te teṣu cāpy aham || (9:29)

Śaṅkara holds to the literal meaning of this verse. God bestows his grace on his devotees who are near to him like fire gives warmth to those nearby. Śaṅkara draws a fundamental distinction, therefore, between those who are devotees and those who are not. It is implied that God is the same to all, because he is available to all. In this sense he is impartial. But it is up to people to avail themselves of God's grace by worshipping him. In short, there is the promise of universal salvation but the initiative belongs to the individual.

In the next verse (9:30) we are told that even if one of very evil conduct (*sudurācāra*) but worships God resorting to none else, such a one is to be deemed righteous (*sādhu*) for such a one indeed is rightly resolved (*samyak-vyavasita*). Śaṅkara glosses *sudurācāra* etc. as "by abandoning evil ways in his external life and by right resolution." *Gītā* 9:31 states in no uncertain terms that:

> Quickly (*kṣipram*) he/she becomes righteous (*dharmātman*) and attains eternal peace (*śaśvac-chānti*). Understand, O Son of Kuntī, that my devotee does not perish.
>
> kṣipraṃ bhavati dharmātmā śaśvacchāntiṃ nigacchati |
> kaunteya pratijānīhi na me bhaktaḥ praṇaśyati || (9:31)

Śaṅkara, in his commentary on this verse, glosses it with much more emphatic language. He begins by saying: "Listen (*śṛṇu*) to the supreme meaning (*parama-artha*)" and then glosses the injunction *pratijānīhi* as "make a proposition with certainty" or "proclaim, assert" (*niścitāṃ pratijānīhi kuru*). Thus, "Listen to the supreme meaning ... Proclaim ... that my devotee does not perish." In the next verse (9:32), we learn the supreme meaning: that women and *śūdras* (along with the third twice-born caste, the *vaiśyas*) are included in this promise of universal salvation that is to be proclaimed everywhere.

> Indeed, O Pārtha, after resorting to Me, even those who [are called] born of evil womb (*pāpa-yonayaḥ*) - women, *vaiśyas* as well as *śūdras* - they attain the supreme goal (*yānti parāṃ gatim*).
>
> māṃ hi pārtha vyapāśritya ye 'pi syuḥ pāpayonayaḥ |
> striyo vaiśyās tathā śūdrās te 'pi yānti parāṃ gatim || (9:32)

Śaṅkara's commentary is worth quoting in full:

> māṃ hi yasmāt pārtha vyapāśritya mām āśrayatvena gṛhītvā ye 'pi syuḥ bhaveyuḥ pāpayonayaḥ pāpā yoniḥ yeṣāṃ te pāpayonayaḥ pāpajanmānaḥ | ke te iti āha-striyaḥ vaiśyāḥ tathā śūdrāḥ te 'pi yānti gacchanti parāṃ prakṛṣṭāṃ gatim ||

Śaṅkara keeps to the literal meaning of the verse except when he comments on *pāpa-yonayaḥ* (those of evil womb). Here he makes the idea tentative rather than absolute by inserting the optative verb *syuḥ*, which he then glosses as *bhaveyuḥ*; thus, "those who *may be* of sinful birth." *Gītā* 9:34 concludes the chapter by saying:

> Be with [your] mind on Me, be devoted to Me, sacrifice to Me, prostrate to Me. Thus steadied, having Me as the supreme goal (*matparāyaṇaḥ*), you will reach Me, the Self.
>
> manmanā bhava madbhakto madyājī māṃ namaskuru |
> mām evaiṣyasi yuktvaivam ātmānaṃ matparāyaṇaḥ || (9:34)

Based on these verses of the *Gītā*, women and *śūdra*s attain the supreme goal after resorting to the Lord. But there are more troublesome verses that must be discussed.

The next obvious question is whether there are any explicit prohibitions against women and *śūdra*s taking *sannyāsa* and attaining salvation. There is considerable discussion over the eligibility of *śūdra*s for *sannyāsa*. As noted, both *śūdra*s and women are considered members of the same category (those who are without knowledge of the Vedas) by this time. I will assume that what is said of *śūdras* applies to women (and vice versa) unless there is specific evidence to the contrary. This relates to the issue of whether knowledge of the Vedas is prerequisite for taking *sannyāsa*.

A key text on this topic is Śaṅkara's commentary on *Vedānta-sūtra* 1:3:34-38. He begins by pointing out that this section was written to remove confusion over whether only twice-born men (*dvijas*) have exclusive access to liberation or whether *śūdra*s (and presumably women) too can claim knowledge of Brahman (*Vedānta-sūtra* 1:3:34). He then offers various arguments made by the opponent (*pūrva-pakṣin*) as to why *śūdra*s have knowledge of Brahman (*brahma-vidyā*). The opponent argues, for instance, that *śūdra*s are eligible because (1) they desire that knowledge; (2) they are capable of having it; (3) there are no specific scriptural prohibitions against them having it analogous to the prohibition that a *śūdra* is unfit for sacrificing (*Taittirīya-saṃhitā* 7: 1.1.6); (4) their dis-qualification from having sacred fires and performing sacrificial works does not invalidate their qualification for knowledge, because knowledge can be apprehended by other means; (5) there is the example of Jānaśruti Pautrāyaṇa who wished to learm from a *śūdra* (according to *Chāndogya-upaniṣad* 4: 2-3), which implies that the *śūdra* knows Brahman; and (6) *smṛti* mentions Vidura and others born of *śūdra* mothers as possessing supreme knowledge. In short, the opponent's view is that *śūdra*s have a claim to knowledge of Brahman (*brahma-vidyā*).

I shall not take up all of Śaṅkara's refutations in detail here. The crux of the matter in his commentary on *Vedānta-sūtra* 1:3:34-38 is that *śūdra*s cannot claim knowledge of Brahman on account of their not studying the Vedas. Mere desire or mundane capability does not suffice, because spiritual capability is required and this involves eligibility to be initiated, to study the Vedas, and to perform sacrifices. Moreover, the reference in *Chāndogya-upaniṣad* 4:2:3 to the fact that Jānaśruti has access to *saṃvarga-vidyā*, which is part of the knowledge of Brahman, argues Śaṅkara, is not to be taken literally or viewed as indicating that *śūdra*s have access to other forms of knowledge. It occurs in a passage of mere praise (*artha-vāda*). Then, too, the reference to *śūdra* in *Chāndogya-upaniṣad* 4:1:3 can be taken in the etymological sense of grief (*suk*) (*Vedānta-sūtra* 1:3:34). In his commentary on *Vedānta-sūtra* 1:3:35, Śaṅkara argues that Jānaśruti is not a *śūdra* but a *kṣatriya*. In 1:3:36 he says that Manu and others say that *śūdra*s are not fit for initiation into study of the Vedas (*upanayana*), and in 1:3:37 that Gautama initiated Jābāla only when he ascertained that he was not a *śūdra*. Finally, *sūtra* 1:3:38 declares that *smṛti* prohibits *śūdra*s from hearing and studying the Vedas and performing Vedic rituals. In the opening line of his commentary on 1:3:38, Śaṅkara repeats the literal meaning of the *sūtra*, supplying the missing words.

Because knowledge of Brahman is usually understood as leading to salvation and because Śaṅkara in his commentary on *Gītā* 9:29-34, as we have seen, has argued that *śūdra*s attain the supreme goal, then it appears contradictory that he assigns here this position to his opponent and proceeds to argue vehemently against it. Just what is going on?

The clue is provided in his commentary on *Vedānta-sūtra* 1.3.38. Just as Śaṅkara completes his rebuttal and seems to demolish any possibility whatsoever that *śūdra*s can attain knowledge of Brahman, he adds a modifying addendum in 1.3.38. He makes two points. First, he argues that because in former lives *śūdras* such as Vidura and Dharmavyādha have acquired good karma from their deeds, the fruition of these impressions (*saṃskāras*) will automatically result in knowledge (sometimes in a subsequent life). Second, all the four castes are qualified (*adhikāra*) for hearing (*śrarana*) the *itihāsas* and *purāṇas* and are to be taught as in the line "he is to teach (*śravayet*) the four castes" (*Mahābhārata*).[2] Śaṅkara then points out that the case is different for knowledge of the Veda, because it is well established that *śūdras* do not possess any such qualification (*na asti adhikāraḥ*) for that.

> yeṣām punaḥ pūrvakṛtasaṃskāravaśād vidura-dharmavyādha-prabhṛtīnāṃ jñānotpattis teṣām na śakyate phalaprāptiḥ pratiṣeddhuṃ jñānas-yaikāntikaphalatvāt | śrāvayeccuturo varṇān iti cetihāsapurāṇādhigame cāturvarṇyasyādhikāras smaraṇāt | vedapūrvakas tu nāsty adhikāraḥ śūdrāṇām iti sthitam ||[3]

Kane points out that Śaṅkara, when commenting on *Vedānta-sūtra* 3:4:36, refers to the

> woman Vācaknavī as one who had the knowledge of brahma 'raikva-vācaknavīprabṛtīnamevaṃbhūtānāmapi brahma-vittvaśrūtyupalabdhe: gārgī vācaknavī figures as a great seeker after brahma in the Br. Up. III.6.1, III.8.1 and 12. The Mahābhārata ways that what it dilates upon as to the *puruṣārthas, dharma, artha, kāma*, and *mokṣa*, is found elsewhere and that what it does not contain on those subjects can be found nowhere else and that the *Mahābhārata* should be listened to by him who desires *mokṣa*, by *brāhmaṇas*, kings and pregnant women (Svargārohaṇaparva 5.50-51).[4]

In other words, eligibility for the twice-born is based on study of the *śruti*, but eligibility for women and *śūdra*s is based on hearing *smṛti*. Śaṅkara glosses the word *paṇḍitā* in his commentary on *Bṛhadāraṇyaka-upaniṣad* 6:4:17 to mean a woman "skilled in household work" instead of the obvious meaning "learned." Because *paṇḍita* denotes a learned person or scholar and may connote one learned in the scripture (including *śruti*) and because Śaṅkara, as

---

[2] The source is not given.

[3] Sanskrit text taken from Kane 1977, vol. 5, 921; note 1468a.

[4] Kane 1977, vol.5, 921; note 1468. It is curious that this extremely important passage is tucked away in a footnote in Kane's final volume whereas in his second volume (p. 943) he says that the first view that only *brāhmaṇas* can be *sannyāsins* is affirmed by the great Śaṃkarācārya in his *bhāṣya* on *Bṛhadāraṇyaka Upaniṣad* 3.5.1 and 4.5.15.

already noted, says that only twice-born men have eligibility to study of Vedas, he obviously does not want to include women in this category (although the orginal Upaniṣadic passaage suggests that women at that time could be scholars).[5] In any case, knowledge through *śruti* is not a problem when knowledge through *smṛti* can be attained.

The final point of the opponent, we recall, was that *smṛti* speaks of Vidura and others such as Dharmavyādha who were born from *śūdra* mothers as having knowledge of Brahman. Now, we know that Śaṅkara agrees that *śūdra*s such as Vidura possess eminent knowledge and have a claim to the knowledge of Brahman but that knowledge is not attained through knowledge of the Vedas. In short, there must be other ways of obtaining knowledge of Brahman and therefore salvation than through the Vedas. Śaṅkara gives us a clue to these alternatives by mentioning deeds in former lives and *smṛti* (non-Vedic scripture). According to Radhakrishnan, this point is also made in Śaṅkara's commentary on *Vedānta-sūtra* 1:1:3 "(*śāstrayonitvāt*: 'from its being the source of Scripture' or 'from Scripture being the source (of its knowledge)'. ... *Śāstra* for S [Śaṅkara] includes the four Vedas, the epics, the *purāṇas* and other branches of learning, *vidyāsthāna*."[6]

Vidyā means knowledge, science, learning, scholarship, and philosophy. Various *vidyā*s are enumerated in the texts. One category is the three (alternatively four) Vedas; another is knowledge of the branches of learning (*vedāṅga*s); and yet another is the knowledge of

---

[5] There were some women who had expertise in the Vedas in ancient times because Kāśikā on Pāṇini IV.1.45 and III.3.21, for example, points out that the formation of the words *ācāryā* and *upādhyāyā* refers to the fact that women were themselves teachers. Because the main body of knowledge at the time was the Veda and its branches *(vedāṅga)*, we can assume that women taught those subjects.

[6] Radhakrishnan 1960, 240-242. Elsewhere Radhakrishnan notes: "As we will see, S. makes out that Suta, Vidura and others, though born on account of the merit acquired in their previous lives, have obtained Brahma-knowledge. The author of Parimala argues that, though the Sudras may not have a right to Vedic study, by listening to the Epics and the Puranas, on account of the strength of their merit previously acquired, they attain to a knowledge of Brahman. Thus knowledge of Brahman is open to all. The ways to it may be different for different people. All human beings by virtue of their humanity are entitled to Brahma-knowledge and salvation" (307).

the soul. Because of the technical nature of the term *vidyā* involving its association with the Vedas and Upaniṣads and because of the importance of the maintenance of Vedic learning for Śaṅkara, it is likely that he chose the opportunity of *Vedānta-sūtra* 3:3:38 to reaffirm the orthodox position that *śūdra*s do not have access to Vedic learning.[7] At the same time, he did not want to close the door on the concept of universal salvation. This takes us to some more questions.

---

[7] There has been considerable scholarly debate over who is eligible for liberation in this life. Those who hold to *śruti* as the source for liberation, think that access is restricted. Those who think experience/intuition (*anubhava*) is most important, consider access open to all.

For another position see Rambachan 1991.50-54. For Rambachan, *anubhava* only supplements *śruti*; it is not an independent means for knowledge of Brahman (114-115). He argues that knowledge of Brahman is through the sentences of *śruti* and not experience (*anubhava*), including meditation (119-123). This position suggests that only those who have access to the Vedas can attain liberation, though he does not explore the restrictions of eligibility.

K.N. Upadhyaya (1991, 123) observes that there is a tension between Śaṅkara's statements that Brahman is known only through scripture and his assertion that this knowledge "culminates in experience (*anubhava*) and 'this experience or realization (*avagati*) of Brahman is the highest end of man' ... Relying on one or the other set of these seemingly conflicting statements, scholars are led into a controversy as to whether, ... scriptural authority or intuitive experience is the authentic and the final way of knowing Brahman or ātman." The author then examines Rambachan's critique of scholars such as S. Radhakrishnan, S.K. Belvalkar, Prabhavananda, N.K. Devaraja, and Ninian Smart who hold to the *anubhava* view as "the ultimately valid source of the knowledge of brahman *(brahma-jñāna)*." He concludes that Śaṅkara considers *śruti* as the valid means of knowledge (*pramāṇa*). "From this it follows that the knowledge derived from it is of an entirely different nature from the realization of Brahman (*Brahma-avagati*) or the Self-knowledge (*ātmānubhava*). *Avagati* or *anubhava* is the very end or the culmination of all *pramāṇa*s in which all *pramāṇa*s are transcended. It cannot, therefore, itself be considered as a *pramāṇa* nor can the eternal *ātman* be ever said to become an object of *pramāṇa*. Unlike *śruti* which ceases when one attains the highest realization, *ātman*, as eternal witness, is ever present whether *pramāṇa*s are operative or non-operative. Hence *ātman* can never be reduced to a *prameya* and come within the purview of a *pramāṇa*" (Upadhyaya 1991, 130).

Andrew Fort, when exploring the idea of liberation within life, looks to *Vedāntasūtra* IV.1.18 which says that "rites like the *agnihotra*, performed with or without meditations (*vidyās*) in this or a prior life, cause brahman realization if done with liberation as the aim. Activities like rites destroy sins acquired because the

Can women and *śūdras* attain salvation in this life or must they await rebirth as *brāhmaṇa* or *dvija* men in another life? If women and *śūdras* can attain salvation in this life, then what is meant by the idea that *brāhmaṇas* and royal sages attain the supreme goal more quickly? The *Gītā*, a text of secondary (perhaps we should say complementary) scriptural status (*smṛti*), has a discussion of how deeds are directly related to salvation.

> Ploughing, cattle-herding, and trade are the duties (*karma*) of the *vaiśyas*, born of innate nature. And of the nature of service (*paricaryātmaka*) is the duty of the *śūdra*, born of innate nature (18:44).

In his commentary on this verse, Śaṅkara gives the opponent's view that doing one's own duties simply leads one to lower heaven (*svarga*) or to a better birth in another caste. To give an example of the opponent's position, he quotes from *Āpastambha-dharmasūtra* 2:2:2-3:

> Those who belong to various castes (*varṇa*) and stages of life (*āśrama*), who are devoted to their own *karma* [i.e. duties], having experienced the results of their actions after death, they then with the residual action (*śeṣa*) attain to births in superior countries, castes (*jāti*), families (*kula*), possessing [superior] *dharma*, span of life (*āyus*), learning, behaviour, wealth, happiness, and intelligence. Also in the *purāṇa* is mentioned [the fact] that various results and worlds are attained by the several castes and orders.

Śaṅkara takes a dramatic stand against this position by arguing: "But on account of a different cause, this result will accrue" (*kāraṇāntarāt tu idaṃ vakṣyamāṇam phalam*). This introduces the next *Gītā* verse.

> Doing one's own duties, a person obtains perfection (*saṃsiddhi*). How one attains success devoted to one's own duty, hear that.

---

realization of Brahman is blocked - that is, certain dharmic actions can remove other actions which block knowledge, so these actions indirectly cause liberation (which arises directly only from knowledge. Rites and actions like hearing, reflection, and devotion are therefore proximate (*antaraṅga*) causes bringing the same result (i.e. liberation) as *brahma-vidyā*" (Fort 1991, 381).

sve sve karmaṇy abhirataḥ saṃsiddhiṃ labhate naraḥ ǀ
svakarmaniratah̤ siddhiṃ yathā vindati tac chṛṇu ǁ (18:45)

Perfection (*saṃsiddhi*) rather than attainment of temporary heaven (*svarga*) or rebirth in a higher caste is the new result. Śaṅkara states that doing one's own duty leads to perfection ordained according to one's qualities (*lakṣaṇa*). Moreover, one who is qualified (*adhikṛta*) attains perfection of the qualities—that is, perfection of the body and the senses when impurity is destroyed because of the performance of one's own duties—which are suitable for *jñāna-niṣṭhā*, that is, devotion to knowledge. In short, perfection in *karmayoga* creates perfection of the qualities suitable for devotion to knowledge. The new cause is doing one's duty for its own sake. By contrast, the old cause was desire (*kāmya*). More details are given in the next *Gītā* verse (18:46):

> After worshipping (*abhyarcya*) Him—from whom there is the evolution of beings and by whom all this is pervaded—through [performance of] his/her own duty, a human being attains perfection (*siddhim*).

yataḥ pravṛttir bhūtānāṃ yena sarvam idaṃ tatam:
svakarmaṇā tam abhyarcya siddhiṃ vindati mānavaḥ ǁ (18:46)

Doing one's duty for its own sake must be transformed into doing one's duty as an act of worship. In his commentary on this verse, Śaṅkara, says by "worshipping (*abhyarcya*, i.e. *pūjayitvā*, i.e. *ārādhya*) Him, that is, the Lord by one's own duty, that is, each according to caste (*varṇa*) as said previously, one attains perfection only (*kevalam*) regarding the qualities suitable for [pursuing] *jñāna-niṣṭhā* (devotion to knowledge)." Thus, Śaṅkara is not talking about ultimate perfection here but only perfection of the body and senses.

In other words, human beings, which by definition includes women and *śūdra*s, can perform their duty to serve as an end in itself and then perform it as an act of worship thereby becoming qualified for the next stage of *jñāna-niṣṭhā*. But it may be argued that Śaṅkara is not talking about women in this context; he is speaking about people of the four *varṇa*s—*brāhmaṇa*s, *kṣatriya*s, *vaiśya*s and *śūdra*s—so why are these passages relevant to the issue of women obtaining the supreme goal, that is, salvation? If this is the question, then the reply is as follows. First of all, Śaṅkara himself understood women and *śūdras* as belonging to the same category—those who may be *pāpa-yonayaḥ*—in *Gītā* 9.32. It is well-known in Mīmāṃsā hermeneutics that a member of a class can serve as the example of the entire class. In other words, *śūdra* can represent the *Gītā* category defined as "who may be *pāpa-yonayaḥ,*" which also includes women according to 9.32. According to *Gītā* 18.44 and the following verses, because *śūdra*s can attain perfection (*saṃsiddhi*) by the performance of their own duty, which is to serve, and thereby are eligible for devotion to knowledge (*jñāna-niṣṭhā*), the same can be argued for women. Not only do women belong to the same category as *śūdra*s, they also have the same definition of their own karma (*svakarma*), that is, to serve. If women serve their husbands as their duty and thereby worship the Lord, they attain the perfection of the qualities necessary to pursue *jñāna-niṣṭhā*. The normative role of women (*strī-dharma*) being a good wife, therefore, qualifies them to pursue *jñāna-niṣṭhā.*

The fruit of *jñāna-niṣṭhā* is *naiṣkarmya-siddhi*, that is, perfection in the form of absolute freedom from action (18:48). Verse 18:49 says

> He whose reason (*buddhi*) is not attached anywhere, whose self is subdued (*jitātman*), from whom desire has fled (*vigata-spṛha*) attains by renunciation (*sannyāsa*) the supreme perfection (*parama*) of being without action (*naiṣkarmya-siddhi*).

> asakta-buddhiḥ sarvatra jitātmā vigataspṛhaḥ ǀ
> naiṣkarmyasiddhiṃ paramāṃ sannyāsenādhigacchati ǀǀ (18:49)

Śaṅkara comments on *Gītā* 18:49 as follows:

> Someone of this type who knows the Self (*ātmajña*) attains to the supreme perfection of freedom from action (*naiṣkarmya-siddhi*) through *sannyāsa*. On account of his knowledge of the unity of the actionless (*niṣkriya*) Brahman and Ātman, all actions have departed from him. This is the state of supreme freedom from action which is a perfection (*siddhi*). *Naiṣkarmya-siddhi* may also mean the attainment of *naiṣkarmya*, the state in which one remains as the actionless self (*niṣkriya-ātma-rūpa*). It is supreme as distinguished from the perfection attainable by that which is born of action (*karma*). It is the state of immediate liberation (*sadyo-mukti*). This state is attained by *sannyāsa* or by right knowledge or, better yet, by the renunciation of all action for which one is prepared by right knowledge.

Here, as in other passages, the masculine pronouns are used, but in Sanskrit (and in English until recent times), the masculine has stood both for human beings and men. This gives the modern interpreter the choice to decide the referent by context. In this context, it is surely human beings—women and men. Several verses later Śaṅkara elaborates on what he means by *sannyāsa*:

> Dwelling in an isolated place, eating little, controlling speech, body and mind, constantly engaged in meditation and taking refuge in dispassion (*vairāgya*). (*Gītā* 18:52)
>
> After abandoning (*vimucya*), egotism, strength, arro-gance, desire, anger, and property, free from possession, and peaceful, one is fit (*kalpate*) for becoming Brahman. (*Gītā* 18:53)
>
> Absorbed in Brahman (*brahmabhūta*), one whose self is tranquil neither grieves nor desires. Treating all beings alike, one attains supreme devotion to Me (*madbhaktiṃ labhate parām*). (*Gītā* 18: 54)

In 18:52 Śaṅkara glosses *vivikta-sevī* (isolated place) as forest, sandbank of a river, cave, and so forth. He glosses "having abandoned" (*vimucya*) in 18:53 as "having become a *sannyāsin* of the highest order (*parama-haṃsa-parivrājako bhūtvā*)." He comments on 18:54 that *bhakti* is *jñāna-niṣṭhā*, the supreme kind of devotion.

In 18:55, he calls again for the renunciation of all actions and cites various scriptural passages such as "*saṃnyāsa* is renunciation of action" (*saṃnyāsaḥ karmaṇām nyāsaḥ*) to uphold this position. Finally, Śaṅkara summarizes the argument by saying that having attained the perfection (*siddhi*), which is the result (*phala*) of *bhaktiyoga*, which is the worship (*abhyarcana*) of the Lord by means of one's own duty (*svakarman*), one has the qualification for *jñāna-niṣṭhā*, which leads to renunciation of the highest order (*parama-haṃsa-parivrājako bhūtvā*) and has its conclusion in the fruit of liberation (*mokṣa*). *Gītā* 18:66, says:

> Completely abandoning all *dharmas*, seek Me as the only refuge; I will liberate you from all sins: do not grieve.
>
> sarvadharmān parityajya mām ekam śaraṇaṃ vraja |
> ahaṃ tvā sarvapāpebhyo mokṣayiṣyāmi mā sucaḥ ||

With regard to the discussion at hand, Śaṅkara makes several important points in his lengthy commentary on this verse. He notes that the word *dharma* here includes also *adharma* because of the meaning of being *naiṣkarmya*, that is, without any action. Later Śaṅkara says that devotion to knowledge (*jñāna-niṣṭhā*) culminates in pure self-knowledge, which is bliss. Because supreme bliss is not an effect to be accomplished by action, actions such as *nitya-*, *naimittika-*, and *kāmya-karma* concern the individual who is ignorant of the Self. Consequently, liberation is attained, according to Śaṅkara, through *jñāna-niṣṭhā* accompanied by renunciation of all works.

To conclude, scrutiny of these passages has failed to turn up any specific statement that women and *śūdra*s are barred from taking *sannyāsa* after attaining eligibility for *jñāna-niṣṭhā*. Indeed the whole discussion begins with the context of the four castes. Nowhere are *brāhmaṇa*s then singled out for special consideration regarding eligibility for *sannyāsa*. Similarly, nowhere is it said that only twice-born men (*dvija*s) are eligible. Moreover, *śūdra*s are not told to do their duty in order to be reborn as *brāhmaṇa*s. Indeed Śaṅkara challenges the view of Āpastamba that one should desire rebirth in a higher caste and with greater learning. We are reminded here that the *Gītā* and Śaṅkara tell us in 9:31 that the one of very evil conduct will *quickly* attain the supreme goal. We assume that this is also the case for those mentioned in the next verse (9:32): women, *vaiśya*s and *śūdra*s. Now, it may be argued that the emphasis on "quickly" suggests that the *Gītā* and Śaṅkara (who follows it literally with his gloss of *śīghram*) hold out eternal peace (*śaśvat-śānti*) in this very life even for one of very evil conduct who becomes righteous not to mention women, *vaiśya*s and *śūdra*s who also are said to attain the supreme goal (*parāṃ gatim*). Because *kṣipram* can mean immediately, the idea of liberation within this life (*jīvan-mukti*) is underscored. We still have to deal with *Gītā* 9:33, however, which says:

> How much more (*kim punar*) the pure *brāhmaṇa*s and devoted royal sages, after attaining this impermanent and unhappy world, worship Me.
>
> kiṃ punar brāhmaṇāḥ puṇyā bhaktā rājarṣayas tathā ।
> anityam asukhaṃ lokam imaṃ prāpya bhajasva mām ॥

[Śaṅkara's commentary] kiṃ punaḥ brāhmaṇāḥ puṇyāḥ puṇyayonayaḥ bhaktāḥ rājarṣayaḥ tathā rājānaś ca te ṛṣayaś ca iti rājarṣayaḥ | yataḥ evam ataḥ anityaṃ kṣaṇabhaṅguram asukhaṃ ca sukhavarjitam imaṃ lokaṃ manuṣyalokaṃ, prāpya puruṣārthasādhanaṃ durlabhaṃ manuṣyatvaṃ labdhvā bhajasva sevasva mām.

Śaṅkara stays with the literal meaning of the verse. Although he comments on all other words, he does not mention *kim punar*. *Kim punar* may be construed, however, with *api* in the previous verse and *kṣipram* in the verse previous to that. It may, therefore, be understood as a synthesizing particle that indicates the relation among these verses which are not otherwise syntactically connected. Accordingly, Śaṅkara contrasts the pure *brāhmaṇa*s and royal sages with the people of the previous verses—that is, (1) the one of very evil conduct and (2) those who may be of evil womb (women, *vaiśya*s, and *śūdra*s)—by saying *kim punar* (how much more). Thus, if those of very evil conduct, women, *vaiśya*s, and *śūdra*s all attain liberation in this very life, how much more quickly the *brāhmaṇa*s and royal sages attain it in this very life.

Here is another problem. If women and *śūdra*s can take *sannyāsa*, how are we to interpret passages which suggest that only *brāhmaṇa*s can take *sannyāsa*? Some may still doubt whether *śūdra*s and women can take *sannyāsa*. Indeed, it may be claimed that Śaṅkara's commentary on *Muṇḍaka-upaniṣad* 1:2:12 and *Bṛhadāraṇyaka-upaniṣad* 3:5:1 and 4:5:15 present quite a different view, for there only *brāhmaṇa*s can take *sannyāsa*. In *Muṇḍaka-upaniṣad* 1.2.12, for instance, it is said:

There is mention of the *brāhmaṇa* because with reference to *brahmavidyā*, the *brāhmaṇa* alone (*eva*) has distinct qualification (*viśeṣataḥ adhikāraḥ*) for [knowledge of] Brahman by means of the renunciation of everything.

brāhmaṇaḥ brāhmaṇasya eva viśeṣato 'dhikāraḥ sarvatyāgena brahmavidyāyām iti brāhmaṇa-grahaṇam

Eva, of course, is a particle of emphasis. Although it can mean "alone," it can also mean "indeed, truly, really," and so forth to strengthen the idea. It can also be a mere expletive without any exact meaning and need not be translated. *Viśeṣataḥ,* also an indeclinable, means according to the difference of, in proportion to, especially, particularly, above all.

Grahaṇam means mentioning with praise. Therefore, alternatively the line may be translated: "There is praise of the *brāhmaṇa especially* because regarding *brahma-vidyā* the *brāhmaṇa especially* has qualification for [knowledge of] Brahman by means of the renunciation of everything." This line can be interpreted in two ways. One is exclusive (that is, only *brāhmaṇa*s) and the other inclusive (though the *brāhmaṇa*s are more qualified). It may be argued, moreover, that there are grammatical problems with the translation "the *brāhmaṇa* alone." *Eva* must be bound by nature or context to mean "only, solely" as in the phrase "a woman alone gives birth" or the "Absolute (Brahman) alone is real." Otherwise, *eva* would be but a particle of emphasis. This seems to be the case here, because it is nowhere well established in *śruti* that only *brāhmaṇa*s can take *sannyāsa*.

If this is the key proof text for the position that Śaṅkara is against the salvation of women and *śūdra*s in this very lifetime, or if there are no other unambiguous proof texts, then it cannot be argued that *only brāhmaṇa*s can know Brahman because of their nature or the context. Moreover, because of the addition of the word *viśeṣataḥ*, which means especially or particularly, *eva* must connote emphasis. If the latter interpretation is what Śaṅkara intends, based on the grammar and his understanding, then the issue may not be whether women and *śūdra*s can attain salvation or take *sannyāsa*, but how *quickly* they attain salvation compared to the *brāhmaṇa*s who are especially qualified. This is the conclusion reached in the prior section (which also referred to royal sages, who are *kṣatriyas* and therefore twice-born). Thus, examination of *Muṇḍaka-upaniṣad* 1.2.12 does not permit us to conclude that Śaṅkara confines *sannyāsa* and knowledge of the Absolute to *brāhmaṇa*s only.

We turn now to a key statement in *Bṛhadāraṇyaka-upaniṣad* 4:5:15, which has also been used to prove that only *brāhmaṇa*s are eligible for *sannyāsa*:

> Or it may be that the injunctions of the *śruti* about the life-long performance of rites concern the other two castes except the *brāhmaṇa*, for the *kṣatriya* and the *vaiśya* are not entitled to monastic life.[8]

---

[8] Madhavananda 1975, 552.

itaravarṇāpekṣayā vā yāvaj jīvaśrutiḥ |
na hi kṣatriyavaiśyayoḥ parivrājyapratipattir asti ||

Śaṅkara's purpose in this section is to summarize the confusion surrounding the issue of renunciation in scripture—whether there is an option with regard to taking renunciation, whether the four stages of life are to be followed in strict succession, or whether there can be the adoption of any one—and to demonstrate that consistency can indeed be found.

There are a number of scriptural statements which prescribe that rituals are to be performed throughout the lifespan. Because scripture also advocates renunciation (which is understood as the non-performance of rituals among other things) this apparent contradiction must be overcome. Śaṅkara's tactic is to suggest that the necessity of performing rituals throughout the lifespan applies only to *kṣatriya*s and *vaiśya*s. (This implies that all the statements regarding renunciation apply only to *brāhmaṇa*s). Because the statements are directed to different groups, there is no contradiction.

Such is the logic. We know that Śaṅkara is a master of clever argumentation. But does he really think that only *brāhmaṇa*s are eligible to take renunciation? If he does, then why does he make this passage hypothetical? "Or it may be ... In that case ..." Surely, the idea of restricting *sannyāsa* to *brāhmaṇa*s is such an important one that had Śaṅkara wanted to make this case, he would have done so on a number of occasions (there are several other scriptural statements that would have provided opportunity). For that matter, he could have taken up the issue anywhere. Then, too, if Śaṅkara really does think that only *brāhmaṇa* men can take *sannyāsa*, why does he make such a point of refuting the position of the opponent in *Gītā* 18:45? That is, one should not do one's duty in order to be reborn in a superior caste with superior learning (according to *Āpastambha-dharmasūtra*). If only *brāhmaṇa*s can take *sannyāsa* and if *sannyāsa* is necessary for enlightenment, then obviously women and *śūdras* should be encouraged to be reborn as *brāhmaṇa*s with superior learning. But, we recall, Śaṅkara counters this position and argues that one should do one's duty for its own sake, for worship, and to gain eligibility for *jñāna-niṣṭhā* which, in turn, should lead one to take *sannyāsa*.

If this argument is not yet convincing, then we have only to look at the conclusion of Śaṅkara's discussion on *Bṛhadāraṇyaka-upaniṣad*

4:5:15. Here he makes the point that there is no contradiction among the three options (renunciation, following the four stages of life in succession, or monasticism) in accordance with a person's capacity, knowledge, non-attachment, and desire. Śaṅkara himself here admits that those who are qualified for rites (and we are to understand the *dvija*s i.e. the *brāhmaṇa*s, *kṣatriya*s, and *vaiśya*s) are eligible for the three orders of life (*brahmacārya, vānaprastha*, and *sannyāsa*) in addition to *gṛhastha*. Surely, then, he cannot hold to his previous position that only *brāhmaṇa*s are eligible for *sannyāsa*. On the contrary, *brāhmaṇa*s, *kṣatriya*s, and *vaiśya*s are eligible. This causes us to pause and take seriously the *hypothetical* nature of Śaṅkara's argument in his commentary on *Bṛhadāraṇyaka-upaniṣad* 1.2.12 that *kṣatriya*s and *vaiśya*s must perform rites throughout their lives. Does he not signal to us with his hypothetical language that he is including this example simply for the sake of demonstrating that consistency in the scriptures can be achieved in this particular manner? In short, is it not an argument for the sake of argument rather than a point central to Śaṅkara's view of who is eligible for *sannyāsa* and salvation?

This is not quite the same, of course, as saying that women and *śūdra*s are eligible for *sannyāsa*. But one could argue that the context here is ritualism. Because Śaṅkara does not think that women and *śūdra*s are eligible for Vedic ritualism (see *Vedānta-sūtra* 1:3:34-38 discussed earlier), his comments in this context are confined to those who are eligible for Vedic rites, that is, the twice-born (*dvija*). There is no reason to bring the salvation and *sannyāsa* of women and *śūdra*s into this particular discussion, because according to his commentary on *Vedānta-sūtra* 1:3:38, the source of knowledge is not the Vedas but *smṛti*. Once again, because the *Gītā* is *smṛti* and it advocates *sannyāsa* for those who do their own duty and offer it as worship, thereby becoming eligible for *jñāna-niṣṭhā* and *sannyāsa*, it can be concluded that women and *śūdra*s, too, are eligible for renunciation.

The matter, however, is not yet completely settled. In *Bṛhadāraṇyaka-upaniṣad* 3:5:1, it is said that having acquired knowledge (about the Self and Brahman), *brāhmaṇas* renounce the desire for sons and wealth (that is, the *gṛhastha* stage of life) and become mendicants. Living with this strength, they become meditative. Eventually they transcend even the opposition of meditativeness and non-meditativeness to become knowers of Brahman.

In his commentary, Śaṅkara says that the word *brāhmaṇa* refers to *brāhmaṇas* of ancient times who were qualified for renunciation because they had renounced *the desire for sons* (that is marriage) as the means of winning this world. Therefore, those knowers of Brahman had nothing to do with rituals. Known as *parama-haṃsas*, they led a mendicant's life, lived by begging, and wore no sign (that is, the sacred thread). The opponent then raises an objection. He argues that there is no injunction for the *brāhmaṇas* to renounce because the present tense is used rather than the imperative, which signifies a command (*vidhi*). Thus, passages such as "the *brāhmaṇa*s renounce ... and live a mendicant life" is a mere eulogy (*artha-vāda*) and abandonment of the holy thread and so forth cannot be urged. The opponent next says that because study of the Vedas is enjoined in the mendicant life, because only one who wears the holy thread may study the Vedas, because one becomes *śūdra* by giving up the study of the Vedas, and because the scriptures condemn giving up the study of the Vedas, only desires are to be renounced but not all rites and their means. Śaṅkara rebuts this position by saying that the monk should not only give up the holy thread but also the study of the Vedas, that the ultimate aim of the Upaniṣads is to teach Self-knowledge, and so forth. Then, too, because the rituals performed by those who wear the sacred thread are within the range of ignorance and forms of desire (for Śaṅkara, everything that is not knowledge of Brahman is ignorance), their renunciation is surely enjoined.

The opponent suggests that the conflict can be resolved not by renouncing desires but by wearing the sacred thread and studying the Vedas. Śaṅkara, however, will have none of this. He mentions that because *brāhmaṇa*s in the past renounced the sacred thread and the Vedas and became mendicants, *brāhmaṇa*s today should do the same, for renunciation is enjoined. Moreover, this is complete renunciation of the highest order of monks rather than *vānaprastha* (withdrawal to the forest along with continued performance of ritual, wearing of the sacred thread, and study of the Vedas). Only then is one a *brāhmaṇa*, a knower of Brahman; for then his status as a knower of Brahman is literally true. Therefore, the text says that the knower of Brahman may behave in any (except reckless) manner—in other words, he may follow any one of the four stages of life.

Now, it is quite obvious that this whole discussion is not about the fact that *only brāhmaṇa*s can take *sannyāsa* as opposed to other castes such as *kṣatriya*s, *vaiśya*s and *śūdra*s. Indeed no other groups are even mentioned. On the contrary, the issue once again is the interpretation of the particle *eva,* which can mean "only" or "especially." When Śaṅkara states that *brāhmaṇa*s are mentioned because they *eva* are qualified for renunciation, it would make more sense to translate *eva* as "especially" because of the same grammatical problems mentioned above and because of the context. Śaṅkara's main concern in his commentary here is to overcome brahmanical objections to the idea of renunciation because of other Vedic statements that *brāhmaṇa*s must wear the sacred thread, perform rituals, and study the Vedas throughout their lives. The entire discussion is to resolve such apparent contradictions of *śruti* for *brāhmaṇa*s. This is hardly an argument for the exclusivity of renunciation for *brāhmaṇa*s. Rather, it is an argument that *brāhmaṇa*s are eligible for renunciation (despite *śruti* statements that seem to be to the contrary) and that the real *brāhmaṇa* is one who knows the Absolute, that is, Brahman. Although Śaṅkara nowhere spells it out, he implies in this discussion that *brāhmaṇa*s are *especially* qualified precisely because of their knowledge of the Vedas.

Finally, we see that people other than *brāhmaṇa*s are instructed in the knowledge of Brahman. In *Bṛhadāraṇyaka-upaniṣad* 4:2:1-4, for instance, Janaka, emperor of Videha (who is presumably a *kṣatriya*), is said to have studied the Vedas and heard the Upaniṣads, but because he still had not attained self-knowledge, he sought instruction from Yājñavalkya. This passage is important because it shows that *kṣatriya*s were eligible to study the Vedas and Upaniṣads and could attain self-knowledge in this very life. If someone were to argue that only *brāhmaṇa*s can take *sannyāsa* because only they are eligible on the basis of knowledge of the Vedas, then we would have to reply on the basis of this passage that *kṣatriya*s also are eligible for Vedic study and if they are not encouraged to take *sannyāsa*, it must be for a different reason.

But we also find that women are eligible for the knowledge of Brahman. Because women and *śūdra*s are associated (as in *Gītā* 9:32), further support for the eligibility of *sannyāsa* and salvation for women is relevant to the argument. Śaṅkara's comments on *Bṛhadāraṇyaka-upaniṣad 2:4* (which is Yājñavalkya's dialogue with his wife Maitreyī) is relevant to this discussion. It is important to note that whereas the Upaniṣad itself is non-committal on the subject of Maitreyī's liberation, Śaṅkara argues the case on her behalf. The passage is not a simple narrative about Yājñavalkya's explanation of why he is leaving her and seeking his own salvation. On the contrary, it is an occasion, according to Śaṅkara, to enlighten her. Thus Maitreyī, a woman, is taught knowledge of Brahman. Śaṅkara assumes that she is not eligible for Vedic rituals, but implies that this does not matter, because in any case rites are not the direct means to immortality. Śaṅkara takes the argument even further by stating that being a *brāhmaṇa* or a *kṣatriya* (or, given the context, a woman) is due to the effects of the consciousness created by ignorance (*avidyā*) and cease when they cease to consider themselves as such a person. Śaṅkara then says that the story of Maitreyī and Yājñavalkya is told with a view to enjoining renunciation of the world as part of the knowledge of the Self. This must mean Maitreyī's renunciation as well as Yājñavalkya's, which is explicitly mentioned. Otherwise, why would Yājñavalkya instruct her on the knowledge of the Self, if she were ineligible for enlightenment?

In his commentary on *Bṛhadāraṇyaka-upaniṣad* 2:4:5, Śaṅkara elaborates. He points out that Yājñavalkya, exceedingly pleased that Maitreyī accepted his argument that rituals are not the means to immortality, tenderly explains to his dear wife, who is desirous of liberation, that knowledge of the Self which confers immortality. He instructs her to reflect steadfastly, that is, meditate, on the meaning of his words. Here, because Yājñavalkya tells Maitreyī to meditate on his words, his instruction can hardly be considered perfunctory but rather intended to achieve the supreme goal of enlightenment. With a view to teaching renunciation as a means to immortality, Yājñavalkya creates a distaste for the lifestyle of having a wife, husband, sons, and so forth, so that they be given up. He says that it is not for the sake or necessity of the husband that he is loved by his wife, but it is for her own sake that he is loved by her and vice versa. Moreover, a wife loves her husband ultimately for her own sake, that is, her own liberation because she recognizes the ultimate identity of her true Self and his true Self. In this passage, Śaṅkara explicitly links his teaching about Brahman and renunciation as a means to immortality to the example of a woman and presents the husband's and wife's orientation to liberation as parallel.

In the same commentary (on *Bṛhadāraṇyaka-upaniṣad* 2:4:5), Śaṅkara provides more detail on how a person achieves realization of the Self. He points out that realization of Brahman begins with hearing about the Self from a teacher and the scriptures but that this must culminate in a combination of hearing, reflection, and meditation for liberation. He then notes that concepts of caste (such as *brāhmaṇa* or *kṣatriya*), stages of life (*āśramas)*, and so on, upon which rites depend, are superimposed falsely on the Self by ignorance. Next he uses the famous analogy of falsely seeing a snake in a rope to illustrate his point. Śaṅkara concludes that through hearing, reflection, and meditation, the Self is realized and all this is known. In other words, Śaṅkara, using the example of Maitreyī, reminds us that different kinds of status (such as the difference between men and women) and eligibility (for Vedic knowledge or not) are superimpositions (*adhyāsa*) on the Self. Therefore, it is suggested that she can be enlightened through hearing, reflection, and meditation (because sexual differences and Vedic eligibility are not essential to the Self and because enlightenment involves the Self, not the categories of the ordinary realm). In his commentary on *Bṛhadāraṇyaka-upaniṣad* 2:4:13, Śaṅkara observes that Yājñavalkya tells Maitreyī that this great, endless, infinite Reality is quite sufficient for knowledge. He does not take this occasion to add qualifications or rebut the position that knowledge of the Vedas or performance of the rituals is necessary as a prerequisite.

Nowhere through these discussions does Śaṅkara hint that Maitreyī is ineligible for salvation or that she must await another life. Moreover, we are told in no uncertain terms that caste identities - and here *śūdra*s an included in the list suggested by *ādi* (which means "and so forth") - belong to the realm of ignorance. In other words, just as Maitreyī can hear, reflect upon, and meditate on Brahman (in other words become eligible for *jñāna-niṣṭhā* and then take *sannyāsa*), so can *śūdra*s. This section of the *Bṛhadāraṇyaka-upaniṣad* is very strong evidence for the position that both women and *śūdra*s are eligible for renuncaition of ordinary life (caste and stages of life) and can achieve enlightenment in this very life.

In any case, is *sannyāsa* the only means for attaining salvation according to Śaṅkara? In his commentary on *Bṛhadāraṇyaka-upaniṣad* 4:5:15, Śaṅkara says that even without any explicit injunction to take *sannyāsa* that enlightened sages can become monastics simply because they are convinced about the immutable identity of ātman and Brahman (which is beyond factors such as rituals or caste identity) or if they desire illumination. This statement suggests that it is an *option* to embrace the monastic life. In other words, we find scope in Śaṅkara's commentary for concluding that he thinks that *śūdra*s can take *sannyāsa,* if they have realized the identity of the Self and Brahman.

The same, of course, can be said for women. The fact that women can attain liberation through hearing, reflection, and meditation without having to leave home to become a mendicant is extremely important, because this means that they do not have to abandon their marriages to seek salvation. Given the normative nature of women's householder status in Hinduism and the perceived threat that their abandonment in large numbers would create for family life, the intergenerational cycle, and society, having access to liberation without formal monasticism is significant, especially because Hinduism had no institutionalized ascetic hermitages for women (unlike Buddhism).[9]

This passage also suggests that there are two kinds of people who may take *sannyāsa*: those who know, i.e. are enlightened and therefore renounce, and those who *seek* to know and therefore renounce. For the latter, renunciation is recommended because it is efficacious for bringing forth Self-knowledge. This statement demonstrates that *sannyāsa* as literal renunciation of the householder's way of life is not mandatory. We are reminded here again of Śaṅkara on *Gītā* 18:49 where he says that this Self-knowledge is attained by *sannyāsa* or right knowledge, or better still, by the renunciation of all actions for which one is prepared by right knowledge. In other words, it is an option whether one pursues renunciation through right knowledge alone or by renunciation of

---

[9] See Young 1987, 68-70.

actions [such as the duties of caste and stage of life]. Even though the latter is preferred, the former is possible.

In his commentary on *Bṛhadāraṇyaka-upaniṣad* 4:5:15, Śaṅkara's states that the knowledge of ātman by the *via negativa* (realizing that the true Self is not this, not this—*neti neti*) and by the renunciation of everything are the only means of attaining immortality. As in the case of Maitreyī, these are independent of any auxiliary means and that even without any explicit injunction to take *sannyāsa*, the enlightened sage can embrace the monastic life. Śaṅkara notes, moreover, that unlike the performance of rituals, knowledge of the Self is not dependent on place, time, circumstances, and so forth because the ātman is an eternal truth. It follows that if Self-knowledge is not dependent on circumstance, it cannot be dependent on renunciation, just as it cannot be dependent on rituals. Although Śaṅkara does not spell out the logic explicitly, it is implied.

The fact that some *kṣatriyas* have attained right knowledge without being renunciates is indicated in Śaṅkara's commentary on *Gītā* 3:20:

> If they [Janaka and others] were persons who had attained right knowledge [of the Self], then the meaning is: for the sake of *loka-saṅgraha* they abided in perfection accompanied with action, that is without renouncing action due to *prārabdha-karma*s.
>
> yadi te prāptasamyagdarśanāḥ tataḥ lokasaṅgrahārthaṃ prārabdhakarmatvāt karmaṇā sahaiva asannyasyaiva karma saṃsiddhim āsthitā ity arthaḥ
>
> [To Arjuna] If you think ... that [action] need not necessarily be done by someone else who has right knowledge and has achieved the goal, even then, being subject to *prārabdha-karma*s, you should perform action having in view *loka-saṅgraha*.
>
> ...atha manyase...nāvaśyamanyena kartavyaṃ samyag-darśanavatā kṛtārtheneti, tathāpi prārabdhakarmāyattaḥ tvaṃ lokasaṃgraham ... saṃpaśyan kartum aharsi

If *sannyāsa* is necessary for enlightenment, an explanation must be given as to why *kṣatriya*s such as Janaka are said to have right knowledge, to abide in perfection (*saṃsiddhi*), and to have attained the goal (*artha*, presumably enlightenment) yet are not ascetics. If only *brāhmaṇa*s can take *sannyāsa* and *sannyāsa* is necessary for enlightenment, then how can *kṣatriya*s be enlightened?

Does this mean that the *kṣatriyas* were enlightened in a previous birth when they were *brāhmaṇa*s who took *sannyāsa*, but were reborn as *kṣatriyas* because of *prārabdha-karma*s (previous karma)? This argument cannot be made because even after entering a higher stage of life—presumably, *sannyāsa*—one never descends to a lower one in another birth (See *Vedānta-sūtra* 3:4:40). Moreover, after enlightenment one is never reborn, though one may live for some time because of *prārabdha-karma*s. Therefore a possible conclusion is that some *kṣatriya*s such as Janaka attained enlightenment without taking *sannyāsa* and continued to act in the world (in accordance with their caste) because of *prārabdha-karma*s.

Further substantiation for the idea that *sannyāsa* is not necessary for salvation is found in Śaṅkara's commentary on *Vedānta-sūtra* 3:4:36-38. *Sūtra* 3:4:36 states that those who are "between," that is, not within the standard stages of life, are qualified for supreme knowledge according to scripture. Śaṅkara observes that the opponent (*pūrva-pakṣin*) argues that they are not qualified because they are not within the stages of life and therefore cannot do the works (rituals and so forth) that characterize these stages and that cause knowledge. Śaṅkara rebuts the opponent's position by arguing that even if a person does not belong to an *āśrama*, such a one is qualified for knowledge because there are scriptural examples to this effect as in the case of Raikva (who as a widower was outside the stages of life and could not perform rituals because he had no wife to accompany him)[10] and Gārgī who possessed knowledge of Brahman (*Chāndogya-upaniṣad* 4:1; *Bṛhadāraṇyaka-upaniṣad* 3: 6; 8).

Śaṅkara elaborates on this idea that widowers such as Raikva and women such as Gārgī may also be competent for knowledge in *Vedānta-sūtra* 3:4:38. He says that for this class of "between" people, prayers, fasts, and performance of duties as worship may substitute for the mandatory actions of the stages of life (presumably the mandatory Vedic rituals of the householder stage were foremost in his mind because they were at the heart of brahmanical orthodoxy and prerequisite for knowledge of Brahman for *brāhmaṇa* men) and

[10] Vedic rituals were to be performed only by a married couple (although there were ways to circumvent this prescription).

quotes Manu 2:87 to this effect. In addition, he argues that the purificatory rituals done in previous births may culminate in spiritual perfection in this life, quoting *Bhagavad-gītā* 6:45 to this effect. He argues that when the lack of ignorance can be seen in these people, there is obviously knowledge and absence of obstacles. For all these reasons, says Śaṅkara, widowers and the like have qualification for the (supreme) knowledge.

This argument reminds us of our earlier discussion based on *Vedānta-sūtra* 1:3:34-38, which concluded that *śūdra*s (and women), though without a right to knowledge through the Vedas, may attain liberation because of knowledge obtained through merit (*prārabdha-karma*s) in previous lives or through the other category of scripture called *smṛti.*[11] At the same time Śaṅkara admits, following *Sūtra* 3:4:39, that the state of belonging to an *āśrama* is better on account of the indicatory marks. This probably refers to the idea that performance of one's caste duty can be the means of liberation if done as worship. As in *Gītā* 9:33 "How much *more* [quickly] the *brāhmaṇas* and royal sages." Because this concept supports the caste system and caste was considered important for an ordered society, Śaṅkara thought caste duties offered as worship is preferred to a society without caste.

There is one last argument on this topic. According to Śaṅkara's commentary on *Vedānta-sūtra* 1:1:2, both scripture and personal experience (*anubhava*) are means of knowing Brahman. Śaṅkara notes that scripture is not the only means of enquiry into Brahman unlike the enquiry into rituals (as in Pūrva- mīmāṃsā). Rather, one may resort to scripture *or* experience (intuition) according to the

---

[11] According to Marcaurelle, "Having 'a perceptible result' seems to define fruition of immediate Self-knowledge into annulment of ignorance and into the ensuing liberation, as wholly different from fruition of rites into results, which are out of immediate perception such as attainment of heaven after death. Since the result of rites is quite different from the result of Self-knowledge, lack of qualification for receiving the result of action does not imply failure to obtain the result of knowledge. Śaṅkara then states that anyone who wishes to obtain the result of knowledge is qualified for the discipline of knowledge and its result. Only a scriptural prohibition could restrict such a universal qualification. But there is none as noted by Śaṅkara" (Marcaurelle 2000, 51).

occasion for two reasons. First, experience (intuition) is the final result of the enquiry into Brahman. Second, because the reference to experience (intuition) makes sense only because the object of knowledge (Brahman) always exists and is not something to be accomplished. According to Arvind Sharma, for Śaṅkara there are two exceptions to the idea that liberation for Śaṅkara occurs through *smṛti*: "one indirect and the other direct .... The indirect exception is that *mukti* is possible through knowledge or *śruti*. The direct exception is that *mukti* is possible through direct intuition or *anubhava*. After all Śaṅkara's basic position is aphoristically stated to be that liberation can't be attained without *jñāna*, not that it can't be attained without *śruti*."[12]

This point is illustrated by an annecdote narrated by K. Satchidananda Murty. Once Śaṅkara came across an outcaste leper in a pitiable state, but who was spiritually advanced. To liberate him from rebirth, Śaṅkara composed for him a verse on the model of the dialogue between Yājñavalkya and Janaka in *Bṛhadāraṇyaka-upaniṣad* 4.3.1 ff.

> What is your Light?
> The sun during the day and lamps etc. during the night.
> Let it be so, but tell me what is the light that beholds (cognises) the sun, moon etc. as shining?
> That is my eye.
> And, when it is closed, what beholds them?
> My mind (reason).
> What is it that behold (cognises) your mind?
> I.
> So, you are the supreme Light?
> That I Am, my Master.[13]

When he heard this, the leper immediately became a knower of the absolute (*brahma-jñānin*) and saw Truth. Murty thinks that this was an ingenious way to circumvent orthodoxy. "If one wishes to enlighten those whom orthodoxy does not permit to hear the holy texts, let one express their meaning in other words. A quiet peaceful revolution,

---

[12] Sharma 1988.
[13] Murty no date 8-9.

indeed! No other great Vedantic teacher of medieval India who commented on the *Brahmasūtra* showed such liberalism and humanism."[14] He concludes that Śaṅkara was a compassionate knower of Brahman.

In this context yet another question comes to mind. Does Śaṅkara use the same language when referring to the goal for women and *śūdra*s as he uses when referring to it for *brāhmaṇa*s or *dvija*s? There are various terms and phrases used in the commentaries by Śaṅkara for liberation: the goal (*artha*) (*Gītā* 3:20); eternal peace (*śāśvat-śānti*) and "does not perish" (*na ... praṇaṣyati*) (*Gītā* 9:31); the supreme goal (*parā gati*) (*Gītā* 9:32); knowledge (*jñāna*); and knowledge of Brahman (*brahma-vidyā*) (*Vedanta-sūtra* 1:3:38); supreme perfection of being without action (*naiṣkarmya-siddhi*) and the state of immediate liberation (*sadyo-mukti*) (*Gītā* 18:49); liberation (*mokṣa*) (*Gītā* 18:55); pure-self-knowledge that is bliss (*Gītā* 18:66); knowledge of the Self and realization of the Self (*Bṛhadāraṇyaka-upaniṣad* 4:5:15); and the highest way (*Vedānta-sūtra* 3:4:38).

The "goal" is mentioned with reference to *kṣatriya*s such as Janaka and is construed with the words perfection (*saṃsiddhi*) and service (*loka-saṅgraha*), which are contrasted with supreme perfection as absolute freedom from action (*naiṣkarmya-siddhi*); Janaka seeks Self-knowledge and attains "that which is free from fear due to birth, death, and so forth." The phrases "eternal peace" and "does not perish" refer to the one of very evil conduct who become righteous. The "supreme goal" is used with reference to women, *vaiśya*s, and *śūdra*s. "*Jñāna*" is connected with *śūdra*s among others. "Knowledge of Brahman" is discussed with reference to *brāhmaṇa*s, *kṣatriya*s, or *dvija*s. The "supreme perfection," "immediate liberation," "liberation," and "pure-self-knowledge which is bliss" conclude a discussion that began with reference to people of the four castes. And references to "knowledge of the Self," and "realization of the Self" are found in Yājñavalkya's dialogue with his wife Maitreyī.

There are no terms that are exclusively associated with one category of person. Women, *vaiśya*s, and *śūdra*s are associated with the supreme goal just as Janaka, a *kṣatriya*, and Maitreyī, a woman,

---

[14] Murty no date, 8-9.

are instructed in knowledge of the Self and realization of the Self. All four castes are included in the *Gītā's* discussion. Only when Śaṅkara talks about *brahma-vidyā* does he exclude *śūdras* when this term is construed as knowledge of the Vedas. Otherwise, there does not seem to be any particular association of *brāhmaṇa*s and liberation or even *dvija*s and liberation in the passages discussed here. The idea that knowledge of Brahman (presumably in the sense of *jñāna-niṣṭhā*) is to lead to renunciation is made explicit in the case of Maitreyī. We can assume, given the importance of *sannyāsa* for Śaṅkara, that if women can take *sannyāsa*, so can *śūdra*s. There is perhaps some reluctance, however, to encourage kings to take *sannyāsa*. This may be a political strategy on Śaṅkara's part. Kings are needed to rule. Therefore, Śaṅkara suggests that they continue to act in the world (*loka-saṅgraha*) because of *prārabdha-karma*s. In this case, practical wisdom takes precedence over spiritual wisdom.

At the very end of the *Vedānta-sūtras* (4:4:22), Śaṅkara says that it is a settled matter that those who through perfect knowledge have dispelled all mental darkness and are devoted to the eternally perfect liberation (*nirvāṇa)* do not return to this world. The same is true for those who resort to knowledge of the qualified Brahman. Finally, we are told that repetition of the words "Non-return, according to scripture," concludes these teachings.

The Salvation of Women and Śūdras *in Historical Perspective*

The term *pāpayonayaḥ* was used in the *Gītā* to describe women, *vaiśya*s, and *śūdra*s. It is well known that women and *śūdra*s were often associated in the *smṛti* because they both were *avaidika* (without knowledge of the Veda, therefore ignorant) and because they both served others (master and husband). Ignorance and service were associated with low status, which was thought to be a product of *pāpa* or bad karma. As a result, women and *śūdra*s were described in some orthodox circles as being those of evil womb or bad birth (*pāpa-yonayaḥ*). Moreover, because many *vaiśyas* were losing status at the time of the *Gītā*, they were included in this category as well. Although the *Gītā* opened the door to the legitimation of the salvation of women and *śūdra*s (9:32), it did so ostensibly as a concession—even (*api*) women, *vaiśya*s and *śūdra*s. Then, too, it did not eliminate the pejorative adjectival phrase: those born of evil womb (*pāpa-yonayaḥ*).

Arvind Sharma[15] has presented evidence for the fact that both women and *śūdra*s once had access to Vedic learning and rituals, at least in some circles. The *śūdra*s, for instance, had a special, positive connection with the *Yajur-veda, Taittirīya-saṃhitā, Vājasaneyī-saṃhitā, Taittirīya-brāhmaṇa, Śatapatha-brāhmaṇa,* and *Bṛhadāraṇyaka-upaniṣad* (though these texts might also contain negative passages). The fact that the term *śūdra*s could refer to another Indo-European group, the *dāsa*s, might explain the ambiguity of their status. As speakers of Sanskrit with a common Indo-European religious heritage, they could be included in some Vedic rituals (perhaps the more archaic, domestic ones), but because they did not belong to the *Ṛgveda/Sāmaveda* tradition, they could be viewed as without knowledge of these Vedas (hence *avaidika*) and therefore without the eligibility for Vedic rituals related to these texts. The development of other "Vedic" texts (such as *Yajur-veda, Tattirīya-saṃhitā, Vājasaneyī-saṃhitā*) might have served to integrate some of the *dāsa*s into the Vedic tradition (causing the non-Vedic *dāsa*s to be considered degraded *brāhmaṇa*s or even *śūdra*s (and hence permanently *avaidika*).

It is not surprising, therefore, to find that *śūdra*s with Vedic learning are also alluded to (as the opposing position) in the Mīmāṃsā literature, though this school itself did not approve of them. It is significant, Sharma argues, that their ineligibility is not mentioned in any Vedic verse. In the *Mānava-dharmaśāstra*, the *Vedānta-sūtras,* and the *Mahābhārata* (Śāntiparvan 181.15), the loss of Vedic rituals or knowledge for *śūdra*s is mentioned, though the *Mahābhārata* mentions the *śūdra*s positively as does the *Atharva-veda,* the fourth or last Veda, which was accepted only about this same time. Sharma argues that according to tradition, Vyāsa (whose other name was Bādarāyaṇa) was the author of the *Mahābhārata* and the *Vedānta-sūtras* and was the same author who created the fourfold division of the Vedas (which suggests that he was instrumental in integrating those groups associated with the *Yajur* and *Atharva* Vedas). Just as he was acknowledging that *śūdra*s were to be debarred from Vedic rituals according to *Vedānta-sūtras,* he was providing another

---

[15] Sharma 2000.

approach to salvation through the *Mahābhārata* (which includes the *Gītā).* I would add that Vyāsa (or a "school" maintaining his tradition) was trying to bridge the conceptual opposition between inclusion and exclusion by defining exclusivity as sole brahmanical expertise in the Vedas and Vedic rituals, which must be protected and honoured, and inclusivity as universal religion based on religious experience, *smṛti* scriptures, and non-Vedic rituals and mantras (which were available to everyone, including women and *śūdra*s). To get the elite to accept, at least nominally, the universalism of the latter (which was important given the popularity of Mahāyāna Buddhism at the time), he gave a slight privileging to the *brāhmaṇa*s and royal sages even in universal passages.

In the centuries after the writing or redaction of the *Gītā*, there remained two views: that women and *śūdra*s were eligible for salvation in this life, and that they were not. The former was promoted in most bhakti circles. That *brāhmaṇa*s were increasingly drawn into these bhakti groups suggests that there was a liberal brahmanical position (the one that had integrated women and *śūdra*s). Other *brāhmaṇa*s, however, were conservative (and exclusive). A case in point is Bhāskara, who may have lived about the time of Śaṅkara or just before. In his commentary on *Gītā* 9:32, he first gives the opponent's view, which upholds salvation for women and *śūdra*s, and then refutes this position.

Śaṅkara no doubt knew of the polarization on this issue in brahmanical circles. If we assume that his aim was to protect the status of the Vedas (and by extension Vedic Religion, which had been under attack by the heterodox religions), then it is likely that his primary interest was to shore up orthodoxy by insisting that *brāhmaṇa*s maintain expertise in and commitment to the Vedas. Many *brāhmaṇa* intellectuals of the period, after all, had become Buddhists: Nāgārjuna, Asaṅga, Vasubandhu, Dignāga, and so forth. Indeed, Śaṅkara must have known that the universal religion promoted by Buddhism could also be countered by a parallel Hindu movement. In fact, there was one already under way and he himself belonged, at least nominally, to it as a South Indian and a Vaiṣṇava.[16] As a result,

[16] See "Relations of Early Advaitins to Vaiṣṇavism" in Hacker 1995, 33-39.

he would have been aware of the power of sectarian proselytizing (as in the Tamil *bhakti* hymns) to women and *śūdras*.

Thus, we conclude that Śaṅkara wanted it both ways. He wanted his philosophical system (*darśana*) to appeal to conservative circles (because he wanted to protect the Vedas) and by extension the Vedic tradition. As a result, he had to define a purpose for knowledge of the Vedas in order to safeguard them, and so he argued that it helped *brāhmaṇas* and royal sages to gain salvation *more quickly*.

But Śaṅkara certainly did not want to close the door on liberal ones. Hence his emphatic endorsement of the salvation of women, *vaiśyas* and *śūdras* in *Gītā* 9:32; his modifying addendum on *Vedānta-sūtra* 1:3:38 where he held out *smṛti* as an alternative to *śruti* (the Vedas); his view that *anubhava* as direct intuition of Brahman was universally available; his understanding that liberation could occur for anyone who had accumulated sufficient merit in previous lives; and his position that doing one's own duty leads to knowledge of Brahman, and so forth. In the final analysis, though, if salvation even for the evil one could be attained *in this very life*, "more quickly" for *brāhmaṇas* and royal sages was hardly something for women and *śūdras* to quibble over!

In sum, the texts ostensibly say different things about who is eligible for salvation and renunciation. Because Śaṅkara is responding to a specific text that comments on a specific context, his specific comments cannot be generalized. Rather, we have had to search for the logic that holds them all together, that is, the fact that he wanted to maintain both exclusivity and inclusivity, and thereby have his cake and eat it too. As such, Śaṅkara was in the tradition of Vyāsa, but even more subtle about revealing his hermeneutical strategies to bridge the yawning gap between inclusiveness and exclusiveness. Even this deliberate opaqueness could be considered a strategy to finesse integration and preempt exploitation of a loophole. But another explanation is that the confusion occurred because of Śaṅkara's disciples.[17] In his commentary on Śaṅkara's commentary on

[17] This position is accepted by Hacker (see Hacker in Halbfass 1995, 27) though he expresses some doubt because an old commentator on one of Sureśvara's works never explicity calls Sureśvara's teacher Śaṅkara (in Halbfass 1995, 43) but only by

Bṛhadāraṇyaka-upaniṣad 3:5:1, Sureśvara, reputed to be a direct disciple of Śaṅkara, said that Śaṅkara held the view that only *brāhmaṇa*s could obtain salvation but he himself thought that any *dvija* was eligible.

First, Sureśvara's debate with Śaṅkara was not over whether women and *śūdra*s can attain salvation, but whether only *brāhmaṇa*s or all *dvija*s (twice-born men) can attain it. Sureśvara attributed the former position to Śaṅkara and argued for the latter. My reconstruction of Śaṅkara's thought shows, however, that he could never have been so exclusive (restricting liberation to *brāhmaṇa*s only) because he accepted arguments for the salvation of women and *śūdra*s according to *svakarma*, *smṛti*, and *anubhava* thereby creating scope for a universal religion, and because he kept to the literal meaning of *Gītā* 9:32.

It seems, then, that Sureśvara was not intimately familiar with Śaṅkara's own thought. It could be that he limited himself to study of Śaṅkara's commentary on *Bṛhadāraṇyaka-upaniṣad* 3:5:1 and 4:5:15 (which could be used to support a more conservative position) and ignored his commentary on the *Vedānta-sūtra*s and *Gītā* (the more liberal one). But that would have been very curious if he were indeed a direct disciple. It is more likely that Sureśvara lived well after Śaṅkara. By that time the conservative position that *sannyāsa* for *brāhmaṇa* men only based on *Bṛhadāraṇyaka-upaniṣad* 3:5:1 and 4:5:15 had been reinforced and was now mainstream as *brāhmaṇas* had become more powerful and caste hierarchy had come to dominate even the devotional (*bhakti*) movement. Sureśvara argued against this tradition by now attributed to Śaṅkara himself to establish that *dvijas* are included in those eligible for salvation, a position that Śaṅkara indeed held—along with others. Moreover, no one had made the effort to read all his works systematically with this issue in mind.

There has also been considerable confusion over the figure of Sureśvara, namely, whether the figure of Viśvarūpa (who upheld the view that only *brāhmaṇa*s can take *sannyāsa*) was the same person as

---

certain titles (albeit ones that are found in the colophons of Śaṅkara's "authentic" works). It is also possible, I think, that the colophons were written later than the text and introduced anachronistic material.

Sureśvara (who argued that all *dvija*s could take *sannyāsa*). P.V. Kane[18] accepts that they are the same person despite the obvious contradiction in their two positions and does not dispute the idea that they are direct pupils of Śaṅkara. Also Kane does not challenge the idea that Śaṅkara established four *maṭha*s for the propagation of his views. But the fact that *ten* orders of *advaitin sannyāsin*s developed, purportedly in succession from Śaṅkara's *four* disciples is curious.[19] Moreover, "pedigrees of teachers and pupils appear to have been fabricated, no two of which agree in toto and in some of them Sureśvara is said to have lived for 700 or 800 years."[20] Surely in the light of such confusion, it is best to rely on Śaṅkara's own works for his views regarding who is eligible for *sannyāsa* and salvation, rather than the works of so-called disciples who may have lived in a later time and had their own views regarding eligibility.[21]

In any case, none of the later medieval works support the idea of *sannyāsa* for women and *śūdra*s (perhaps because of growing conservatism in the society at large on account of the Muslim invasions) except the *Jīvan-muktiviveka*, which says that women and *śūdra*s are eligible for *tyāga* (renunciation) following the example of Maitreyī (*Bṛhadāraṇyaka-upaniṣad* 4:5:3-4). This text makes a distinction between informal renunciation (*tyāga*) and formal renunciation (*sannyāsa)*, which was probably associated with the Śaṅkara *maṭhas:* women and *śūdra*s may abandon all actions, though they could not adopt the peculiar ascetic mode of life with its outward symbols.[22] (This text also says that the "mother and the wife of a *sannyāsin* will not be born again as women, but they may be born as men." This does not suggest that women *must* be reborn as men to seek liberation. On the contrary, it accounts for an anomaly. Because wives and mothers are told to be devoted to their husbands and sons,

---

[18] Kane 1973, vol. 1, 562-3.

[19] Hacker notes that there is no epigraphic evidence for Śaṅkara *maṭha*s before the fourteenth century (in Halbfass 1995, 29).

[20] Kane 1974, vol.2, 948-949.

[21] Stanzas 1-2 that mention Śaṅkara in Sureśvara's *Pañcīkaraṇavārttika* are "apparently spurious (cf. P. Tuxen in: Aus Indiens Kultur, Festgabe R. v. Garbe dargebracht, Erlangen, 1927, p. 134)" in Halbfass 1995, 55 note 12.

[22] Kane 1974, vol. 2:946.

but because their husbands and sons can renounce them to seek salvation—which gives them an anomalous status and perhaps subjects them to hardship as well—these women are automatically given the reward of being reborn as men in the next life. This might have had some appeal in conservative circles).

One last passage in this context is worthy of mention. According to Śrīkara's *bhāṣya* on *Vedānta-sūtra* I.3.34, *sannyāsa* as defined by Vedic texts is only for the *dvijas,* whereas mere abandonment of worldly pleasures and desires (*nyāsa*) is for women, *śūdras* and mixed castes.[23] In other words, a distinction is also made here between Vedic and non-Vedic types of renunciation.

By the Moghul period, however, some of the ten orders accepted women ascetics. This development is related to the activities of Madhusūdana Sarasvatī who introduced a liberalization in the ascetic orders by initiating *kṣatriya*s, *vaiśya*s, and *śūdras* to counter the proselytism of the Muslim fakirs. Because of the close association of *śūdra*s and women, it does not surprise us to find that women were now accepted into some of these orders. (Today, there are female and *śūdra sannyāsins* in six and half of the ten orders.)[24] And women and *śūdras* are studying the Vedas and performing Vedic rituals in other contexts.

BIBLIOGRAPHY

1. *Primary texts*

Bhagavadgītā Bhāṣya by Bhāskarācārya (Sanskrit text). 1965. In *Sarasvati Bhav Granthamala.* vol. 94. ed. Baladeva Upadhyaya. Varanasi.

Brahmasūtra-Śaṅkarabhāṣya (Sanskrit text). 1980. ed. J.L. Shastri. New Delhi: Motilal Banarsidass.

Śaṅkara. *Bṛhadāraṇyakopaniṣadbhāṣya* 1891. Ānandāśrama Sanskrit Series, no. 15. Poona: Ānandāśrama Press.

Śrīmadbhagavadgītā. 1910-1911. Sanskrit text. With commentaries by Rāmānuja, Vedānta Deśika, Śaṅkara, Ānandatīrtha, Jayatīrtha. 3 vols. ed. A.V. Nara-siṃhācārya. Madras: Ānandāśrama Press.

---

[23] Kane 1974, vol. 2:946.

[24] Ojha 1981, 261.

2. *Secondary sources*

Gambhīrānanda, Swami. trans. 1973. *Eight Upaniṣads*. With the Commentary of Śaṅkarācārya. vol. 2. Calcutta: Advaita Ashrama.

______. trans. 1965. *Brahmasūtra-bhāṣya of Śaṅkarācārya*. Calcutta: Advaita Ashrama.

Halbfass, Wilhelm. 1988. *India and Europe: An Essay in Understanding*. Albany: State University of New York Press.

______. 1991. *Tradition and Reflection*. Albany: State University of New York Press.

______. 1995. *Philology and Confrontation: Paul Hacker on Traditional and Modern Vedānta*. Albany: State University of New York Press.

Hino, Shoun. 1991. *Sureśvara's Vārtika on Yājñavalkya Maitreyī Dialogue*. 2nd ed. Delhi: Motilal Banarsidass.

Hume, Robert Ernest. trans. [1877]. 1968. 2nd. ed. *The Thirteen Principal Upanishads*. Oxford: Oxford University Press.

Kalyanasundara Sastri, V.R. 1989. "Śaṅkara on jñāna-yoga." *Perspectives of Śaṅkara*. Rashtriya Śaṅkara.

Jayantī Mahotsava Commemoration Volume. 297-306. Department of Culture. Ministry of Human Resource Development Government of India.

Kane, P.V. 1973-1977. (reprint). *History of the Dharmaśāstra*. 5 vols. Poona: Bhandarkar Oriental Research Institute.

Madhavananda, Swami. trans. 1975. *The Bṛhadāraṇyaka-upaniṣad*. With the commentary of Śaṅkarācārya. Calcutta: Advaita Ashrama.

Mahadevan, M.P. 1961. *Collected Papers of Professor S.S. Suryanarayana Sastri*. Madras: University of Madras.

Mayeda, Sengaku. "Ādi-Śaṅkarācārya's Teaching on the Means to Mokṣa: Jñāna and Karman." *Journal of Oriental Research* vol. 34-35. 1964-1966, 66-75,.

______. 1973. *Śaṅkara's Upadeśasāhasrī* (crit. ed.) Tokyo: Hokuseido Press.

Marcaurelle, Roger. 2000. *Freedom Through Inner Renunciation: Śaṅkara's Philosophy in a New Light*. Albany: State University of New York Press.

Monier-Williams, Sir Monier. [1899] 1970. *A Sanskrit-English Dictionary*. Oxford: Clarendon Press.

Murty, K. Satchidananda. 1974. *Revelation and Reason in Advaita Vedānta*. Delhi: Motilal Banarsidass.

______. [no date] *Rashtriya Sri Shankaracharya Jayanti Mahotsava. Inauguration Address*. New Delhi: Vigyan Bhavan.

Ojha, C. 1981, "Feminine asceticism in Hinduism: its tradition and present condition," *Man in India*, vol. 61/3. 1981, 254-85.

Potter, Karl H. "Śaṅkarācārya: The Myth and the Man." *JAAR Thematic*

Studies vol. 18/3-4. 1982, 111-125.

Radhakrishnan, S. trans. 1960. *The Brahma Sūtra: The Philosophy of Spiritual Life*. London: George Allen & Unwin.

Rambachan, Anantanand. 1991. *Accomplishing the Accomplished: The Vedas as a Source of Valid Knowledge in Śaṅkara.* Mongraphs of the Society for Asian and Comparative Philosophy, no. 10. Honolulu: University of Hawaii Press.

Rukmani, T.S. "Śaṅkara's Views on Yoga in the Brahmasūtrabhāṣya in the Light of the Authorship of the Yogasūtrabhāṣya-vivaraṇa." *Journal of Indian Philosophy* vol. 21. 1993, 395-404.

Sastri, A. Mahadava. 1972. *The Bhagavad-Gītā.* With the commentary of Śrī Śaṅkarāchārya. Madras: V. Ramaswamy Sastrulu & Sons.

Sastri, C. Markandeya. 1973. *Sureśvara's Contribution to Advaita.* Guntur: Sundari Samskrita Vidyalaya.

Sharma, Arvind. "Śaṅkara's Attitude to Scriptural Authority as Revealed by His Gloss on Brahmasūtra 1.1.3" *Journal of Indian Philosophy* vol. 10. 1982, 179-186.

______. 1986. *The Hindu Gītā: Ancient and Classical Interpretations of the Bhagavadgītā.* London: Gerald Duckworth & Co.

______. [1988] "Śaṅkara on the Indispensability and Inaccessibility of Śruti." Paper delivered to the American Oriental Society, Chicago.

______. "Of Śūdras, Sūtas, and Ślokas: Why is the Mahābhārata Preeminently in the Anuṣṭubh Metre?" *Indo-Iranian Journal.* vol. 43. 2000, 225-278.

Taber, John. "Reason, Revelation and Idealism in Śaṅkara's Vedānta." *Journal of Indian Philosophy* vol. 9. 1981, 283-307.

Thibaut, George. [1890;1896] 1962. *The Vedānta Sūtras of Bādarāyaṇa.* With the commentary by Śaṅkara. 2 vols. New York: Dover Publications.

Upadhyayay, K.N. "Śaṅkara on Reason, Scriptural Authority and Self-Knowledge" *Journal of Indian Philosophy* 19:121-132. 1991.

Vetter, T. 1979. *Studien zur Lehre und Entwicklung Śaṅkaras.* Vienna: De Nobili Research Library.

Yoshitsugu, Sawai. "Rāmānuja's Hermeneutics of the Upaniṣads in Comparison with Śaṅkara's Interpretation." *Journal of Indian Philosophy* vol. 19. 1991, 89-98.

Young, Katherine K., 1987. "Women in Hinduism." *Women in World Religions.* Arvind Sharma, ed. (Albany: SUNY Press. 59-105).

______. ed. 1994. *Hermeneutical Paths to the Sacred Worlds of India.* Atlanta: Scholar's Press.

______. "Theology Does Help Women's Liberation: Śrīvaiṣṇavism: a Case Study." The *Journal of Vaiṣṇava Studies.* vol. 3, no. 4. 173-233.

INDEX